INDIA'S REFORMS

Series Editors' Note

With this volume, we are pleased to launch the series Studies in Indian Economic Policies. The series is intended to bring out scholarly studies of the past and future economic policies and their impact on India. It will include volumes authored by single or paired authors as well as collections of essays by different authors devoted to closely related themes. The series is not wedded to any specific method of analysis or viewpoint but does seek a policy focus and high standards of economic and political analysis.

The initial impetus for the series came from the Columbia Program on Indian Economic Policies, generously funded by the John Templeton Foundation. Since it began on October 1, 2009, the program has undertaken a series of research projects. We plan to bring out several volumes based on the research undertaken by this program and to include other studies relevant to assessing Indian economic policies and proposals. We thank the John Templeton Foundation for supporting the Columbia Program and Oxford University Press, especially Terry Vaughn and Catherine Rae, for making this series possible.

Jagdish Bhagwati and Arvind Panagariya
Columbia University
September 2011

INDIA'S REFORMS: HOW THEY PRODUCED INCLUSIVE GROWTH

Edited by

Jagdish Bhagwati

AND

Arvind Panagariya

OXFORD
UNIVERSITY PRESS

OXFORD
UNIVERSITY PRESS

Oxford University Press, Inc., publishes works that further
Oxford University's objective of excellence
in research, scholarship, and education.

Oxford New York
Auckland Cape Town Dar es Salaam Hong Kong Karachi
Kuala Lumpur Madrid Melbourne Mexico City Nairobi
New Delhi Shanghai Taipei Toronto

With offices in
Argentina Austria Brazil Chile Czech Republic France Greece
Guatemala Hungary Italy Japan Poland Portugal Singapore
South Korea Switzerland Thailand Turkey Ukraine Vietnam

Published by Oxford University Press, Inc.
198 Madison Avenue, New York, New York 10016

www.oup.com

Oxford is a registered trademark of Oxford University Press

Library of Congress Cataloging-in-Publication Data
India's Reforms : How they Produced Inclusive Growth/ edited by Jagdish Bhagwati, Arvind Panagariya.
p. cm.
Includes bibliographical references and index.
ISBN 978-0-19-991518-7 (cloth : alk. paper) 1. Poverty—India.
2. Equality—India. 3. India—Commercial policy.
4. India—Economic conditions. 5. India—Social conditions.
6. India—Politics and government. I. Bhagwati, Jagdish N., 1934– II. Panagariya, Arvind.
HC440.P6I5323 2012
330.954—dc23 2011040814

9 8 7 6 5 4 3 2 1

Printed in the United States of America
on acid-free paper

CONTENTS

PART TWO
TRADE, POVERTY, AND INEQUALITY

PREFACE

This volume constitutes the first crop of research from the Columbia Program on Indian Economic Policies, housed in the School of International and Public Affairs (SIPA) and the Institute for Social and Economic Research and Policy (ISERP). It contains six original essays on issues related to poverty, inequality, and democracy in India and how they have interacted with the recent economic reforms, especially with trade openness.

Initially some scholars, such as Bradford DeLong of University of California, Berkeley and Dani Rodrik of Harvard University, had argued that the systematic reforms that began in 1991 had contributed little to growth in India, since growth acceleration had already begun in the 1980s. But the jump in the growth rate to the 8 to 9 percent range in the 2000s from below 6 percent in the 1980s; the success of such sectors as telecommunications, airlines, and automobiles; the tripling of the trade-to-GDP ratio since 1991; and the gigantic expansion of foreign investment, all of which can be directly linked to the reforms, have laid that debate to rest.

The debate has therefore shifted to whether reforms have helped the poor and the socially disadvantaged, whether people themselves feel that their lot has improved, and whether voter behavior has begun to respond to the changed prospects for a better future. The essays in this volume address these issues using extensive empirical evidence. The introduction provides a summary of the contributions.

The essays in the volume have benefited greatly from presentations at two major conferences that the Columbia Program organized. The first one was held at Columbia University in New York on November 4–6, 2010, and the second one under the joint auspices of Columbia University and the National Council on Applied Economic Research (NCAER) in New Delhi on March 31–April 1, 2011. We are most grateful to Dr. Rajesh Chadha, Senior Fellow, NCAER, who collaborated with us for the second conference and oversaw its superb execution. Thanks also go to Dr. Shashanka Bhide, NCAER's Acting Director General at that time, for facilitating the event.

We were lucky to have leading scholars, policymakers, and journalists at both conferences. We take this opportunity to thank Shankar Acharya, former Chief Economic Advisor, Government of India; Jay Panda, Member of the Lok Sabha; and Y. V. Reddy, former Governor of the Reserve Bank of India, for undertaking the long journey from New Delhi to New York and offering their thoughtful commentaries at the first conference. At the Delhi conference, we were privileged to have the participation of Sunil Jain, Opinion Editor, *Financial Express*; Bimal Jalan, former Governor of the Reserve Bank of India and Member of the Rajaya Sabha; Vijay Kelkar, Chairman of the Twelfth Finance Commission; Pradeep Mehta, Secretary General of CUTS; Rakesh Mohan, Professor at Yale University; Nandan Nilekani, Chairman of the Unique Identification Authority of India; T. N. Ninan, Chairman of the Business Standard Ltd.; Jay Panda, Member of the Lok Sabha; Sharad Raghavan, Reporter, *Financial Express*; Govinda Rao, Director of the National Institute of Public Finance and Policy; and N. K. Singh, Member of the Rajya Sabha.

We also thank the discussants of these essays in New York and New Delhi, including Surjit Bahlla, Oxus Investments; Pradeep Chhibber, University of California, Berkeley; Rana Hasan, Asian Development Bank; Amartya Lahiri, University of British Columbia; K. Sundaram, Delhi School of Economics; and Ashutosh Varshney, Brown University. We note with regret that Professor Suresh D. Tendulkar, who also offered his excellent comments at the Delhi conference, passed away on June 21, 2011. We shall miss him.

Jagdish Bhagwati and Arvind Panagariya
Columbia University

CONTRIBUTORS

Jagdish Bhagwati, University Professor at Columbia University, New York, NY

J. Cain, Graduate Student, University of Missouri, Columbia, MO

Poonam Gupta, Reserve Bank of India Professor, National Institute of Public Finance and Policy, New Delhi

Rana Hasan, Principal Economist, India Resident Mission, Asian Development Bank, New Delhi

Pravin Krishna, Chung Ju Professor of International Economics and Professor of Economics, Johns Hopkins University, Washington, DC

Devashish Mitra, Professor of Economics and Gerald B. and Daphna Cramer Professor of Global Affairs, Syracuse University, Syracuse, NY

Megha Mukim, PhD Candidate, London School of Economics, London and Visiting Scholar, Columbia University, New York, NY

Arvind Panagariya, Professor of Economics and Jagdish Bhagwati Professor of Indian Political Economy, Columbia University, New York, NY

Guru Sethupathy, Assistant Professor of International Economics, Johns Hopkins University, Washington, DC

Alfred Stepan, Wallace S. Sayre Professor of Government, Columbia University, New York, NY

INDIA'S REFORMS

Chapter 1

Introduction
Trade, Poverty, Inequality, and Democracy

JAGDISH BHAGWATI AND ARVIND PANAGARIYA

The Indian economy grew at the impressive annual average rate of 8.5 percent during the eight-year period from 2003–4 to 2010–11.[1] This miracle-level performance of the economy has come on the heels of slower but accelerating growth.

India became independent in 1947 and launched its development program in 1951 with its First Five Year Plan (1951–56). Although the country was quickly able to break out of the British-era stagnation, growth remained slow during the first three decades following the launch of the development program. During these decades, India adopted and nurtured the elements of a liberal democracy: a parliamentary democracy, an efficient bureaucracy, an independent judiciary, a free press, and a civil society (constituted by a growing number of nongovernmental organizations [NGOs]).

But these political triumphs were offset by India's dismal economic record, not merely in its growth rate but also in its objective of reducing India's appalling poverty, which every leader during the fight for Independence had highlighted as India's foremost challenge. It is now widely agreed, after extensive analyses, that this failure was caused by the command-and-control economic-policy regime, reinforced by a highly inward-looking trade policy, which India adopted and intensified starting in the late 1950s. In accord with the predictions of the analysts who had correctly diagnosed the failings of India's economic policy framework, India failed to deliver sufficiently rapid growth to make a dent on poverty: the trend poverty rate during these three decades remained stubbornly unchanged.

An ad hoc and piecemeal process of liberalization began in the second half of the 1970s and continued through the 1980s, with some acceleration in the second half of the 1980s. This liberalization, combined with an expansionary fiscal policy, led to some acceleration in growth, especially toward the end of the 1980s (Table 1.1). But the external debt, incurred to finance the fiscal expansion, and limited export earnings due to a relatively inward-looking trade regime culminated in a balance of payments crisis in 1991. The GDP growth plummeted to 1.4 percent in 1991–92.

Table 1.1 GROWTH IN THE GROSS DOMESTIC PRODUCT (GDP) AT FACTOR COST

Period	*Annual Growth Rate*
1951–52 to 1980–81	3.6
1981–82 to 1987–88	4.6
1988–89 to 1990–91	7.2
1991–92 (crisis)	1.4
1992–93 to 2002–3	5.8
2003–4 to 2010–11	8.5

Source: Calculations by Arvind Panagariya using the CSO data.

The Congress government that came to the helm under the leadership of Prime Minister Narasimha Rao in 1991 quickly responded to the crisis, which required immediate attention. Toward that end, it launched important systematic and systemic reforms that addressed both the immediate crisis and fundamental flaws in the policy framework, which had handicapped India's economic performance. The government substantially ended the investment and import licensing, opened the economy to foreign investment, and launched the process of fiscal consolidation.

While some critics on the left have contended that the reforms were imposed by the United States and the Bretton Woods institutions, which extended funds to tide over the payments crisis forthwith, it is entirely wrong to assume that these reforms had not long been seen as desirable within India itself if India was to begin delivering on its promise of superior economic performance. This is evident from the fact that, while the crisis was essentially over in less than two years, the government did not revert to the old ways but instead pushed ahead with financial sector reforms, entry of private players in the telecom and airline industries, divestment from public sector enterprises, and tariff liberalization.

Though the growth rate had plummeted to just 1.4 percent during the crisis year of 1991–92, the reforms quickly returned the economy to the higher growth path and helped sustain a growth rate of 5.8 percent between 1992–93 and 2002–3.

The final push to India's growth came from reforms under the Bhartiya Janata Party (BJP)-led government of Prime Minister Atal Bihari Vajpayee, which deepened and widened the reform process. It completed the telecom reform, which helped unleash explosive growth in telecommunications: the number of phones per 100 individuals rose from just three at the end of March 1999 to sixty-one at the end of September 2010. The government deregulated almost all interest rates, made large cuts in import tariffs on industrial goods, opened trade in services through liberalization of foreign investment, embarked upon a program of genuine privatization, and introduced major reforms in areas of indirect taxation, electricity, banking, and infrastructure. As we have noted, these reforms delivered on their promise: there has been substantial acceleration in India's growth rate since 1980, and more than 200 million individuals have been lifted out of abject poverty, whereas the pre-reforms period had seen both dismal growth and abysmal reduction of poverty.

Despite this dramatic turnaround in the economic performance and the fortunes of the poor, economic reforms in India have met with skepticism, even hostility, from a few determined economists, mostly from the populist left. They have questioned the wisdom of the policy changes every step of the way. Let us consider and refute each of their objections.

They initially argued that the shift in growth was not impressive when compared with that in the 1950s (Nayyar 2006). When this argument could not be maintained with plausibility, the opponents shifted ground and began to argue that the reforms had little to do with the accelerated growth (DeLong 2003; Rodrik 2003; Rodrik and Subramanian 2005; Kohli 2006). Neither of these lines of attack on the reforms can survive scrutiny; Arvind Panagariya (2008, pp. 16–21) has systematically dissected these criticisms and decisively laid them and associated concerns to rest.

A brief recapitulation of this refutation of both arguments is useful.

First, now that the economy has decisively shifted to 8–9 percent growth on a long-sustained path, the argument that the acceleration is unimpressive relative to the 1950s shift in the growth rate loses its salience.

Second, the link between reforms and the explosive growth seen in many sectors is too tight to deny credibly. Can one imagine that the telecom revolution would have happened without the mega-reforms instituted first under the Rao government and then under the Vajpayee government? Or that air travel could have progressed so far in terms of both quality and quantity without the grant of free entry to private carriers? Or that the annual production of automobiles could have risen from just 180,000 in 1990–91 to 2 million in 2009–10, and that of two-wheelers could have grown from 1.8 million to 10.5 million over the same period, without import and investment delicensing and without opening to foreign investment? Or that banking services could have become as widespread and customer friendly as they are today without freer entry of private domestic and foreign banks? In a similar vein, the argument that the exports of goods and services and foreign investment could have expanded as much as they have without external trade and investment liberalization is *prima facie* implausible.

Having lost both arguments, therefore, most skeptics, who cannot reconcile themselves to their loss of credibility and their face, have shifted ground again. Thus, they no longer insist that growth has not accelerated and that the acceleration, if any, has little to do with the reforms. Instead they have shifted to issues of poverty, inequality, and voter response. They argue that although reforms have helped generate growth, they have not helped the poor in general and the socially disadvantaged groups in particular (Mehta et al. 2011). They say that the vast majority of Indians, especially among the socially disadvantaged and marginalized groups, have failed to see their fortunes improve even as the economy has grown faster. Even if overall poverty may have declined, the impact of openness has been to increase it (Topalova 2007, 2010). The critics also routinely blame trade openness for increasing inequality.

The present volume is devoted to a systematic examination of these and related critiques, using the available data and analysis. The investigation proceeds along three broad lines.

First, it focuses on how individuals themselves view the reforms or their outcomes both in their direct responses when surveyed and indirectly through votes in favor of performing versus nonperforming incumbents. Second, we use the National Sample Survey (NSS) data to measure poverty among various social groups over time and to see whether the assertions that poverty has continued to rise among the socially disadvantaged groups—the Scheduled Castes and Scheduled Tribes—are grounded in empirical reality. Finally, we also investigate whether openness has indeed been detrimental to the fortunes of the poor and whether it has led to increased inequality.

The eminent Columbia University political scientist Alfred Stepan analyzes the subjective responses of individuals when asked how their conditions have changed and how they see the future without necessarily connecting them to the policies. His findings unequivocally show that a rising proportion of the people say their fortunes are improving, while a declining proportion say the opposite. This trend carries over to their expectations for the future economic prospects. In their contribution, Poonam Gupta and Arvind Panagariya assess how these perceptions are feeding into electoral process. They find that voters today pay much greater attention to the economic outcomes that the ruling party in the state delivers than they did in the past. The voters reward chief ministers who deliver superior economic outcomes and punish those responsible for the inferior ones.

The remaining chapters in the volume assess the impact of trade openness on poverty and inequality in the general population as well as in specific social groups. Jewel Cain, Rana Hasan, and Devashish Mitra study the effect that increased openness has had on poverty. They argue that openness lowers poverty by increasing employment in the export industries, which tend to be labor-intensive in the labor-abundant economies, and by stimulating growth. Their econometric analysis broadly confirms this conjecture. In particular, they find no evidence whatsoever in favor of the oft-repeated claim that increased openness increases poverty. Megha Mukim and Panagariya assess the assertions that despite rising incomes in general, poverty among the disadvantaged social groups—the Scheduled Castes (SC) and Scheduled Tribes (ST)—has increased and that openness is detrimental to the economic fortunes of these social groups. They squarely reject both these claims and show that openness has in fact been beneficial to the SC. Finally, Pravin Krishna and Guru Sethupathy study the trend in inequality and fail to find in it either a perceptible increase or a detectable decrease. They also reject the hypothesis that openness by itself has led to increased inequality.

In chapter 2, Stepan, who has worked intensively on election data both in India and worldwide, analyzes voluminous cross-section data from the National Election Studies (NES) and the State of the Nation Surveys coordinated by the Center for the Study of Developing Societies over six national elections between 1971 and 2009. He focuses on issues relating to evolving economic fortunes, support for democracy, and political participation among different groups in India. He concentrates on seven marginalized groups: Scheduled Caste, Scheduled Tribe, Muslim, very poor, poor, illiterate, and female.

The NES asks respondents questions about their household financial well-being in the previous five years and about their financial expectations for the next five years. Consistent with the rising rates of growth over the years as described above, Stepan finds that nationally the ratio of those saying their financial situation has improved to those saying it has worsened rose from 1.3 in 1996 to 1.5 in 2004 and 4.2 in 2009. The percentage of those saying their situation has worsened dropped from 19 percent in 1996 to 11 percent in 2009.

Stepan also examines the responses of the marginalized groups to this question. Here the data for the 2009 elections are not yet available, so Stepan compares the responses of the marginalized groups to the national average in the year 2004. He finds that the "poor," "Scheduled Tribe," and "female" respondents are within 3 percentage points of the national average of the percentage stating that their fortunes have improved in the last five years. The results are less encouraging for "Muslim" and "very poor" respondents, who were 8 percentage points below the national average. This broad pattern carries over to the question about whether respondents expect their fortunes to improve over the next five years.

Stepan also finds that the support for democracy is stronger in India than in most other countries of the world and that it cuts across all religious lines. The percentage of those having a "preference for democracy as opposed to any other system" is very high among all four of the religious groups in India: Hindus, Muslims, Sikhs, and Christians. Dropping the "don't know" responses from the sample, the percentage of respondents expressing a preference for democracy in 2004 was 88 among Hindus, 87 among Muslims, 88 among Sikhs, and 91 among Christians.

Coming from a different angle in chapter 3, Gupta and Panagariya ask whether voters are reacting to the rural-urban divide by voting out governments sympathetic to reforms, as argued by critics such as Salman Rushdie (2004), or responding to prospects of rapid improvements in their economic fortunes by returning the governments that deliver superior economic outcomes while voting out those failing to deliver, as suggested by Jagdish Bhagwati and Panagariya (2004) and elaborated by Panagariya (2009). To inform this debate, Gupta and Panagariya offer an in-depth analysis of the 2009 election.

The authors first offer detailed data showing that the election results do not reflect the rural-urban divide predicted by the reform critics. Parties that win in the rural constituencies of a state also win in the urban constituencies of the same state. The authors then proceed to assess whether economic performance as captured by growth plays a major role in determining the election outcomes. They hypothesize that since voters rarely come in contact with central government officials and see the state- or lower-level officials as crucial to determining their fortunes, any influence of growth on voter behavior will correlate with state-level measures of growth. Therefore, they divide the states into high-, medium-, and low-growth categories. They then ask how the candidates of the incumbent parties performed in the 2009 parliamentary elections in the three categories of states. Remarkably, they find that incumbent parties in the high-growth states won 85 percent of the seats they contested, while in the medium- and low-growth states the incumbent parties won 52 and 40 percent of the seats contested. In a separate, more technical article, these authors show that this relationship between growth performance and election outcomes survives every model they test econometrically.

A popular theme among reform critics is that openness is harmful to the interests of the poor. In the first serious study on this subject in the Indian context, Patia Topalova (2007) tested whether openness had indeed adversely impacted poverty. Using the NSS survey data, she studied the impact of openness on the incidence of poverty at the district level separately in rural and urban India. She measured openness by employment-weighted average of tariffs, assigning zero tariffs to exportable and nontraded sectors and positive tariffs to sectors producing importables. She found that increased openness led to increased incidence of poverty in the rural districts but had no statistically significant effect in the urban districts. She found no evidence in either rural or urban India that openness helped poverty alleviation.

Because it is contrary to economic logic—insofar as openness stimulates growth in general and the expansion of labor-intensive industries in labor-abundant countries in particular, it should reduce rather than increase poverty—these were intriguing results. Therefore, Hasan, Mitra, and Beyza Ural (2006–7) revisited this question in a follow-up article. They began by noting that the study of this issue at the district level posed several problems. For example, the data from the 1993–94 NSS survey do not readily allow the identification of urban districts. District boundaries also shift over time. There are also questions of randomness of the sample at the district level. Finally, sometimes the number of observations in a district is insufficiently large to yield a tight estimate of poverty.

Therefore, Hasan, Mitra, and Ural chose to study the question at the level of the state and NSS-identified regions within states. Because there are one or more regions within a state, regions are larger in number than states and therefore allow larger degrees of freedom. As such, they offer a good compromise between districts and states: they allow tighter estimation of poverty than districts do, and they allow tighter estimation of regression equations than states do.

These authors also noted that assigning zero tariffs to nontraded sectors in measuring openness, as done by Topalova, is erroneous. Many goods and services may be nontraded precisely because the barriers to trade are prohibitive. Hasan, Mitra, and Ural define openness at the state and regional levels as an employment-weighted sum of tariffs such that only exportable products are assigned zero tariffs, with nontraded sectors entirely excluded from the calculation. These authors also take into account nontariff barriers, which Topalova ignored.

In sharp contrast to Topalova (2007), Hasan, Mitra, and Ural fail to encounter a single case in which reductions in trade protection worsen poverty at the state or regional level. Instead, they find that states with greater exposure to foreign competition to have lower rural, urban, and overall poverty rates and that this beneficial effect is more pronounced in states that have more flexible labor market institutions. The authors also find that trade liberalization led to greater poverty reduction in states with greater exposure to foreign competition. The results hold for overall, urban, and rural poverty, with varying strengths and statistical significance.

In chapter 4, Jewel Cain, Hasan, and Mitra revisit the analysis in Hasan, Mitra, and Ural, using data from a more recent round of the sample survey conducted in 2004–5. They find that every percentage point reduction in the weighted tariff rate led to an average .57 percent reduction in the poverty ratio. This implies that of the overall reduction in poverty during 1987–2004, 38 percent can be attributed to change in the exposure to foreign trade. Since the authors control for time-fixed effects and poverty has declined over time, they are able to infer that the greater exposure of the labor force to foreign competition speeded up poverty reduction. The magnitude of impact and its statistical significance vary across rural, urban, and the two regions taken together, and across tariff and non-tariff measures used, but in no case do the authors find increased openness to result in increased poverty.

Chapter 4 analyzes poverty by aggregating over all social groups. Critics argue, however, that even as poverty has fallen in aggregate, it has risen among the socially disadvantaged groups. For example, in a January 14, 2011, submission to the House of Commons of the UK Parliament, the National Campaign on Dalit Human Rights noted, "In spite of high economic growth rate the poverty rate among excluded communities in India has increased, coupled with the insecurity of livelihoods."[2] In a similar vein, journalist Praful Badawi wrote in the *Financial Chronicle* dated December 29, 2010, "Rising inequalities highlight what is wrong with India's growth trajectory, driven as it is by elite consumption and sectoral imbalances, which exclude disadvantaged groups from the benefit of rising GDP, while aggravating income disparities."

Motivated by these criticisms, Mukim and Panagariya distinguish among the SC, ST, and Nonscheduled (NS) castes and study the evolution of poverty within each group over the four thick National Sample Surveys conducted in 1983, 1987–88, 1993–94, and 2004–5. Contrary to the above assertions, they find that poverty ratio actually fell for every single group between every two successive surveys.

During the twenty-one years covered by the study, poverty declined by twenty percentage points for the SC and eighteen percentage points for both the ST and the NS. The authors also study the pattern of poverty at the state level. They find that in every one of the ten largest states according to the SC population, SC poverty fell by at least ten percentage points between 1983 and 2004–5. Each of these states experienced a decline in poverty between 1993–94 and 2004–5. Poverty also declined significantly among the ST in every one of the ten largest states by the ST population between 1983 and 2004–5. Thus, the assertion that the recent high-growth period has seen poverty rise among the socially disadvantaged groups finds no support in the data.

Mukim and Panagariya also study the relationship between poverty and per capita income, on the one hand, and poverty and openness, on the other, for individual social groups. They find no evidence whatsoever to support the hypothesis that rising incomes or openness has adversely impacted poverty within any one of the groups. As in chapter 4, they find that one or more measures of openness have had a statistically significant and favorable impact on poverty levels in the SC and NS in rural and urban regions and both regions taken together. Regarding the ST, they find statistically significant effect of openness on poverty in urban areas only.

In chapter 6, Krishna and Sethupathy take up the relationship between openness and inequality. For the first time, they measure inequality in India using the Theil index. This index allows them to distinguish between within-group and between-group inequality levels. Using the expenditure data from surveys conducted in 1987–88, 1993–94, 1999–2000, and 2004–5, they show that inequality between states and between urban and rural areas is dwarfed by the inequality across households within these aggregates. The within-group inequality accounts for well over 80 percent of overall inequality and persists in this magnitude throughout the period of this study.

According to Krishna and Sethupathy, the overall inequality shows only modest variation over the period, rising slightly between 1987–88 and 1993–94 and again between 1993–94 and 1999–2000, but falling by 2004–5 to roughly the 1987–88 level. The authors also find that inequality fell in most states and within rural and urban areas in most states between 1987–88 and 2004–5. Finally, they find no correlation between the change in inequality across households within states and the change in state-level measures of tariff and non-tariff protection.

The research in this volume thus shows that, contrary to popular assertions, reforms and the economic growth they spawned have helped address various social groups' concerns about poverty, inequality, and the well-being of the disadvantaged. The lesson, therefore, is that the conventional or Stage 1 reforms in the terminology introduced by Bhagwati (2010), begun in earnest in the early 1990s postcrisis, have been beneficial not just in terms of overall economic prosperity but also, for the most part, to the poor and the disadvantaged. This fairly remarkable assessment is based on scholarly examination of the empirical data and overturns the prevailing presuppositions against the reforms.

The increased revenues accompanying higher incomes made possible by Stage 1 reforms have now opened up the possibility of what Bhagwati calls Stage 2 reforms, for these revenues finally mean that we can spend more on better provision of education and health. But essential to such programs is the reform of delivery mechanisms. Simply spending more on the government provision of education and health, as suggested by many, is going to be far from sufficient to accomplish these goals. Instead, we must pay attention to the details of social engineering involved in the delivery of high-quality health and education to the masses. This is one of the subjects subsequent volumes in this series will attempt to address.

NOTES

1. Indian data are usually reported according to its fiscal year, which begins on April 1 and ends on March 31. For example, "2003–4" refers to the period from April 1, 2003, to March 31, 2004.
2. The submission is available online at http://www.publications.parliament.uk/pa/cm201011/cmselect/cmintdev/writev/616/m8.htm (accessed March 25, 2011).

REFERENCES

Bhagwati, Jagdish (2010). "The 3rd Professor Hiren Mukerjee Memorial Annual Parliamentary Lecture." Lecture delivered to a joint session of the Indian Parliament on December 2, 2010. Available at http://www.columbia.edu/~jb38/papers/pdf/Lok-Sabha-speech-FINAL-EXPANDED-Deceber-14.pdf (accessed November 24, 2011)

Bhagwati, J., and A. Panagariya (2004). "Great Expectations." *Wall Street Journal*, May 24.

DeLong, J. Bradford (2003). "India since Independence: An Analytic Growth Narrative." In Dani Rodrik (ed.), *In Search of Prosperity: Analytic Narratives of Economic Growth*. Princeton, NJ: Princeton University Press, 183–204.

Hasan, Rana, Devashish Mitra, and Beyza P. Ural (2006–7). "Trade Liberalization, Labor Market Institutions, and Poverty Reduction: Evidence from Indian States." *India Policy Forum, 2006–7*.

Kohli, A. (2006). "Politics of Economic Growth in India, 1980–2005 I." *Economic and Political Weekly* 41(13), April 1–7, 1251–59.

Mehta, A. K., A. Shephard, S. Bhide, A. Shah, and A. Kumar (2011). *Chronic Poverty Report*. New Delhi: Indian Institute of Public Administration.

Nayyar, D. (2006). "Economic Growth in Independent India: Lumbering Elephant or Running Tiger?" *Economic and Political Weekly* 41(15), April 15–21, 1451–58.

Panagariya, Arvind (2008). *India: The Emerging Giant*. New York: Oxford University Press.

——— (2009). "Is Anti-incumbency Really Passé?" *Economic Times*, May 28.

Rodrik, Dani (2003). "Institutions, Integration, and Geography: In Search of the Deep Determinants of Economic Growth." In Dani Rodrik (ed.), *In Search of Prosperity: Analytic Narratives of Economic Growth*. Princeton, NJ: Princeton University Press, 1–19.

Rodrik, Dani, and Arvind Subramanian (2005). "From 'Hindu Growth' to Productivity Surge: The Mystery of the Indian Growth Transition." *IMF Staff Papers* 52/2, 193–228.

Rushdie, Salman (2004). "India's New Era." *Washington Post*, May 14, http://www.washingtonpost.com/wp-dyn/articles/A25770-2004May13.html.

Topalova, Petia (2007). "Trade Liberalization, Poverty and Inequality: Evidence from Indian Districts." In Ann Harrison (ed.), *Globalization and Poverty*. Chicago: University of Chicago Press, 291–336.

——— (2010). "Factor Immobility and Regional Impacts of Trade Liberalization: Evidence on Poverty from India." *American Economic Journal: Applied Economics* 2(4), 1–41.

PART ONE

REFORMS AND DEMOCRACY

Chapter 2

Views from the Indian Electorate
Satisfactions and Dissatisfactions with Democracy, Politics, and the Economy

ALFRED STEPAN

In this chapter I present findings from chapters 2 and 3 of the book by Alfred Stepan, Juan J. Linz, and Yogendra Yadav titled *Crafting State-Nations: India and Other Multinational Democracies.* The results presented here are largely drawn from responses to the National Election Studies (NES) and the State of the Nation Surveys coordinated by the Center for the Study of Developing Societies (CSDS), India, over six national elections between 1971 and 2009.[1] We focus on questions as they pertain to support for democracy, political efficacy, and political participation in India. In particular, I focus on the responses of the seven most marginalized groups in the country based on their caste, religious, economic, and gender status. These groups are Scheduled Caste, Scheduled Tribe, Muslim, Very Poor, Poor, Illiterate, and Female respondents.

The first section of the chapter outlines the details of CSDS surveys: how they were conducted and how they compare to alternative national surveys in India and elsewhere. Subsequent sections delve into why India makes a critical case for the "state-nation" model in our book and the results of the surveys. In the final section of the chapter I present results from questions on the Indian economy and discuss how economic change has affected people's perception of their well-being.

ABOUT OUR DATA AND THE INDIAN CASE

Surveys by CSDS are distinctive for their large cross-section samples of Indian voters and are based on demographic information provided by the Census of India and electoral information provided by the Election Commission of India. The surveys are designed by employing multistage stratified random sampling techniques with the unit of analysis beginning with the state and then randomization being employed at the national, state, polling booth, and individual voter levels (using electoral rolls provided by the Election Commission). At every level efforts are made to ensure representation of social, cultural, and political groups in the country. The final surveys are conducted face to face using a structured questionnaire and in the local dialect. Consequently, these surveys are some of the most ambitious surveys ever undertaken on any single national polity. For example, the American National Election Studies (ANES) had 1,807 respondents for the US election survey of the 2000 presidential elections. By contrast, the National Elections Studies of 2004 in India had 27,189 respondents and was conducted in twenty-two Indian languages. In comparison, the World Values Survey (WVS) of India conducted in 2006 had 2,000 respondents and was administered in only ten major Indian languages.[2] Compared to the 172 Muslim, 370 Scheduled Caste, 186 Scheduled Tribe, and 610 illiterate respondents surveyed by the WVS, the NES 2004 sampled 3,254 Muslim, 4,319 Scheduled Caste, 4,274 Scheduled Tribe, and 8,416 illiterate voters. These large size differences mean we can do more statistically with the responses at a disaggregated level.

India's democracy is of particular interest to contemporary social scientists because it has developed in the context of *deep diversity*. One of the greatest points of conflict in multicultural and multinational societies, federal or not, is language. In India, at Independence, ten different languages were spoken by at least 13 million to 33 million people, many of them with mutually unintelligible alphabets. In descending order of number of speakers (excluding Hindi), Telugu, Bengali, Marathi, Tamil, Urdu, Gujarati, Kannada, Malayalam, and Oriya were all spoken by between 32 to 13 million inhabitants of India.[3] In addition, another seventeen languages were spoken by at least 1 million people.[4] The largest language, Hindi, according to the 1961 census of India, was only spoken by 30.37 percent of the total population. This proportion has gradually risen to 41.03 percent in the 2001 census but is still short of anything like a majority.[5] What would John Stuart Mill have said in 1947 about India's chances of building a democracy under such conditions?[6] How has this "Millsian" problem been managed democratically?

Indian society has large communities of almost every major world religion—Hindu, Islamic, Buddhist, Sikh, and Christian. Even after Partition in 1947, India had a large Islamic population. In 2009, India's Muslim population constituted a "minority" of approximately 161 million people, which made it the world's third largest Islamic population in any country in the world, exceeded only by Indonesia's 203 million and Pakistan's 174 million.[7]

Conceptually and comparatively India's poverty also raises important intellectual challenges, especially for those who might think that democratic norms are a luxury of wealthy countries. Of course, India would be significant on grounds of population alone. With its population of slightly over 1.1 billion, it is almost *four times* more populous than any other democracy in the world.[8] The next most populous democracy is the United States, which has a population of 300 million. The combined population in 2006 of the only other long-standing multinational federal democracies—Spain, Canada, and Belgium—was less than 85 million, which is less than half the population of Uttar Pradesh, the most populous of India's twenty-eight states.

Stepan, Linz, and Yadav (2011) argue that given its extraordinary diversity, India cannot create a nineteenth-century French-style democratic "nation-state" with one official language and one curriculum throughout the country in the foreseeable future. Nevertheless, we believe that India has already managed to create what we call a democratic "state-nation." The difference between a "nation-state" and a "state-nation" is depicted in Table 2.1.

In our book, we argue that as a diverse polity approximates the state-nation ideal type, we expect it to have the following four empirically verifiable patterns. First, despite multiple cultural identities among the citizens of the polity, there will be at the same time a high degree of *positive identification* with the state, and pride in being citizens of that state. Second, citizens of the state will have *multiple but complementary* political identities and loyalties. Third, there will be a high degree of *institutional trust* in the most important constitutional, legal, and administrative components of the state. Fourth, by world democratic standards, there will be a comparatively high degree of positive *support for democracy* among all the diverse groups of citizens in the country, for the specific statewide democratic institutions through which the multicultural and possibly multinational polity is governed.

To be sure, these patterns do not simply exist right from the beginning. It is all about crafting and is very much an outcome of deliberate policies and designs. On theoretical and empirical grounds we make the case in the book (but do not have space in this chapter to develop here) that there can be a nested set of seven state-nation

Table 2.1 TWO IDEAL TYPES OF DEMOCRATIC STATES: "NATION-STATE" AND "STATE-NATION"

	Nation-State	*State-Nation*
	PREEXISTING CONDITIONS	
Sense of belonging / "we-feeling"	Awareness of, and attachment to, one major cultural civilizational tradition. With minor exceptions, this cultural identity corresponds to existing state boundaries.	Awareness of, and attachment to, more than one cultural civilizational tradition within the existing boundaries. However, these attachments do not preclude identification with a common state.
	STATE POLICY	
Cultural policies	Homogenizing attempts to foster one core cultural identity, particularly one official language; nonrecognition of multiplicity of cultures. Unity in oneness.	Recognition and support of more than one cultural identity (particularly recognition of more than one official language), even more than one cultural nation, all within a frame of some common politywide symbols. Unity in diversity.

(*continued*)

Table 2.1 (*continued*)

	Nation-State	*State-Nation*
	INSTITUTIONS	
Territorial division of power	Unitary states or symmetrical federations	Federal system. Often de jure or de facto asymmetrical. Can even be a unitary state if aggressive nation-state policies are not pursued and de facto state multilingual areas are accepted. Federacies possible.
	POLITICS	
Ethnocultural or territorial cleavages	Not very salient	Salient and recognized and democratically managed
Autonomist and/or secessionist parties	Autonomist parties are normally not "coalitionable." Secessionist parties are outlawed or marginalized in democratic electoral politics.	Autonomist parties can govern in federal units and are "coalitionable" at the center. Nonviolent secessionist parties can sometimes participate in the democratic political process.

(*continued*)

Table 2.1 (*continued*)

	Nation-State	*State-Nation*
	CITIZEN ORIENTATION	
Political identity	Single identity as citizens of the state and overwhelmingly as members of the same cultural nation	Multiple but complementary identities
Obedience/loyalty	Obedience to the state and loyalty to the nation	Obedience to the state and identification with institutions, neither based on a single national identity

policies that reinforce each other and help facilitate the emergence and persistence of a state nation. These seven state-nation policies are:

1. An asymmetrical, "holding together" federal state, but *not* a symmetrical, "coming together" federal state, or a unitary state
2. Individual rights *and* collective recognition
3. Parliamentary *instead of* presidential or semi-presidential systems
4. Politywide *and* "centric-regional" parties and careers
5. Politically integrated but *not* culturally assimilated populations
6. Cultural nationalists in power mobilizing *against* secessionist nationalists
7. A pattern of complementary *but* multiple identities

Metaphorically, we say these policies are "nested" because the second policy, "group recognition," is normally nested within the first, federalism (especially asymmetrical federalism). The fourth policy, involving the coalitionability of what we call centric-regional parties, is greatly facilitated if the choice of the third policy is parliamentarianism because the executive is a sharable good, and successful achievement of the seventh policy, multiple but complementary identities, is heavily dependent on the prior success of the previous six policies. In chapters 4 and 5 in our book, we show how all of these policies were applied in Tamil Nadu, India, and helped turn potential separatist sentiments among Tamils into multiple but complementary identities and the potential issue of separatism in Tamil Nadu became a nonissue. In sharp contrast, when Sri Lanka attempted to impose nation-state policies on Sri Lanka's Tamils what had been a nonissue of separatism became a Cambodian killing field.

We are very aware of India's continuing problems with poverty and with low levels of literacy, nutrition, basic sanitation, Maoist-style violence (by the "Naxalites," so named after Naxalbari, the place where Maoist militancy was born in India), and violation of human rights and periodic communal riots. Table 2.2 makes some of these comparative problems abundantly clear. We also recognize that these facts are very relevant to an overall assessment of the quality of democratic governance in India and believe that policies and outcomes in these areas should be, and could be, substantially improved.

However, this essay and our book are not about democracy and its links to development per se but about whether India, despite its deep diversity, has been able to at least create the minimal degree of identification and trust in the state of India that a democracy requires. Obviously, the USSR or Yugoslavia were not able to do so. Let us see how India has fared in creating a sense of common identity among a population of so many different languages, religions, and culturally diverse regions.

Table 2.2 COMPARATIVE INDICATORS OF INDIA'S HUMAN AND INCOME POVERTY

Average GDP per capita in Purchasing Power Parity (PPP) in 2000 US dollars among Arend Lijphart's universe of the thirty-six continuous democracies of the world from at least 1977 to 1996	$20,252
India's GDP per capita in PPP in 2007 US dollars	$2,753
India's Human Development Index (HDI) ranking among the 173 countries of the world ranked by the United Nations Development Programme (UNDP)	134th out of 182
India's HDI ranking among Arend Lijphart's thirty-six continuous democracies	34th out of 36
India's Human Poverty Index (HPI-1) ranking among 135 ranked states	88th out of 135
Adult female literacy rate in India	54.50%
Percentage of underweight children in India at age five	46.00%
"Great poverty" level	
All India	22.70%
Muslims	31.00%
States with more than twenty deaths due to Naxalite violence in 2008	6 (18%)

Sources: UNDP, *Human Development Report 2009: Overcoming Barriers: Human Mobility and Development* (New York: Palgrave Macmillan, 2009), pp. 173, 177, and 181–84; Government of India, Prime Minister's High Level Committee, "Social, Economic, and Educational Status of the Muslim Community of India," Sachar Report, November 2006; and Arend Lijphart, *Patterns of Democracy: Government Forms and Performance in Thirty-Six Countries* (New Haven, CT: Yale University Press, 1999).

Table 4.1 shows Lijphart's universe of the thirty-six countries in the world, including India, that were continuous democracies in his judgment from at least 1977 to 1996. For information on Naxalite violence in India, see Ministry of Home Affairs, Government of India, Naxal Management Division, http://mha.nic.in/uniquepage.asp?ID_PK=540

PRIDE IN BEING INDIAN

One important indicator of identification of a citizen with the society and the state is the sense of pride, in this case the pride of being Indian. The pride question has been asked in the widely used comparative public opinion survey European and World Values Survey (World Values Survey, or WVS), under the direction of Ronald Inglehart et al., based at the University of Michigan. To date there are four rounds of these surveys available for our comparative analysis. India has been included in all four rounds.[9] The World Values Survey allows us to place these figures in a comparative perspective. Table 2.3 presents responses to the pride question across eleven long-standing democracies from the latest comparable wave of the World Values Survey. This wave of WVS (1999–2002, held in India in 2001) showed that only in the United States (71 percent) and Australia (70 percent) was the proportion of those who feel "very proud" marginally higher than in India (67 percent). When we look at Brazil, Spain, Austria, and Belgium, the proportion of respondents saying "not very" and "not at all" proud ranges from 8 percent to 22 percent, compared to 7 percent in India.

While it is important to understand the views of the citizenry as a whole, it is equally important to look at the views of any significant minority who may vary from this response. Therefore it is important to ask if the conclusion about the high level of national pride holds across the different sections of society. We thus need a disaggregated picture of national pride for some of the most salient marginal groups in India: Muslims (largest and most disadvantaged religious minority), Scheduled Castes or Dalits (the ex-untouchable community that has historically suffered social exclusion), Scheduled Tribes (forest-dwelling indigenous communities that have remained on the periphery of modern development), and nonliterates.

As Table 2.4 makes clear, Muslim respondents and Scheduled Caste respondents feel no different from the average national

Table 2.3 PRIDE IN NATIONALITY IN THE ELEVEN LONG-STANDING FEDERAL DEMOCRACIES (FIGURES IN %)

	Very Proud	*Quite*	*Not Very*	*Not at All*	*Don't Know / Not Applicable*	*Total*
USA	71	23	4	0	2	100
Australia	70	23	2	0	5	100
India	67	21	5	2	5	100
Canada	65	28	3	2	2	100
Argentina	65	24	4	3	5	100
Brazil	64	19	14	2	1	100
Spain	51	36	6	3	4	100
Austria	50	37	6	2	5	100
Belgium	20	46	15	7	11	100
Switzerland	23	47	16	7	7	100
Germany	15	46	22	7	9	100

Source: The data for all countries is from response to the question "How proud are you to be (nationality)?," in *Human Beliefs and Values: A Cross-Cultural Sourcebook Based on the 1999–2002 Values Survey*, ed. Ronald Inglehart et al. (Mexico City: Siglo XXI Editores, 2004).

response on this question. The respondents from Scheduled Tribes and those without any formal education do report lower levels of pride, possibly because a larger proportion among these groups fail to understand the question itself (this itself reflects the uneven dissemination of the idea of nationalism in modern India) and partly because their level of enthusiasm for Indian nationalism is indeed lower. Yet this lower level of enthusiasm does not lead to any significant

Table 2.4 PRIDE IN INDIA FOR ALL CITIZENS AND FOR MARGINAL GROUPS, 2005 (FIGURES IN %)

	All India	*Muslim*	*Scheduled Caste*	*Scheduled Tribe*	*Nonliterate*
Very proud / proud	89	88	85	81	78
Not proud	3	3	5	3	5
Don't know / No answer	8	9	10	15	17
Total	100	100	100	100	100
N	5,227	636	901	427	1,964

Source: State of Democracy in South Asia: A Report (Delhi: Oxford University Press, 2008).

rejection of the national identity: in none of these groups does the proportion of those who do not feel proud at all exceed 5 percent. Thus, notwithstanding the variations in the reception of and enthusiasm for the national identity, there is no noticeable rejection of the national identity in any minority group for which we have information.

SUPPORT FOR DEMOCRACY

In many countries survey respondents are asked to choose which of the following phrases they most agree with: "Democracy is preferable to any other form of government," "In some circumstances an authoritarian government can be preferable to a democratic government," and "For someone like me a democratic or nondemocratic regime makes no difference"; in addition, the surveys allow for no answers and "don't know." This question has been asked in India in two waves of the National Election Study held in 1998 and 2004 by CSDS.

Table 2.5 reports the findings of both these surveys with those of some other important counties that figure prominently in the democratization literature, such as Spain, Korea, Uruguay, Brazil, and Chile. The level of support for democracy in India varies from 60 percent in the 1999 survey to 70 percent in the 2004 survey. This is substantially higher than in ex-authoritarian regimes like Chile, Brazil, and Korea but clearly behind Spain and Uruguay. It might seem that the support for democracy is moderately high in India. But it is important to notice that those who do not fall in this category are not opposed to democracy. The proportion of Indians who support authoritarianism (6 percent and 4 percent in 1999 and 2004, respectively) or are indifferent to this choice (7 percent and 6 percent in 1999 and 2004, respectively) is very small, even when compared to Spain and Uruguay. The unusually large proportion of the "don't know" response (27 percent and 20 percent in 1999 and 2004, respectively), the highest recorded in any country for this question, accounts for the rest. As we have documented elsewhere, the "don't know" answer correlates highly with illiteracy.

Table 2.6 shows responses to this question by four major disadvantaged groups: Scheduled Castes, Scheduled Tribes, Poor, and Very Poor. The most striking thing about the data is that there is not a single exception to the norm of very high support for a democratic political system. In no group does support for democracy fall below the 60 percent level, and nowhere does support for authoritarianism reach double digits. At first sight some groups appear to deviate slightly from the national norm: the support for democracy among the Scheduled Castes, the Scheduled Tribes, and the Very Poor is about five to ten percentage points lower than the national average.

Table 2.5 ATTITUDES TOWARD DEMOCRACY AND AUTHORITARIANISM IN INDIA AND FIVE IMPORTANT "THIRD WAVE" DEMOCRACIES

	Uruguay	*Spain*	*India 1999*	*India 2004*	*Korea*	*Chile*	*Brazil*
Democracy is preferable to any other form of government (% of valid responses excluding "Don't know")	80 (85)	78 (83)	60 (83)	70 (88)	58 (62)	52 (54)	41 (48)
In some circumstances an authoritarian government can be preferable to a democratic government.	8	9	6	4	27	18	21
For someone like me, a democratic or a nondemocratic regime makes no difference	6	7	7	6	8	25	23
Don't know / No answer	6	6	27	20	7	4	15
N	–1,213	–1,000	–8,133	–27,148	–1,037	–1,200	–1,240

Source: The data for India are from the National Election Study, 1999 and 2004, of the Center for the Study of Developing Societies, Delhi. Data for Uruguay, Brazil, and Chile are from the Latino Barometer 1996, directed by Marta Lagos. The Spanish data are from the Eurobarometer 37 (1992). The Korean data is from the Korea Democracy Barometer, 2004, directed by Doh Chull Shin.

Table 2.6 SUPPORT FOR DEMOCRACY IN INDIA BY DISADVANTAGED SOCIAL GROUPS, NES 2004 (FIGURES IN %)

	All India	*Scheduled Caste*	*Scheduled Tribe*	*Poor*	*Very Poor*
Democracy is always preferable	70 (88)	65 (87)	61 (81)	71 (88)	61 (87)
Sometimes authoritarianism is preferable	4	3	5	4	3
No difference	6	6	8	6	6
Don't know / No answer	20	25	26	19	30
Total	100	100	100	100	100
N	27,145	4,967	2,356	9,409	8,117

Figures in parentheses in the first row are for percent of valid responses if the "Don't knows" are treated as missing data.
Source: National Election Study [India] 2004.

But much of this is a function of larger proportion of "don't know" answers among these groups, which is directly associated with lower levels of educational attainment. Once we control for "don't knows"—by examining the valid percentages after treating "don't know" as missing data—most of the apparent, even if minor, differences among various groups and states disappear.

The NES surveys have also been using a somewhat different question to tap the support of the need for elections in the Indian polity. The question they use is "Suppose there were no parties or assemblies and elections were not held, do you think that the government in this country could be run better?" Answers to this question are available for several points in the last four decades. This question is valuable for double-checking the conclusions drawn above: it has the advantage of measuring popular attitudes to democracy, without using the "D" word, and also of avoiding a lazy "yes" by requiring the supporters of democracy to disagree with the statement.

Table 2.7 shows the results of this question over time, and the trend shows that the support for one of the key democratic institutions, elections, has steadily increased. In a poll given before the last parliamentary elections held in 2004, as many as 91 percent of those who gave a valid response rejected the idea of government generated without parties, electorate, or assemblies (legislatures). These answers are obviously quite consistent with the commitment to democracy we have just noted: in both these questions, the proportion of antidemocrats is barely 10 percent of the citizenry.

Table 2.7 GROWING SUPPORT FOR DEMOCRATIC POLITICAL INSTITUTIONS IN INDIA, 1971, 1996, AND 2004

	NES 1971	*NES 1996*	*NES 2004*
"Do you think that the government in this country could be run better if there were no parties or assemblies and elections were not held?" (those who said no)	43 (74)	69 (86)	72 (91)
N	NA	9,614	27,189

Note: All figures of all respondents, in percentages. Figures in parentheses are for valid responses, if "Don't know" answers are treated as missing values. All the NES data are from the Centre for the Study of Developing Societies.

RELIGION AND DEMOCRACY

When we examine all of India's major religions, do we find comparable consensual support for democracy? Or is it an area of great dissensus and polarization, as the "clash of civilizations" literature would suggest? India has traditionally been a country with high levels of religious heterogeneity, coupled with high levels of religious practice and belief. According to the 2001 Government of India Census, India had approximately 805 million Hindus, 138 million Muslims (making it, after Indonesia and Pakistan, the third most populous Muslim country in the world), 2.3 million Christians (approximately 60 percent Catholic and 40 percent Protestant), 800,000 Buddhists, 400,000 Jains, 600,000 "other religions," and only 100,000 people who did not state a religion.[10] India also has some of the highest levels of religious belief and practice in the world; 93 percent of the population describe themselves as believing in God, 87 percent as being "very" or "somewhat" religious, 53 percent as praying daily, and almost half (at least 400 million people) say they have gone on a pilgrimage or traveled to another place for religious purposes in the last ten years. Finally, against this very high base, 3.9 times as many respondents say that in the last ten years their "family's engagement in religious activities" has *increased* as say they have *decreased*.[11] In recent decades, contrary to classic modernization theories, in India the steadily increasing levels of education and urban living have co-occurred with sharply increasing self-reported levels of religious practice, especially among the more urbanized and more educated. For example, 46 percent of villagers say they pray daily, whereas 65 percent of those in towns, and 77 percent in large cities, say they pray daily. The same trend is visible in education: 44 percent of illiterates say they pray daily, but 56 percent of university graduates say they do, and whereas 18 percent of illiterates were classified as "high participants" in public religious activities, 24 percent of university graduates were so classified.[12]

The model of state religion relations crafted by the Indian Constituent Assembly and developed later was a highly original model with strong affinities to our state-nation model. All religious communities were recognized and respected by the state. All religious communities, for example, could run schools, organizations, and charities eligible for state financial support. The norms and practices of this model are so pervasively accepted that the Hindu nationalist Bharatiya Janata Party (BJP) did not dare, when it was the head of a ruling coalition, not to honor the tradition of giving extensive state subsidizes to help Muslim citizens make the hajj to Mecca.

We do not want to make the case that the Indian model of secularism, by itself, created the attitudinal and behavioral patterns we are about to present, but we believe that the state-nation-like policies and values of India's secular model helped Indians address their great religious heterogeneity, and their great intensity of religious practice, and help constitute the remarkable consensus among all religions concerning democracy we will document.

The first point I would like to stress is that the percentage of members of *all* four of the major religions in India who self-identify themselves as having a "preference for democracy as opposed to any other system" is very high by world standards: Muslims (86 percent), Hindus (88 percent), Sikhs (89 percent), and Christians (93 percent). Muslims, the largest and the most disadvantageous religious community in India, thus have about the same figures as the national norm for all four of the categories concerning democracy. See Table 2.8.

Because of the self-reported increasing religious practice in India, we constructed an index of religious intensity going from "low" to "medium" to "high" to see if the trend toward growing intensity of religious practice correlated with growing undemocratic attitudes and practices as some feared. From our data the exact opposite has occurred. For *all* four major religions in India, a steady counterintuitive

Table 2.8 SUPPORT FOR DEMOCRACY IN INDIA AS A WHOLE AND BY FOUR MAJOR RELIGIONS

	All India	*Hindu*	*Muslim*	*Christian*	*Sikh*
Democracy is always preferable	70 (88)	71 (88)	71 (87)	74 (91)	71 (88)
Sometimes authoritarianism is preferable	4	4	4	3	4
No difference	6	6	7	5	6
Don't know / No answer	20	19	18	18	19
Total	100	100	100	100	100
N	27,145	21,626	3,103	838	687

Source: National Election Study [India], 2004. All figures in the columns are percentages. Figures in parentheses in the first row are for percentage of valid responses if the "Don't knows" are treated as missing data. According to a Pearson's chi-square test, the findings for all religious communities are statistically significant (p-value < .001). Thus, the probability of this occurring by chance is less than one in 1,000.

trend is discernible; for each increase in religious intensity, there is an increase in support for democracy. See Figure 2.1.

In the *State of Democracy in South Asia:* 2005 we constructed a battery of questions exploring the relationship between religion and democracy. Unfortunately, our sample size (5,387, compared to the 27,189 for the 2004 National Election Study) permits us to do detailed comparative study of only the two largest religions in India, Hinduism and Islam. The sample size for other minority religions is too small for a robust analysis. A key question we wanted to explore

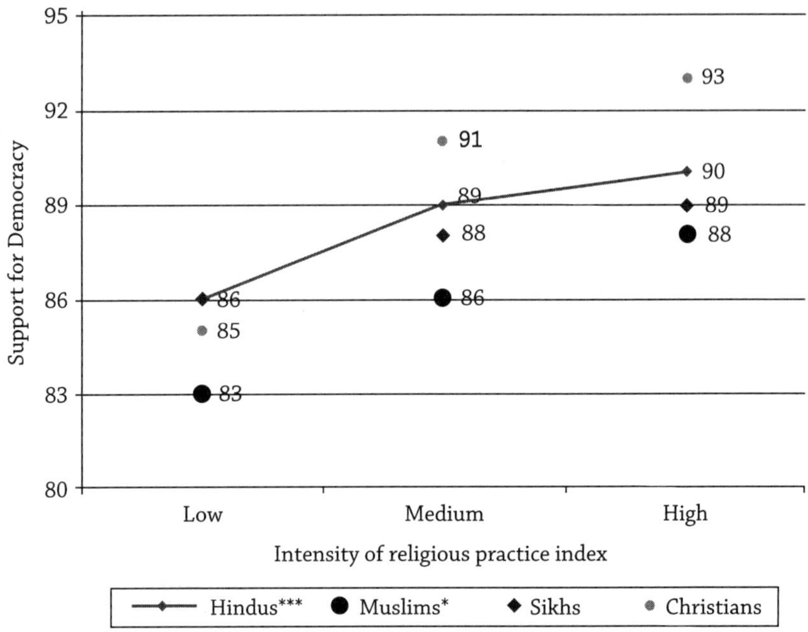

Figure 2.1. India: Religion and Democracy. In all four of India's major religions, the greater the intensity of religious practice, the greater the support for democracy.

was the relationship of increased levels of "the intensity of religious practice," our independent variable, to four critical components of democratic political society that will be our dependent variables: "political efficacy," "overall trust in political institutions," "satisfaction with the way democracy works in this country," and "voting ratios." As Table 2.9 makes clear, again counterintuitively for much of the literature, on all eight observations (Hindus and Muslims on each of the four variables) the group with "high religiosity" has higher scores on each of the four variables than does the group with "low religiosity."

The findings of our surveys indicate that among all four major religions in state-nation India, at the aggregate level, there is a relative consensus among devotees that both their practice of religion and their practice of democracy are integral and valued parts of their public and private lives.

POLITICAL EFFICACY

Perhaps the most important aspect of citizens' perceptions regarding the legitimacy of the democratic system is citizens' sense of whether or not their votes matter. This is a classic question asked in political science and is called the "political efficacy" question. The National Election Studies series in India asks the following question for measuring political efficacy: "Do you think your vote has an effect on how things are run in this country or do you think your vote has no effect?" The Indian NES offers three observation points—1971, 1996, and 2004—that allow us to read the following trend: 48 percent of the respondents felt their vote was efficacious in India in 1971, 59 percent in 1996, and 68 percent in 2004. India's 30 percent increase in the national average of the self-reported sense of efficacy between 1971 and 2004 contrasts sharply with the US sense of efficacy, which dropped from a pooled 70 percent average in 1952–1964, to a pooled average of only 40 percent from 1994 to 2000.[13] But do India's most marginalized groups share in this sense of growing efficacy and support for democracy?

Table 2.10 presents the citizens' self-reported sense of the "political efficacy" of their vote, and their support for the democratic system of elections, among India's seven most significant marginalized groups from 1971, 1996, and 2004. Between 1971 and 2004 *all seven* of these marginalized groups reported a major increase in their perception of the efficacy of their vote and of their support for democracy.

Table 2.9 RELATIONSHIP BETWEEN INTENSITY OF RELIGIOUS PRACTICE AND SUPPORT FOR POLITICAL INSTITUTIONS

	Low Intensity	Medium Intensity	High Intensity	Net Gain from Low to High
TRUST IN PUBLIC INSTITUTIONS (% OF RESPONDENTS WHO REPORTED THEY HAD A HIGH DEGREE OF TRUST IN PUBLIC INSTITUTIONS)				
Hindus	31	35	38	7
Muslims	39	40	48	9
SATISFACTION WITH “THE WAY DEMOCRACY WORKS IN INDIA” (% OF RESPONDENTS WHO REPORTED THAT THEY ARE “VERY SATISFIED” OR “SATISFIED”)				
Hindus	76	82	80	4
Muslims	71	83	84	13

POLITICAL EFFICACY: "DO YOU THINK YOUR VOTE HAS AN EFFECT ON HOW THINGS ARE RUN IN THIS COUNTRY?" (% OF RESPONDENTS WHO SAID YES)				
Hindus	76	81	81	5
Muslims	75	80	77	2
FREQUENCY OF VOTING (% OF RESPONDENTS WHO REPORTED THAT THEY HAD "VOTED IN EVERY ELECTION SINCE THEY BECAME ELIGIBLE FOR VOTING")				
Hindus	64	76	79	15
Muslims	60	72	86	26

Sources: Based on the 2005 survey conducted for the State of Democracy in South Asia Survey: A Report, for "trust" (Question C-13 battery), voting (Question C-8), and "satisfaction" (Question C-12). "Efficacy" is based on the National Election Study [India]—2004 (Question 21). The findings for "efficacy" and "trust," among both Hindus and Muslims, are statistically significant using the Pearson's chi-square test (p-value < .001), which means that the possibility of the findings occurring by chance are less than one in 1,000. "Trust in public institutions" is an index created by adding the responses to the frequency of self-reported trust in "central government" (C-13a), "provincial government" (C-13b), "local government" (C-13c), "civil service" (C-13d), "police" (C-13e), "army" (C-13f), "courts" (C-13g), "Parliament" (C-13h), "political parties" (C-13i), and "Election Commission" (C-13j). The findings for "voting" are statistically significant for Hindus (p-value < .001) and for Muslims (p-value < .050). The findings for "satisfaction" for Hindus are statistically significant (p-value < .001), while the findings for Muslims are positive but not statistically significant.

Table 2.10 SENSE OF POLITICAL EFFICACY AND SUPPORT FOR DEMOCRACY AMONG MARGINALIZED GROUPS IN INDIA IN 1971, 1996, AND 2004

	Political Efficacy			*Support for Democracy*		
Group	*1971*	*1996*	*2004*	*1971*	*1996*	*2004*
National average	48	59	68	43	69	72
ST	31	48	59	41	66	68
Women	36	51	61	32	64	67
Illiterate	36	47	55	31	62	61
Very Poor	38	51	60	32	64	66
SC	42	60	65	38	67	69
Poor	43	55	68	37	68	71
Rural	44	57	66	39	69	70
Muslims	50	60	66	40	72	73

Source: NES = National Election Studies, CSDS, Delhi. The efficacy question was "Do you think your vote has effect on how things are run in this country or do you think your vote makes no difference?" The support for democracy question was "Do you think that the government in this country can be run better if there are no parties or assemblies or elections?"

Views on the Economy

The National Election Studies ask respondents questions on their household financial well-being in the previous five years and on their financial expectations for the next five years. Table 2.11 shows that the ratio of respondents saying their financial situation has *improved,* to those saying it has *worsened,* has grown from 1.3 in 1996 to 1.5 in 2004 to 4.2 in 2009.

Table 2.11 VIEWS ON HOUSEHOLD FINANCIAL SITUATION IN THE PREVIOUS FIVE YEARS, 1996–2009

	NES 1996	*NES 2004*	*NES 2009*
Improved	25	27	46
Same	56	52	34
Worsened	19	17	11
Ratio of improved to worsened	1.3	1.5	4.2
N	9,614	27,189	34,000+

Source: NES = National Election Studies, CSDS, Delhi. The questions from the 1996 and 2004 surveys asked respondents to pick between "improved," "same," and worsened," but the 2009 survey asks respondents to pick between "much better," "better," "same," "worse," and "much worse." We have combined the "much better" and "better" categories to create "improved" and similarly combined the "worse" and "much worse" categories to create "worsened."

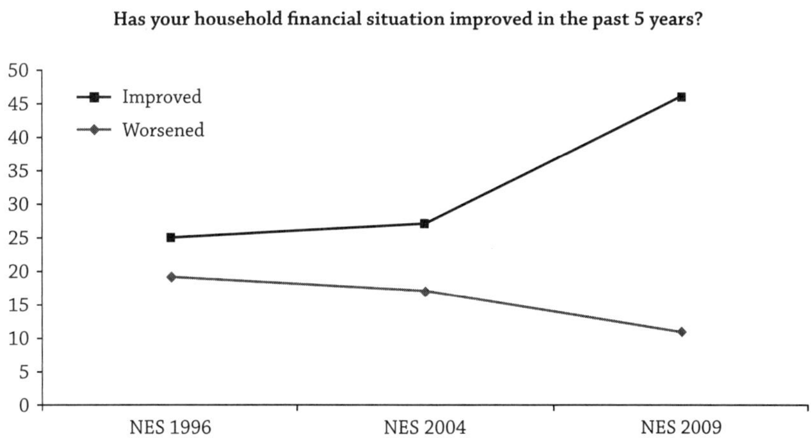

Figure 2.2. India: Household Financial Situations. According to self-reporting, household financial situation has improved in the previous five years (1996, 1998, and 2005).

Table 2.12 VIEWS ON HOUSEHOLD FINANCIAL SITUATION IN THE PREVIOUS FIVE YEARS BY MARGINALIZED GROUPS, NES 2004

	National Average	*Schedule Caste*	*Schedule Tribe*	*Muslim*	*Very Poor*	*Poor*	*Female*	*Illiterate*
Improved	27	22	24	19	19	25	24	20
Same	52	51	54	53	54	54	53	54
Worsened	17	24	16	24	24	18	18	21
Don't know	4	3	5	5	3	4	4	5
N	27,189	4,319	4,274	3,254	8,097	9,550	12,410	8,416

Table 2.13 VIEWS ON HOUSEHOLD FINANCIAL SITUATION IN THE NEXT FIVE YEARS, 1996–2009

	NES 1996	*NES 2004*	*NES 2009*
Improved	48	51	50
Same	27	19	20
Worsened	9	6	10
Don't know	16	25	22
Ratio of improved to worsened	5.3	8.5	5
N	9,614	27,189	

Source: NES = National Election Studies, CSDS, Delhi. The questions from the 1996 and 2004 surveys asked respondents to pick between "improved," "same," and "worsened," but the 2009 survey asks respondents to pick between "much better," "better," "same," "worse," and "much worse." We have combined the "much better" and "better" categories to create "improved" and similarly combined the "worse" and "much worse" categories to create "worsened."

The overall percentage of respondents saying their situation has worsened has also declined from 19 percent in 1996 to 11 percent in 2009. Figure 2.2 presents the same information but in graphical form.

Again, we examine the responses to the same question across the most marginalized groups in the country. While we would ideally like to present the data for these groups for the 2009 elections, those numbers are not yet available. Instead, we present the results for the 2004 elections. The results in Table 2.12 show that the Poor, Scheduled Tribe, and Female groups are within three percentage points of the national average of percentage of people who say their situation has improved. However, Muslim and Very Poor respondents were eight points below the national average.

Table 2.14 VIEWS ON HOUSEHOLD FINANCIAL SITUATION IN THE PREVIOUS FIVE YEARS BY MARGINALIZED GROUPS, NES 2004

	National Average	*Schedule Caste*	*Schedule Tribe*	*Muslim*	*Very Poor*	*Poor*	*Female*	*Illiterate*
Improved	51	47	49	43	45	51	49	42
Same	19	19	20	18	21	19	20	21
Worsened	6	8	5	9	6	6	5	6
Don't know	25	27	26	31	27	24	26	31
N	27,189	4,319	4,274	3,254	8,097	9,550	12,410	8,416

Table 2.13 shows the results of the questions asking respondents to project their future household financial prospects. The proportion who say their future condition will improve are five times larger than the proportion who say their situation will worsen. The results in Table 2.14 show that Scheduled Caste, Scheduled Tribe, Poor, and Female are within four percentage points of the national average percentage of people who say their situation will improve. However, Muslim, Very Poor, and Illiterate respondents were between six and nine percentage points below the national average.

NOTES

This chapter is largely based on Stepan, Linz, and Yadav 2011. Research assistance for revisions to this book and this chapter were done with the excellent support of Pavithra Suryanarayan, a doctoral student in the Political Science Department at Columbia University. The financial support for the research for the book on which this chapter is based comes from the Ford Foundation, the Carnegie Corporation of New York, and the Henry R. Luce Initiative of Religion and International Affairs. Additional work on this chapter has been supported by Columbia University's Program on Indian Economic Policies, funded by a generous grant from the John Templeton Foundation. The opinions expressed in the chapter are those of the author(s) and do not necessarily reflect the views of the John Templeton Foundation, the Ford Foundation, the Luce Foundation, or the Carnegie Corporation of New York.

1. The Center for the Study of Developing Societies is a think tank based in New Delhi, India. I thank Yogendra Yadav for the datasets for the NES All-India postpoll surveys conducted in 1996, 1998, 1999, 2004, and other CSDS data. I was on the advisory committee that helped draft questions on identities, and religion and politics, for the Center for the Study of Developing Societies in 2008 and other surveys.
2. See Shastri 2007.
3. For an analytic discussion of these figures, see Das Gupta 1970.
4. Ibid.
5. Census of India 2001.
6. His oft-cited judgment about the impossibility of having more than one important functioning language and significant nationality in a democratic

polity was "free institutions are next to impossible in a country made up of different nationalities. Among a people without fellow-feelings, especially if they read and speak different languages, the united public opinion necessary to the working of representative institutions cannot exist." See Mill 1861 (p. 393).

7. See Pew Forum on Religion in Public Life 2009.
8. India will surpass China as the most populous country in the world by 2040 according to the 2004 revision of World Population Prospects by the Population Division of the United Nations.
9. See Norris and Inglehart 2004. Also see www.worldvaluessurvey.org.
10. See Census of India 2001.
11. The above percentages concerning religious beliefs and practices are found in State of the Nation Survey (2007), Lokniti, CSDS, New Delhi. The sample size is 15,373, and the questions are B5, B3, B11, B6, and B17, respectively.
12. Ibid. For a rich analysis of the data in this report see Kumar 2008.
13. Virginia Sapiro, Steven J. Rosenstone, and National Election Studies, Center for Political Studies, University of Michigan, American National Election Studies Cumulative Data File.

REFERENCES

Census of India (2001). "Statement 6," Office of the Registrar General of Census. http://censusindia.gov.in/Census_Data_2001/Census_Data_Online/Language/Statement6.htm (accessed March 29, 2010).

Center for the Study of Developing Societies (2008). *State of Democracy in South Asia*. Delhi: Oxford University Press.

Das Gupta, Jyotirindra (1970). *Language Conflict and National Development: Group Politics and National Language Policy in India*. Berkeley: University of California Press.

Kumar, Sanjay (2008). "Religious Practices among Hindus: Does This Influence Their Political Choices?" CSDS Working Paper, 3–9.

Mill, John Stuart (1993 [1861]). "Considerations on Representative Government." In *Utilitarianism, On Liberty, Considerations on Representative Government*, ed. Geraint Williams. London: Everyman.

Norris, Pippa, and Ronald Inglehart (2004). *Sacred and Secular: Religion and Politics Worldwide*. Cambridge: Cambridge University Press.

Pew Forum on Religion in Public Life (2009). "Mapping the Global Muslim Population. A Report on the Size and Distribution of the World's Muslim Population," p. 14. Available at http://www.pewforum.org (accessed March 29, 2010).

Shastri, Sandeep (2007). *World Values Survey—Wave V 2005–2010 India Segment-Questionnaire Codebook*. Bangalore: World Values Survey

Stepan, Alfred, Juan J. Linz, and Yogendra Yadav (2011). *Crafting State-Nations: India and Other Multinational Democracies*. Baltimore: Johns Hopkins University Press.

Chapter 3

Economic Reforms and Election Outcomes

POONAM GUPTA AND ARVIND PANAGARIYA*

The National Democratic Alliance (NDA), which introduced wide-ranging economic reforms between 1998 and 2004, lost the 2004 Lok Sabha election.[1] Consistent with the conventional wisdom at the time, the Bhartiya Janata Party (BJP), which led the NDA, had taken the view that the electorate welcomed its reforms and therefore fought the election on the now derided "India Shining" platform. Confident of a victory, it even called the elections four months earlier than the due date. Yet not only did it lose the Lok Sabha election, but its close ally Chandra Babu Naidu, who had been seen as the face of the reforms, modernization, and urban growth, also suffered a crushing defeat in the legislative assembly elections in the state of Andhra Pradesh.

Critics of economic reforms immediately sought to capitalize on the defeat of the NDA and its allies by celebrating it as a vote against the reforms. Distinguished author Salman Rushdie expressed this view in an opinion piece in the *Washington Post* on May 14, 2004, in these words:

> The Indian battle for centrality in the debate about the country's future has always been, to some degree, a battle between the city and the village. It is between, on the one hand, the urbanized,

> industrialized India favored by both the socialist-inclined Jawaharlal Nehru and the free-market architects of the "India Shining," the new India in which a highly successful capitalist class has transformed the heights of the economy, and, on the other hand, the agricultural, homespun India beloved of Mahatma Gandhi, the immense countryside India where three-quarters of the population still lives and which has not benefited in the slightest from the recent economic boom.

Rushdie continued,

> It's no accident that the ruling alliance lost heavily in Andhra Pradesh and in Tamil Nadu, precisely the states that wooed information technology giants such as Microsoft to set up shop, turning sleepy "second cities" such as Madras, Bangalore and Hyderabad into new-tech boom towns. That's because while the rich got richer, the fortunes of the poor, such as the farmers of Andhra, declined year by year.

Coming from the proreform angle, Bhagwati and Panagariya (2004) argued that the defeat of the NDA reflected a fundamental change in the attitude of voters: having experienced the benefits of reforms, henceforth they would not tolerate incumbents that did not deliver rapid improvements in their fortunes. With per capita income growth of 1.5 percent per year during the 1950s through the mid-1980s, people saw no perceptible change in their lives. This fact made the electorate pessimistic insofar as their economic fortunes were concerned. Resigned that a perceptible change in the economic conditions was impossible, they repeatedly returned the ruling Indian National Congress party (the Congress) to power. The sole exception was the 1977 election following the Emergency Rule, in which the electorate handed the outgoing prime minister, Indira Gandhi, a crushing defeat for trampling the *political* freedoms that it had come to cherish.

But the liberal reforms that began in an ad hoc fashion in the 1980s and became systematic in 1990s changed this ethos. Incomes began to grow at higher rates on a sustained basis and poverty began to decline. This fundamentally altered people's aspirations: having experienced change for the better, they wanted more of it and sooner than later. And if an incumbent government would not deliver it, they would look for another one. In the words of Bhagwati and Panagariya (2004), "Perhaps, when little progress takes place all around, the centuries-old Indian fatalism takes over. But when the poor begin improving, then the 'revolution of rising expectations' is likely to arise. This is a direct result of the perception of real possibilities."

The hypothesis here is that the voting behavior has undergone change over time, as voters have become more and more conscious of the potential for better life offered by economic reforms leading to faster growth and improved economic fortunes. Until the 1980s, voters saw little improvement in their economic prospects so that they voted based on other factors such as candidate characteristics, caste considerations, and specific local issues. Occasionally, issues of national importance, such as the imposition of emergency rule, ongoing war or victory in war, and sympathy waves resulting from the assassination of a popular ruler, played a decisive role as well. These special circumstances usually resulted in unusually large voter turnouts as well as more than usual victory margins. Thus the Indian voter was primarily a partisan voter except when there was a wave of nationalism or sympathy. According to the Bhagwati-Panagariya hypothesis, this trend has been broken in recent years as economic growth has become an important factor.

In this context, it is interesting to note that the 2009 national election produced an outcome opposite of the 2004 election: it returned the ruling coalition, the United Progressive Alliance (UPA), to power.

On the surface, this seemed to undercut the bias against incumbency observed in the 2004 election. But as Panagariya (2009) explained, a more nuanced analysis suggested otherwise. He noted, "The key feature of anti-incumbency in India is that it strikes with potency at the level of the state. The electorate rewards the party of a performing chief minister and punishes that of nonperforming one in not just state assembly elections but national parliamentary ones as well." Thus, in the 2009 election, the Congress, which led the UPA and was the national incumbent, won just nine out of seventy-two seats in the states of Bihar, Orissa, and Chhattisgarh, which all had performing non-Congress governments. On the other hand, Delhi and Andhra Pradesh had performing Congress chief ministers, and the party respectively bagged seven out of seven and thirty-three out of forty-two seats in those two states. In Rajasthan, where an outgoing BJP chief minister had performed less than spectacularly, the Congress had trounced her party in the state elections held less than six months prior to the national elections. In the national election, the Congress went on to win twenty out of twenty-five seats in that state.

Against this background, the primary aim of this chapter is to test the validity of the contrasting hypotheses offered by Salman Rushdie, on the one hand, and Bhagwati and Panagariya, on the other. More broadly, we assess the role of economic performance in determining the election outcomes in India. While taking a brief look at some of the earlier elections as well, we mainly focus on the latest parliamentary elections (2009). There are two main reasons for this choice. First, shifts in the voter attitudes resulting from reforms are likely to be reflected in the most recent election, which has taken place against the backdrop of miracle-level growth of 8 to 9 percent nationally. Second, the data for the 2009 election, especially those relating to the candidate characteristics, are more readily available.

As a concomitant to the analysis of the implications of growth, we consider in detail the role the personal characteristics of the candidates such as wealth, education, and pending criminal charges play in determining the election outcomes. We also consider the role incumbency plays at the level of the candidate as well as the party. That is to say, we analyze whether outgoing members have a higher frequency of election than other candidates and whether the candidates of incumbent parties at the center and in the states do better than those of the opposition parties. In the present chapter, we study these issues only in terms of unconditional probabilities, leaving the task of more rigorous analysis using an econometric model in a companion article (Gupta and Panagariya 2011).

Our main result may be summarized as follows. First, we find no evidence of a rural-urban split in the election outcomes predicted by the Rushdie hypothesis. If the candidates of the state ruling party win in the rural areas, they also win in the urban areas. Likewise, if they lose in the urban areas they also lose in the rural areas. Second, in the 2009 parliamentary election, on average, candidates of the incumbent party in a state had a better chance of scoring a victory if that state exhibited higher growth than those in a state exhibiting lower growth. Compared with the candidates in the lowest-growth states, the advantage to candidates of the ruling party in the state was higher at the top end of the growth distribution than in the middle. Third, on average, incumbency was helpful in winning the 2009 election. That is to say, on average, an incumbent candidate and the candidates of the ruling parties at the center and states had better chances of victory than other candidates.[2] Fourth, on average, better-educated and wealthier candidates had a better chance of victory than their less well educated and less wealthy counterparts. Finally, a key source of the victory for the UPA in the 2009 election was its superior performance in the states with nonperforming governments headed by parties outside of the UPA.

The chapter is organized as follows. In the next section, we summarize the literature on elections, especially as it relates to India. In the third section, we describe some salient features of the last three Lok Sabha elections held in 1999, 2004, and 2009. In the fourth and fifth sections, we describe the relevant characteristics of the constituencies and candidates, respectively. In the sixth section, we present our main result on the role of growth in determining the election outcome. In the seventh section, we explain the sources of the Congress gains in the 2009 election. Our main point here is that the UPA made large gains in the states that had nonperforming governments headed by non-UPA parties. In the final section we discuss our conclusions.

THE RELEVANT LITERATURE

Only a small body of the literature on elections focuses on the subject central to our chapter: the role of economic performance in determining the electoral outcomes. The relevant studies include Fair (1978), Lewis-Beck (1988), Powell and Whitten (1993), Alesina and Rosenthal (1989), and Brender and Drazen (2008). Among the early studies, few find a statistically significant effect of economic performance on the election outcomes, the major exception being Fair (1978), which finds a positive and significant effect of growth on the prospects of victory in the United States. A more recent and important exception is Brender and Drazen (2008), which offers an analysis of the role of growth in elections using comprehensive cross-country data and distinguishes between developed and developing countries. These authors find that while faster growth helps incumbents win elections in the developing countries, it has no such effect in the developed countries. Our main result conforms most closely to the one found by these authors though we arrive at it through a comparison of states within a single developing country, India.

A different strand of the literature on elections, developed exclusively in the context of the western democracies and employing the principal-agent framework, focuses on the impact the desire to win elections has on the behavior of the incumbent politician. The central question here is how political incumbents manipulate the tax and expenditure policies, manage their legislative votes, and exchange political favors to maximize the chance of electoral victory.[3] Given that our objective is to study the determinants of electoral outcomes rather than how the objective of electoral victory conditions political behavior, this literature is at best indirectly relevant to our work.

A final body of the relevant literature on elections examines whether incumbency by itself is an asset or liability in elections. This literature is narrowly focused on the identification of the incumbency advantage. It begins by recognizing that a higher unconditional probability of victory of an incumbent over non-incumbent may be the result of selection bias and therefore need not represent incumbency advantage per se. Conversely, a lower unconditional probability of victory of the incumbent may not represent incumbency disadvantage. Incumbents may win more frequently simply because they happen to be better candidates or have more resources to spend on campaigns. Alternatively, if incumbents lose more frequently than non-incumbents, this may be simply because they fail to keep a number of inconsistent promises made in the prior election or because they prove themselves to be inept during their terms. Therefore, the observed frequencies of losses and wins by incumbents are by themselves insufficient to infer the effect of incumbency. The most compelling approach to identifying the impact of incumbency is regression discontinuity, which tries to identify incumbents and non-incumbents who are otherwise identical in all respects and compares their probabilities of victory in election.[4]

In the specific Indian context, the literature on the incumbency advantage or disadvantage is relatively new. Linden (2004) uses the regression discontinuity approach and finds that prior to 1991, incumbents had enjoyed an advantage over non-incumbents. But beginning in 1991, this relationship reversed with incumbents suffering a disadvantage. For the elections from 1991 to 1999, he estimates that on average incumbents were fourteen percentage points less likely to be elected than similar non-incumbents.[5] He reaches this conclusion by comparing the probabilities of victory of candidates in an election that had barely won (incumbents) to those of the candidates who barely lost (non-incumbents) the prior election. The underlying assumption is that the candidates that just win and those that just lose an election are identical in all respects and any advantage or disadvantage to a victorious candidate (incumbent) in the following election must result from incumbency.

While Linden (2004) studies incumbency disadvantage at the level of the candidate, a number of descriptive analytic studies following the 2004 election have focused on the disadvantage arising from association with an incumbent party. In an early analysis immediately following the 2004 election, Panagariya (2004) pointed out that the election outcome exhibited a strong anti-incumbency pattern that punished the main ruling party in the state: candidates of the party in power in a state faced a higher risk of defeat than the candidates of the main opposition party in the constituencies located in that state. For example, the Telugu Desham Party (TDP), which ruled in Andhra Pradesh, overwhelmingly lost to the Congress in that state. In three other states—Rajasthan, Madhya Pradesh, and Chhattisgarh—the BJP and its allies had defeated the ruling Congress governments in the state assembly elections held in December 2003, and they also overwhelmingly defeated the latter's candidates in these states in the Lok Sabha election of April–May 2004.

In a more comprehensive analysis, Yadav (2004) also notes that on average the state ruling parties performed poorly in the 2004 national elections in the constituencies located in their own states but with one major exception: candidates of parties that had defeated the party in power in a just-held state election also did well in the national election. Yadav characterizes the one to two-year period between the state and national elections as the "honeymoon" period during which the candidates of the incumbent party in the state enjoy a positive advantage. Our definition of the incumbent party in a state takes into account this difference between the "entrenched" and "recent" incumbent, focusing principally on the former.

Ravishankar (2009) carries out a quantitative analysis of the prospects of victory for the incumbent candidates of the main party in power relative to the incumbent candidates of the main opposition party using the national and state election data from 1977 to 2005. Because her analysis is strictly restricted to incumbent candidates, it does not compare incumbent and non-incumbent candidates. She finds that setting aside the parties in their honeymoon period, incumbent candidates of the main party in power in both national and state elections face higher probability of loss in their re-election bids than the incumbent candidates of the main opposition party. Ravishankar (2009) also finds a cross effect flowing from party incumbency at the national level to state elections and vice versa. Once again, setting aside the parties in their honeymoon period, incumbent candidates of the main party in power at the center face a higher probability of defeat than the incumbent candidates of the main opposition party at the center. Symmetrically, incumbent candidates of a party in power in a state face a higher probability of defeat in the national election than the incumbent candidates of the main opposition party within that state.

A key shortcoming of Ravishankar (2009) is that it excludes non-incumbent candidates. If the incumbency effect is related to the party in power, there is no reason why it should not apply to non-incumbent candidates contesting the election on the incumbent party's ticket. Our data set, though confined to the 2009 national elections, includes all candidates and therefore allows for more complete test of the incumbency effect at the level of the party in the companion paper mentioned above.

SALIENT FEATURES OF THE PAST THREE ELECTIONS

Table 3.1 reports the broad results of the elections held in 1999, 2004, and 2009. It shows that the national parties numbering six or more have won only a little more than two-thirds of the seats in each of the three elections.[6] Unsurprisingly, the party winning the largest number of seats has fallen well short of the majority so that each government has been based on a multi-party coalition. Because the party with the second most seats ends up in the opposition, state parties, which together account for approximately 30 percent of the seats have come to acquire great salience.

Led by the Bhartiya Janata Party (BJP), the National Democratic Alliance (NDA) had ruled from 1999 to 2004. Counting on its popularity at the time, it called for an early election. But, the BJP suffered major losses shrinking its tally from 182 to 138 seats, whereas the Indian National Congress (INC) or simply the Congress improved its tally from 114 to 145 seats.[7] Though the latter still fell well short of the 272 seats necessary to form a government, remarkably, it was successful in cobbling together a majority coalition that came to be known as the United Progressive Alliance (UPA). The UPA government successfully served its entire term until 2009. At one level, it could be argued that neither the decline in the seats held by the BJP from 182 to 138 nor the rise in the seats held by the Congress from 114 to 145 represented a major shift away from the incumbent towards the opposition. Yet, given the expectations of a clear mandate in favor of a very popular prime minister, the media uniformly described the outcome as a decisive vote against the incumbents.

The 2009 national election was different from the 2004 election in one fundamental sense: it returned the main ruling party, the Congress, to power with a larger number of seats as well as with a larger victory margin. Beating even the most optimistic predictions, the

Table 3.1 BROAD RESULTS OF THE NATIONAL ELECTIONS IN 1999, 2004, AND 2009

Party	*1999*	*2004*	*2009*
National Parties	369	364	376
Indian National Congress	114	145	206
Bharatiya Janata Party	182	138	116
Bahujan Samaj Party	14	19	21
Nationalist Congress Party		9	9
Communist Party of India	4	10	4
Communist Party of India (Marxist)	33	43	16
Rashtriya Janata Dal		24	4
State Parties	158	159	146
Samajwadi Party		36	23
Janata Dal (U)		8	20
All India Trinamool Congress		2	19
Dravida Munnetra Kazhagam		16	18
Biju Janata Dal		11	14
Shiv Sena		12	11
All India Anna Dravida Munnetra Kazhagam		0	9
Telugu Desam Party		5	6
Janata Dal (S)		4	3

continued

Table 3.1 (*continued*)

Party	*1999*	*2004*	*2009*
Other (Unrecognized) Parties	10	15	12
Independent candidates	6	5	9
Total	543	543	543

Congress increased its tally yet again from 145 to an impressive 206 seats. The Marxist Communist Party suffered the worst losses shrinking from 43 to 16 seats. The BJP also declined from 138 to 116 seats. Thus between 1999 and 2009, the Congress and the BJP had more or less exchanged their positions.

Among the national parties, the Marxist Communist Party of India, the Communist party of India, and the Rashtriya Janada Dal (RJD) suffered the largest losses besides the BJP. RJD even lost its status as a national party after the elections. Among the state parties, Samajwadi Party suffered the largest losses. Those making major gains other than the Congress were the Congress ally in West Bengal, All India Trinamool Congress, and opposition parties JD (U) and AIADMK. The other myriad state parties and unrecognized parties broadly maintained their positions.

One immediate reaction to the results in the press was that incumbency had helped rather than hurt in this election, though some observers did question this conclusion. Our own view is that the picture is more nuanced with incumbency at the state government level in conjunction with economic performance playing a decisive role. We return to the study of this idea, closely related to the Bhagwati and Panagariya (2004) hypothesis discussed in the introduction, in a later section.

CHARACTERISTICS OF THE CONSTITUENCIES

Table 3.2 shows the salient features of the constituencies, taking all constituencies in the country into account. The averages we report in the table are virtually unchanged when we limit the sample to the nineteen major states on which our subsequent analysis will be based.

A total of 8,071 candidates contested the 2009 election. Of these, as many as 3,825, or 47.4 percent, were independent, another 30 percent were affiliated with the national or regional parties and the rest belonged to the unrecognized parties. In the 2009 election, in all, 372 parties fielded one or more candidates. Party affiliations in general and with a national or state party in particular played a crucial role in determining the outcome: candidates with a party affiliation accounted for more than 98 percent of the top four candidates and for the majority of the winning candidates. 534 winning candidates out of a maximum possible of 543 had some party affiliation. Only nine winning candidates had contested as independents.

The average number of candidates per constituency was fifteen; the maximum and minimum number of candidates in any constituency were forty-three and three, respectively. Remarkably, as the latter figure indicates, there was not a single constituency with direct contest between two candidates. Countrywide, 59.4 percent of the voters turned up to vote. The maximum turnout was 90.4 percent (in Tamluk constituency in West Bengal) and the minimum 25.6 percent (in Srinagar constituency in Jammu and Kashmir). Constituencies near the higher limit were in West Bengal, followed by the northeastern and southern states (Andhra Pradesh, Kerala, Tamil Nadu). Those near the lower end were in the states of Jammu and Kashmir (J&K), Bihar, Uttar Pradesh, and Rajasthan.

On average, the winning candidates secured about 44 percent of the votes cast and the second candidate from top obtained about

Table 3.2 DESCRIPTION OF THE CONSTITUENCIES ACROSS ALL STATES

	Average	*Minimum*	*Maximum*
Number of voters	1,319,916	45,981	2,343,012
Number of candidates	15	3	43
Voter turnout (%)	59.4	25.6	90.4
Votes obtained by the top candidate (%)	43.9	21.3	78.8
Votes obtained by the second candidate (%)	34.3	8.7	48.7
Victory margin	9.7	0.04	70.1
Votes obtained by the top four candidates (%)	93.8	62.6	100

34 percent of the total votes. Sushma Swaraj of the BJP won with the highest proportionate majority in Vidisha constituency of Madhya Pradesh, claiming 78.8 percent of the total votes cast. The simple average of the percentage-point victory margins across all constituencies was 9.7, and the margins ranged from .04 to 70 percentage points.

The top four candidates summing to 2,170 out of a total of 8,071 candidates accounted for the bulk of the votes polled in most constituencies. In aggregate, these candidates accounted for more than 90 percent of the total votes polled. This can be gleaned from the fact that the density of votes in Figure 3.1 is heavily concentrated in the first four candidates.

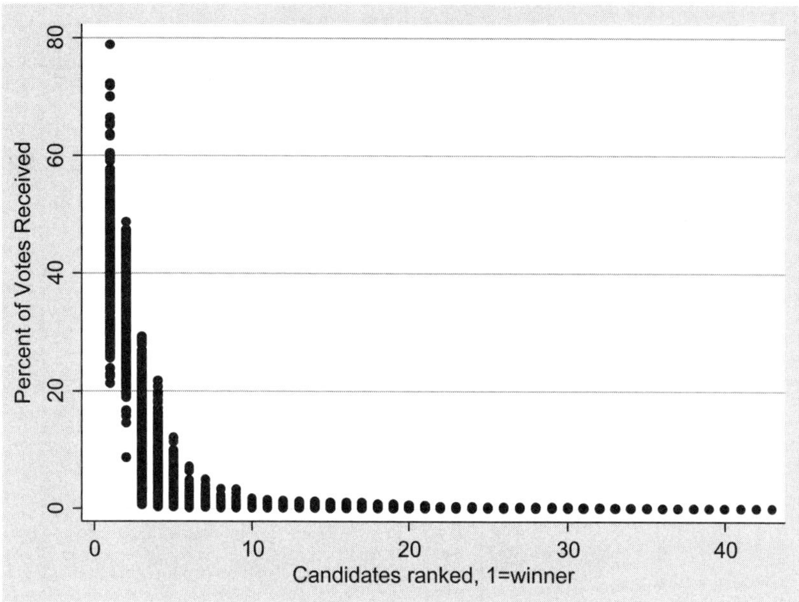

Figure 3.1. Percentage Votes Obtained by Candidates at Different Ranks

CHARACTERISTICS OF THE CANDIDATES

We now turn to a consideration of some key characteristics of the candidates that have implications for the electoral outcomes. These relate to wealth, education, pending criminal cases distinguished by the seriousness of the charges, gender, and incumbency status. We provide the data for all candidates, the top four candidates and the victorious candidates.

Wealth

Table 3.3 provides the distribution of candidates by wealth across five different wealth categories. For each wealth category, column 4 shows the top four candidates as a proportion of the total number of

Table 3.3 DISTRIBUTION OF CONTESTING AND WINNING CANDIDATES ACCORDING TO WEALTH (CANDIDATES IN ALL INDIAN STATES)

Wealth Category	*Wealth (million rupees)*	*Number of Candidates (% of total)*	*Number of Top Four Candidates*	*Number of Candidates Winning*	*Probability of Being in the Top Four Candidates*	*Probability of Victory*
		I	*II*	*III*	*IV: (II/I) x 100*	*V: (III/1) x 100*
1	0–0.5	3,176 (39%)	274	14	8.6	0.4
2	0.5–5	2,835 (35%)	642	134	22.6	4.7
3	5–9	700 (8.7%)	329	89	47	12.7
4	9–50	896 (11%)	629	194	70.2	21.7
5	50-higher	464 (5.8%)	296	112	63.8	24.1
Total	All wealth categories	8,071	2,170	543	26.9	6.7

candidates in the given wealth category. Similarly, column V shows the number of winning candidates as a proportion of the total number of candidates.

Two features of the table stand out. First, candidates from all wealth categories are able to participate in elections and make it to the list of the top four candidates; nearly half of the top four candidates come from the lowest wealth category of 5 million rupees or less. The system does seem to offer an opportunity to run for election without regard to wealth status. Second, the unconditional probability of victory rapidly rises with wealth: while three-fourths of the candidates belong to the lowest two wealth categories, only a little more than a quarter of the elected candidates come from them. Alternatively stated, 56 percent of the winning candidates possess at least INR 10 million in declared wealth (and perhaps much more in reality). The contrast is brought out most sharply by a comparison of unconditional probability of victory of a candidate in the highest wealth category (24.1 percent) to that of the lowest wealth category (.4 percent). It bears cautioning, of course, that no causal relationship between wealth and election outcome can be drawn from these data. Wealth can very well be positively correlated with other attributes defining a good candidate in the eyes of the electorate.

Education

Next, we consider the distribution of candidates by education level. Once again, we identify five education levels, the lowest one being no formal education and the highest one a postgraduate or higher or a technical degree. Table 3.4 reports the frequency distribution and unconditional probabilities of being in the top four and the winning candidate.

Three features of the table are noteworthy. First, contrary to the common impression, most candidates contesting elections have some formal education. Indeed, the vast majority of those contesting

Table 3.4 DISTRIBUTION OF CONTESTING AND WINNING CANDIDATES ACCORDING TO THE LEVEL OF EDUCATION (CANDIDATES IN ALL INDIAN STATES)

Education Category	*Education Level*	*Number of Candidates*	*Number of Top Four Candidates*	*Number of Winners*	*Probability of Being in Top Four*	*Probability of Victory*
		I	*II*	*III*	*IV: (II/I) x 100*	*V: (III/1) x 100*
0	No formal education	134	5	0	3.7	0
1	Up to Class V	964	106	15	11	1.6
2	Middle or high school	2,665	495	104	18.6	3.9
3	Undergraduate	1,623	603	157	37.2	9.7
4	Postgraduate or higher or technical	1,984	875	260	44.1	13.1
Total	All education levels	7,370	2,084	536	28.3	7.3

have at least gone through the middle school. Second, while the proportion of those with an undergraduate or higher degree is approximately half among those contesting, it is more than 80 percent among those winning. Four out of every five members in the 2009 Lok Sabha boast of an undergraduate or higher degree. At the other extreme, while 134 candidates with no formal education contested elections, none actually won. Finally, the unconditional probability of getting elected consistently rises with the education level. The biggest jump takes place as we move from high school to a college degree. We remind, however, that as in the case of wealth, this fact need not reflect causation if education is correlated with other factors that make a candidate attractive to the electorate.

Criminal Cases

Perhaps the most interesting characteristic relates to criminal cases pending against the contesting and winning candidates. Table 3.5 documents the relevant data. In constructing the table, we identify five categories based on the number of pending cases against a candidate.

Two features of the table stand out. First, as many as 14 percent of the candidates have criminal cases pending against them. And a much larger percentage of elected members of Lok Sabha—30 percent—have such cases. Even if we exclude the candidates with just one case since the prospects of frivolous cases are high against those in politics, more than eighty members of the current Lok Sabha, accounting for 15 percent of total members, have two or more criminal cases pending against them. Second, somewhat disconcertingly, the within group probability of victory rises steadily with the number of pending criminal cases.

We note that closer examination leads to a more nuanced picture from the one emerging from the aggregate data shown in Table 3.5. The criminal charges against the candidates range from the

Table 3.5 DISTRIBUTION OF CONTESTING AND WINNING CANDIDATES ACCORDING TO CRIMINAL CASES (CANDIDATES IN ALL INDIAN STATES)

Crime Category	*Number of Criminal Cases*	*Number of Candidates*	*Number of Top Candidates*	*Number of Winners*	*Probability of Being in Top 4 Candidates*	*Probability of Victory*
		I	*II*	*III*	*IV: (II/I) x 100*	*V: (III/1) x 100*
0	0	6,894	1,578	381	22.9	5.5
1	1	627	286	76	45.6	12.1
2	2 to 4	392	212	59	54.1	15.1
3	5 to 9	92	61	16	66.3	17.4
4	>10	44	30	11	68.2	25
Total	All Crime Categories	8,049	2,167	543	26.9	6.7

benign such as participation in rallies declared unlawful to more serious ones such as kidnapping, extortion, and murder. To understand the true picture, we must disaggregate the data further. To economize on space, we relegate this task to an appendix available upon request from the authors. Here we simply note that the probability of a serious crime by a contestant rises with the number of criminal cases registered against him or her. Whereas only 40 percent of the candidates with one case registered against them had been accused of a serious crime, nearly 90 percent of those with ten or more pending cases had one or more serious criminal charges against them.

Detailed examination also reveals a significant degree of concentration of criminal cases against candidates by state. The state that tops the 2009 chart is Bihar, where more than a quarter of the candidates have at least one criminal case and more than 17 percent having at least one serious charge against them. Other states, which exhibit large proportions of candidates with criminal cases, include Jharkhand, Orissa, Uttar Pradesh, Gujarat, West Bengal, and Maharashtra. We have an interesting case in Kerala, where 22 percent of the candidates have criminal cases registered against them but the vast majority of them involve benign charges such as participation in demonstration. Only a third of the cases against the members from Kerala involve serious crimes.

Distribution of Candidates by Gender

Table 3.6 reports the gender distribution of contesting and victorious candidates. The data show the expected pattern. Much fewer women than men contest election. As a result, there are many more male members in the Lok Sabha. One mildly interesting feature is that the unconditional probability of a woman winning the election is higher than that of a man.

Table 3.6 GENDER COMPOSITION OF CONTESTING AND WINNING CANDIDATES (CANDIDATES IN ALL INDIAN STATES)

Gender	*Total Candidates*	*Top Four Candidates*	*Number of Winning Candidates*	*Probability of Being in Top Four*	*Probability of Victory*
	I	*II*	*III*	*IV: (II/I) x 100*	*V: (III/I) x 100*
Women	556	183	58	32.9	10.4
Men	7,515	1,987	485	26.4	6.5
Total	8,071	2,170	543	26.9	6.7

Incumbents and Non-incumbents Compared

We may now compare the incumbent and non-incumbent candidates within the populations of all, top four and victorious candidates. As Table 3.7 shows, while non-incumbent candidates far outnumber incumbent ones, virtually all of the latter are among the top four. With fifteen candidates per constituency on average, it should be no surprise that even if half of the incumbents were voted out, the unconditional probability of their victory relative to non-incumbents would be very high. Therefore, losses to a large number of incumbents are quite consistent with the incumbents having a strong showing in a statistical sense. In a similar vein, even as the main parties such as the Congress and the BJP might experience a decline in their tally of seats, the statistical probability of their candidates winning would still remain very high relative to the rest of the main parties taken together.

Table 3.7 INCUMBENTS AMONG ALL CONTESTANTS, TOP FOUR AND WINNERS (CANDIDATES IN ALL INDIAN STATES)

Incumbency Status	*Total Candidates*	*Top Four Candidates*	*Number of Winning Candidates*	*Probability of Being in Top Four*	*Probability of Victory*
	I	*II*	*III*	*IV: (II/I) x 100*	*V: (III/I) x 100*
Incumbents	387	376	184	97.2	47.5
Non-incumbents	7,684	1,794	359	23.3	4.7
Total	8,071	2,170	543	26.9	6.7

The Profile of an "Average" Candidate

Finally, we provide the average of each characteristic across all, top four and winning candidates in Table 3.8. If we could construct a winning candidate with these average characteristics, he would be a wealthy male (with mean assets worth 59 million rupees and median assets worth 12 million rupees) in his mid-fifties with at least an undergraduate degree. He would come from one of the main political parties. There is a 30 percent chance that he would have at least one criminal case against him and a 15 percent chance that he will have two or more criminal cases against him, and a 14 percent chance that the case would involve a serious crime. There is also 34 percent probability that he had served as an MP in the previous parliament.

Table 3.8 AVERAGE OF THE CHARACTERISTICS ACROSS VARIOUS CANDIDATES (CANDIDATES IN ALL INDIAN STATES)

Characteristics	*All Candidates*	*Top Four Candidates*	*Winning Candidates*
Age	46	51	53
Wealth category	2.1	3	5
(Average wealth in million rupees)	-17	-41	-59
Criminal record (probability in %)	14	27	30
Serious crime (probability)	7.4	13	13.8
Member, national party (probability in %)	20	60	69
Member, state party (probability)	9	19	27
Male (probability in %)	93	92	89
Education (category)	2.6	3.1	3.2
Incumbent (probability in %)	4.8	17.3	34

RURAL-URBAN DIVIDE VERSUS ECONOMIC PERFORMANCE

Having analyzed the role of candidate characteristics, we now turn to a consideration of the key question raised at the beginning of this chapter. Are the critics right in their claim that the reforms have exclusively benefited the urban capitalists and done precious little for the masses in the countryside thereby leading the latter to vote out governments sympathetic to growth-oriented reforms? Or is it that they are now more inclined to pay attention to the economic performance and vote out the governments that fail to deliver good economic performance, as the reform advocates argue?

That the case of the reform critics is weak is readily shown. There is now compelling evidence (including in chapters 3 and 4 of this volume) that the reforms that led to accelerated growth on a sustained basis had actually led to a significant decline in poverty in both rural and urban areas by 2004. The decline in poverty has also been across the board extending to the socially disadvantaged, Scheduled Castes, and Scheduled Tribes. Therefore, the very premise on which the critics' argument is based is empirically invalid.

Equally important, an analysis of 2009 election results reveals that the voting pattern exhibits no urban-rural divide. In Table 3.9, we report the number of urban and rural constituencies and the rates of victory of the state incumbent party in the state as a whole and in urban and rural regions separately. We define a constituency to be urban if less than 60 percent of its population is rural. The table includes the nineteen major states on which our subsequent analysis will focus. The main point to note is that proportions of victories of the state incumbent party in the rural and urban areas closely match. For example, the incumbent party, which did well overall in Tamil Nadu and Andhra Pradesh, did well in both rural and urban constituencies. In Uttar Pradesh, the incumbent party did poorly overall and in rural and urban constituencies taken separately. In Gujarat, the results were moderate for the incumbent party overall as well as separately in rural and urban regions. If the assertion by Rushdie quoted in the introduction that the election was a contest between cities and countryside were right, we would find a divide in the vote across rural-urban boundaries.

Table 3.9 VICTORY PROPORTIONS OF STATE INCUMBENT PARTY IN RURAL AND URBAN CONSTITUENCIES

State	Urban Constituencies	Rural Constituencies	Incumbent Party Candidates Elected (as % of total)		
			Statewide	Urban Constituencies	Rural Constituencies
Andhra Pradesh	5	37	79	80	78
Bihar	2	38	80	100	79
Chhattisgarh	0	11	91	NA	91
Goa	2	0	100	100	NA
Gujarat	11	15	58	55	60
Haryana	1	9	90	100	89
Himachal Pradesh	0	4	75	NA	75
Jharkhand	3	11	67	100	56
Kerala	3	17	29	0	36

Madhya Pradesh	4	25	55	100	48
Maharashtra	18	30	54	72	43
Delhi	7	0	100	100	NA
Orissa	1	20	78	100	76
Punjab	4	9	40	0	57
Rajasthan	4	21	16	0	19
Tamil Nadu	24	15	82	77	89
Uttar Pradesh	8	72	25	13	26
Uttarakhand	0	5	0	NA	0
West Bengal	9	33	28	0	36

Note: "NA" stands for "not applicable."

The case of the critics is, thus, decisively refuted. To establish the case of the reform advocates that poor economic performance contributes negatively to the election outcome and good performance positively, we measure the economic performance in terms of the gross state somestic product (GSDP). Our approach is to divide the states into three groups of high, medium and low growth and then ask how the candidates of incumbent party in each of these groups of states do in relation to one another.

To make this approach operational, we must first identify the group of states to be included in the sample. We note at the outset that center-administered union territories do not have territory-level governments by definition. Therefore, the concept of incumbent versus non-incumbent territory-level government is redundant for them and they are automatically excluded from the sample. In addition, we exclude Jammu and Kashmir, and the seven northeastern states (including Assam) and Sikkim. These states have a very strong presence of the central government, which a priori undermines the idea of the electorate seeing the state government as being the principal entity responsible for the economic outcomes. Finally, due to multiple turnovers of the government, we are unable to determine the incumbent government in Karnataka. These exclusions limit the sample to 19 states already introduced in Table 3.9. These 19 states include 478 out of the total of 543 constituencies and 90 percent of the eligible voters. Of the included constituencies, 364 are in general categories, 78 are reserved for the Scheduled Caste candidates, and 36 are reserved for the Scheduled Tribe candidates.

We measure economic performance in terms of the average growth in the GSDP from the beginning of the fiscal year 2004–5 to the end of 2008–9.[8] This period approximately coincides with the period between the May 2004 and May 2009 general elections and also defines the approximate period of the incumbent rule in the states. We rank the states in the declining order of the average growth rate

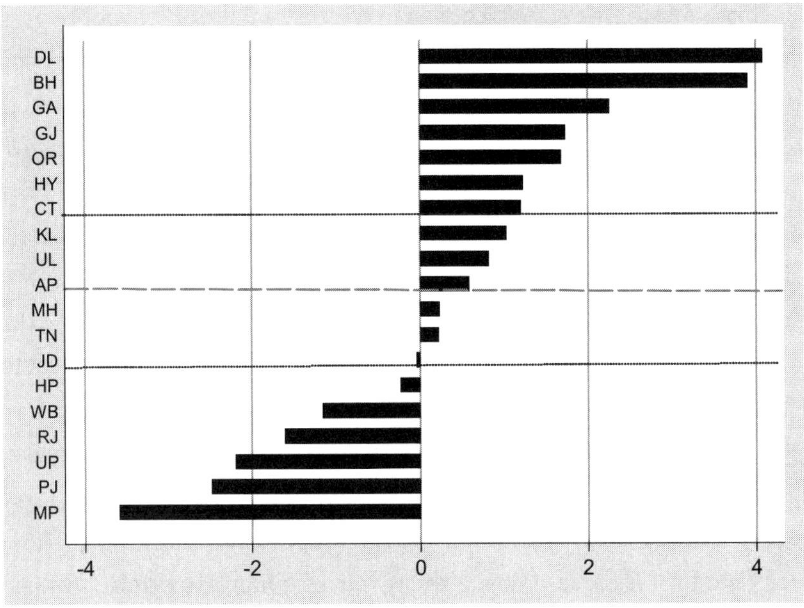

Figure 3.2. Difference between the Average Growth Rate of State Domestic Product and the GDP Growth Rate (2004–2008)

and divide them into three groups: high, medium, and low growth. In Figure 3.2, we depict the deviation of the average growth in the GSDP from that in the GDP for each of the nineteen states, with the states stacked in order of declining growth rates to accomplish this task. The dotted lines in turn divide the nineteen states into a high-growth group with seven states and low- and medium-growth groups of six states each.

We define the incumbent party as the main ruling party (or two main ruling parties when power is shared) in 2007 and in at least two consecutive preceding years. If there was an election for the state legislative assembly in 2008 or 2009 and the party ruling until 2007 lost this election, it was still considered the incumbent party for purposes of the national elections held in April–May 2009. The underlying logic is that the electorate would treat the party that was in government for several years prior to 2009 responsible for the policies and performance of the state rather than the party that took over the government in the year just preceding the general election.

Armed with this classification of the states and the definition of the incumbent party, we can ask the following key question: what proportion of the candidates fielded by the state incumbent party in the Lok Sabha constituencies located in that state won the national election? The outcome is depicted in Figure 3.3. Remarkably, on average, incumbent parties in the high-growth states won 85 percent of the seats they contested. In contrast, those in medium- and low-growth states could win on average only approximately 52 and 40 percent of the seats contested, respectively. This strong relationship between growth performance and election outcomes handsomely survives every model we test econometrically in Gupta and Panagariya (2011).

One final issue remains: if the reward for high growth in the elections is a recent phenomenon since the exception growth of 8 to 9 percent itself took root only recently, a pattern similar to Figure 3.3

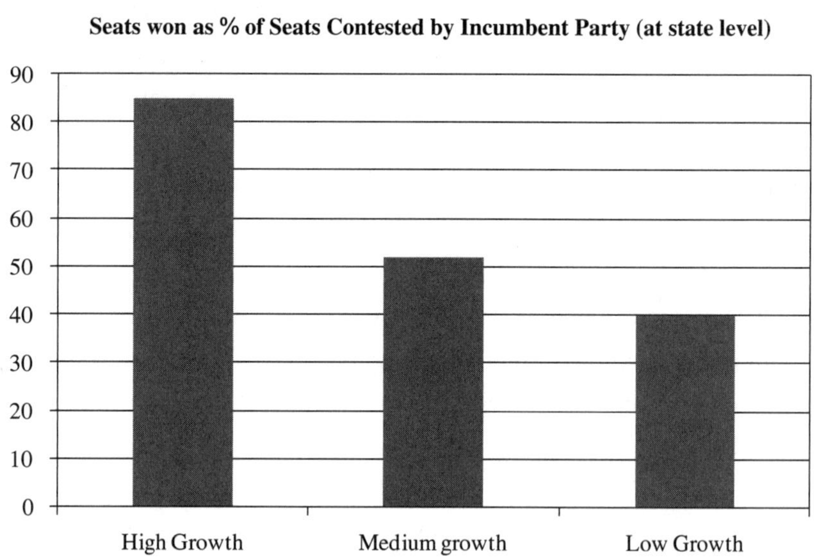

Figure 3.3. Proportion of the Candidates of the Incumbent Party in the State Winning the National Election (sorted by the states' growth rates)

will not obtain in the prior elections. This indeed turns out to be the case. Without reproducing the detailed calculations, we note that in the 2004 election, percentages of candidates of the incumbent parties winning were on average 11, 72, and 39, respectively, in high-, medium-, and low-growth states. The same lack of pattern existed in the 1996 elections with winning candidates of the state incumbent parties being on average 26, 56, and 25 percent of the contesting candidates in high-, medium-, and low-growth states, respectively.[9]

EXPLAINING THE SUPERIOR PERFORMANCE OF THE UPA[10]

The 2009 parliamentary election returned the UPA to power with more seats than even the most optimistic predictions. From 145 seats in 2004, the Congress increased its tally to 206 seats. Attributing this gain to the stellar growth performance at the national level, as done by some in the Indian press, is too simplistic. After all, the Congress performance varied widely across the states in the elections. For instance, as previously noted, it won just nine out of seventy-two seats in the states of Bihar, Orissa, and Chhattisgarh. Despite the high growth they experienced, these states voted overwhelmingly against the Congress. Clearly we need a more nuanced analysis to explain the increase in the Congress and UPA tallies.

Our analysis in the previous section offers a part of the explanation: states where the Congress ruled and growth performance was superior, it was able to retain and perhaps even increase its tally. For example, in Haryana and Delhi, two of the fastest-growing states, where the Congress was the incumbent party, it won most of the parliamentary seats, increasing its tally from 15 seats in 2004 to 16 seats in 2009 out of a total of 17 seats. But this factor by itself is not sufficient to explain the rise of the Congress tally from 145 in 2004 to 206 in 2009.

The larger part of the gains to the Congress and its allies came from states that had non-Congress governments and did not perform economically well. In these states, the state incumbent parties lost large number of seats, which the Congress and its allies were able to pick up. Table 3.10 provides the full details of the gains made by the Congress. In the states of Madhya Pradesh, Punjab, Rajasthan, and Uttar Pradesh, where the Congress was in the opposition and the growth record of the incumbent state governments turned out to be poor, it made huge gains, picking up forty-two extra seats. The Congress ally Trinamool Congress (AITC) made similar gains in West Bengal, another slow-growing state ruled by a rival party. The AITC added seventeen seats to its tally in the state, making it easier for the Congress to put together a coalition government. The Congress more or less maintained its 2004 position in most of the medium-growth states; Kerala is the major exception. In that state, the Congress added as many as thirteen states, though it also lost three between Jharkhand and Uttarkhand.

Table 3.10 ADDITIONS TO THE CONGRESS TALLY IN 2009 OVER 2004 ELECTION

	High-Growth States	*Medium-Growth States*	*Low-Growth States*
Congress government	1 (Delhi, Haryana)	8 (Andhra Pradesh, Maharashtra)	
Non-Congress government	2 (Bihar, Orissa, Chhattisgarh, Gujarat)	10 (Jharkhand, Kerala, Uttarakhand)	42 (Madhya Pradesh, Punjab, Rajasthan, Uttar Pradesh)

Our analysis to date does not allow us to explain why the Congress was the major beneficiary of the losses incurred by the incumbent parties in states with non-Congress governments that performed economically poorly. Our analysis predicts the losses to the incumbent party but does explain why the voters then choose the candidates of one or the other party. There is some tentative evidence that the main opposition party is the major beneficiary, but further work is required to establish this hypothesis more definitively.

CONCLUDING REMARKS

The issue of how the changes in the economic fortunes induced by policy changes affect election outcomes has been a long-standing one. In India, some analysts have argued that the liberal economic reforms of the 1990s and beyond hurt the vast majority of the poor residing in rural India. As a result, the electorate votes out the governments that try to implement such reforms. An alternative view is that voters reward governments that adopt policies that deliver better economic outcomes as reflected in faster economic growth. In this chapter, we have provided evidence contradicting the first hypothesis and prima facie supporting the second hypothesis. In Gupta and Panagariya (2011), we carry out detailed econometric analysis, which robustly established this hypothesis.

In addition to this key result, we have also noted the role the candidate-specific characteristics might play in the election outcomes. Once again, our results in this chapter are tentative, but we give them further rigor in the companion article mentioned in the previous paragraph. We offer data showing that educated and wealthy candidates win disproportionately. Moreover, incumbents have had much higher rates of victory than non-incumbents. These results, of course, do not establish causation, since wealth and education may be correlated with other unobserved characteristics that the voters prefer. We conclude with a word of caution. Growth itself may be correlated with several attributes that the voters value. For example, superior growth performance may be positively correlated with good governance including law and order. It may also be associated with reduced levels of poverty. Therefore, there remains scope for differences of opinion on whether the voters rewarded growth in the 2009 elections or other variables with which it might be correlated. From a policy perspective, however, we do not see this as a major issue. Even if the voters value these other variables over growth per se, growth would serve as a reasonable target variable for the state politicians to win the elections.

NOTES

* The authors are at National Institute of Public Finance and Policy, New Delhi, and Columbia University, New York. They can be reached at pgupta@nipfp.org.in and ap2231@columbia.edu, respectively. Work on this chapter has been supported by Columbia University's Program on Indian Economic Policies, funded by a generous grant from the John Templeton Foundation. The opinions expressed in the chapter are those of the authors and do not necessarily reflect the views of the John Templeton Foundation. The authors are indebted to the participants of Columbia-NCAER Conference on Trade, Poverty, Inequality and Democracy on March 31–April 1, 2011, for many helpful comments and to Ganesh Manjhi for his excellent research assistance.

1. Lok Sabha, translated as "Assembly of the People," is the lower house of the Indian Parliament. For purposes of elections to Lok Sabha, the country is divided into 543 constituencies, principally on the basis of population, with each constituency electing one member. Elections to the upper house, called Rajya Sabha and translated as "state Assembly," are indirect with the vast majority of its members elected by the state legislative assemblies.
2. This incumbency effect could be due to a variety of reasons, such as the incumbent candidates and parties having more resources to spend on election campaigns, having better name recognition, or even being more charismatic. Our results here do not separate the pure incumbency effect on which a great deal of the political science literature focuses.

3. For example, Rogoff and Sibert (1988) and Alesina and Rosenthal (1989) analyze the use of fiscal and monetary policy actions, and Besley and Case (1995) analyze the use of tax-expenditure choices by incumbents to gain electoral support. Levitt and Poterba (1999) study the effect of congressional representation on state economic growth. Levitt (1994), Baron (1989), and Snyder (1990) examine the response of politicians to campaign contributions. Lee (2001) provides additional references.
4. An excellent example of this analysis is Lee 2001. A vast body of political science literature is devoted to the analysis of the incumbency effect in election outcomes. For example, see Erikson 1971, Collie 1981, Garand and Gross 1984, Jacobson 1987, Payne 1980, Alford and Hibbing 1981, and Gelman and King 1990.
5. Uppal (2009) also finds that incumbency has hurt the candidates in recent Indian elections.
6. India has more than one thousand registered political parties. These are divided into national parties, state parties, and unrecognized parties. Any registered party that lacks the status of state or national party is an unrecognized party. The Election Commission confers the status of state party on any party that meets certain thresholds in terms of votes received and seats won in an election. A state party acquires monopoly on the use of its party symbol in the state. A party qualifying as state party in four states gets the national status and then has the monopoly over the use of its election symbol over the entire country. It is not unusual for parties to lose the national status if they lose the qualifications for it.
7. Virmani (2004) offers an analysis of the voter behavior in the 2004 election.
8. Data in India typically relate to its fiscal year, which begins on April 1 and ends on March 31. Therefore, fiscal year 2004–5 refers to the period from April 1, 2004, to March 31, 2005.
9. We do not do this calculation for the 1998 and 1999 elections because they took place as a result of the fall of unstable coalition governments, which fell well before their full five-year terms ended. Because the state elections in the majority of states had taken place in 1996 or before, the identification of the incumbent parties in the states for these years is not a clean affair.
10. This section draws heavily on Gupta (2011).

REFERENCES

Alesina, A., and H. Rosenthal (1989). "Moderating Elections." NBER Working Papers 3072.

Alford, J. R., and J. R. Hibbing (1981). "Increased Incumbency Advantage in the House." *Journal of Politics* 43, 1042–61.

Baron, David (1989). "Service-Induced Campaign Contributions, Incumbent Shirking, and Reelection Opportunities." In P. C. Ordeshook, ed., *Models of Strategic Choice in Politics*, 93–120. Ann Arbor: University of Michigan Press.

Besley, T., and A. Case. (1995). "Does Electoral Accountability Affect Economic Policy Choices? Evidence from Gubernatorial Term Limits." *Quarterly Journal of Economics* 110(3), 769–98.

Bhagwati, J., and A. Panagariya (2004). "Great Expectations." *Wall Street Journal*, May 24.

Brender, A., and A. Drazen (2008). "How Do Budget Deficits and Economic Performance Affect Reelection Prospects?" *American Economic Review* 98(5), 2203–20.

Collie, M. P. (1981). "Incumbency, Electoral Safety, and Turnover in the House of Representatives, 1952–1976." *American Political Science Review* 75, 119–31.

Erikson, Robert S. (1971). "The Advantage of Incumbency in Congressional Elections." *Polity* 3, 395–405.

Fair, Ray C. (1978). "The Effect of Economic Events on Votes for President." *Review of Economics and Statistics* 60(2), 159–73.

Garand, James C., and Donald A. Gross (1984). "Change in the Vote Margins for Congressional Candidates: A Specification of the Historical Trends." *American Political Science Review* 78, 17–30.

Gelman, A., and G. King (1990). "Estimating Incumbency Advantage without Bias." *American Journal of Political Science* 34, 1142–64.

Gupta, Poonam (2011). "For Performers, Incumbency Helps." *Financial Express*, April 19.

Gupta, P., and A. Panagariya (2011). "Growth and Election Outcomes in a Developing Country." Columbia Program on Indian Economic Policies, Working Paper no. 2011-8.

Jacobson, Gary C. (1987). "The Marginals Never Vanished: Incumbency and Competition in Elections to the U.S. House of Representatives, 1952–1982." *American Journal of Political Science* 31, 126–41.

Lee, David S. (2001). "The Electoral Advantage to Incumbency and Voters' Valuation of Politicians' Experience: A Regression Discontinuity Analysis of Elections to the US House." NBER Working Paper no. W8441.

Levitt, S. D. (1994). "Using Repeat Challengers to Estimate the Effect of Campaign Spending on Election Outcomes in the U.S. House." *Journal of Political Economy* 102(4), 777–98.

Levitt, S. D., and J. M. Poterba (1999). "Congressional Distributive Politics and State Economic Performance." *Public Choice* 99(1–2), 185–216.

Lewis-Beck, Michael S. (1988). *Economics and Elections*. Ann Arbor: University of Michigan Press.

Linden, L. (2004). "Are Incumbents Really Advantaged? The Preference for Non-incumbents in Indian National Elections." Unpublished ms., Columbia University.

Panagariya, A. (2004). "Vote against Reforms?" *Economic and Political Weekly* 39(21), May 22, 2079–81.

——— (2009). "Is Anti-incumbency Really Passé?" *Economic Times,* May 28.

Payne, J. L. (1980). "The Personal Electoral Advantage of House Incumbents." *American Politics Quarterly* 8, 375–98.

Powell, G. B., Jr., and G. D. Whitten (1993). "A Cross-National Analysis of Economic Voting: Taking Account of the Political Context." *American Journal of Political Science,* 37(2), 391–414.

Ravishankar, N. (2009). "The Cost of Ruling: Anti-incumbency in Elections." *Economic and Political Weekly* 44(10), 92–98.

Rogoff, K., and A. Sibert (1988). "Elections and Macroeconomic Policy Cycles." *Review of Economic Studies* 55(1), 1–16.

Rushdie, Salman (2004). "India's New Era." *Washington Post,* May 14, http://www.washingtonpost.com/wp-dyn/articles/A25770-2004May13.html

Snyder, J. M., Jr. (1990). "Campaign Contributions as Investments: The U.S. House of Representatives, 1980–1986." *Journal of Political Economy* 98, 1195–227.

Uppal, Y. (2009). "The Disadvantaged Incumbents: Estimating Incumbency Effects in Indian State Legislatures." Public Choice 138(1), 9–27.

Virmani, Arvind (2004). "Economic Growth, Governance and Voting Behavior: An Application to Indian Elections." ICRIER Working Paper no. 138.

Yadav, Y. (2004). "The Elusive Mandate of 2004." *Economic and Political Weekly* 39(51), December 18, 5383–95.

PART TWO

TRADE, POVERTY, AND INEQUALITY

Chapter 4

Trade Liberalization and Poverty Reduction

New Evidence from Indian States

J. CAIN, RANA HASAN, AND DEVASHISH MITRA

International trade leads to gains in aggregate welfare or average real incomes through various channels. It generates efficiency gains from specialization and exchange based on comparative advantage. It also leads to higher welfare and productivity due to the availability of larger varieties of final and intermediate goods. These are aggregate effects and do not automatically translate into a reduction in poverty, as trade does create winners and losers.

Under fairly plausible conditions, trade theory tells us that the winners from trade liberalization are the owners of the factor(s) of production a country is relatively abundant in, and the losers are the owners of the scarce factor(s). Most poor countries are relatively abundant in unskilled labor. This fact should lead us to expect that unskilled workers will benefit from trade liberalization in such countries. As a result, trade reforms should help with poverty reduction in poor, unskilled-labor-abundant countries. However, what can come in the way of the prediction regarding the poverty reducing effect of trade to hold is the lack of mobility of factors, including labor, from one sector to another. The reasons are twofold. First, the gains from specialization work through the reallocation of factors from one sector to another. Second, the prediction that all unskilled workers gain from trade in a country that is abundant in them requires the equalization of their wages across sectors. In the absence of intersectoral labor mobility, such equalization will not take place, and workers who are not able to get out of sectors that are forced to shrink upon trade liberalization will see a decline in their incomes (and even an adverse change in their employment status in the presence of other labor market rigidities).

Based on the arguments above, the effect of trade on poverty is an empirical question. The two studies that have examined the impact of trade reforms on poverty in the Indian context are Topalova (2005) and Hasan, Mitra, and Ural (2007). Topalova examined the impact of trade liberalization on district-level poverty in India. Her main findings can be summarized in three short quotes from her paper: (1) "rural districts where industries more exposed to trade liberalization were concentrated experienced a slower progress in poverty reduction"; (2) "compared to a rural district experiencing no change in tariffs, a district experiencing the mean level of tariff changes saw a 2 percentage points increase in poverty incidence and a .6 percentage points increase in poverty depth. This setback represents about 15 percent of India's progress in poverty reduction over the 1990s"; (3) there is "no statistically significant relationship between trade exposure and poverty in urban India," but point estimates are still in the same direction in urban poverty as in rural poverty.

The results from Hasan, Mitra, and Ural (2007) are quite different from those of Topalova (2005). In no case do they find reductions in trade protection to have worsened poverty at the state or region level. Instead, they find that states whose workers are on average more exposed to foreign competition tend to have lower rural, urban, and overall poverty rates (and poverty gaps), and this beneficial effect of greater trade openness is more pronounced in states with more flexible labor market institutions. They also find that trade liberalization has led to poverty reduction to a greater degree in states more exposed to foreign competition by virtue of their sectoral composition. Their results hold, at varying strengths and significance, for overall, urban, and rural poverty. In addition, they find some evidence that industrial delicensing has had a more beneficial impact on poverty reduction in states with flexible labor institutions, consistent with the findings of Aghion et al. (2008) on the relationship between delicensing and performance in the registered manufacturing sector across Indian states.

Unlike Topalova, who restricts her analysis to tariffs, Hasan, Mitra, and Ural look at both tariffs and nontariff barriers (NTBs). Just the way Topalova arrives at her district-level measure of tariffs, Hasan, Mitra, and Ural weight tariffs and alternatively NTBs by sectoral employment to arrive at the state-level inverse measure of the trade exposure of the labor force. But unlike Topalova, they refrain from using nontradable employment weights (where Topalova sets zero sectoral tariffs) in the aggregation of protection, since a commodity not being traded means the trade costs are prohibitive (not zero). They allow for the transmission of changes in protection rates to domestic prices to vary by state in some of their analysis. Third, in order to avoid sampling related issues, they work with state-level measures of urban, rural, and overall poverty (see Hasan, Mitra, and Ural 2007 for details), whereas Topalova uses district-level measures of urban and rural poverty.[1] They also complement their analysis with robustness checks using region-level measures of poverty, where regions are those defined by the National Sample Survey (NSS). As in Topalova's analysis, the poverty measures used in Hasan, Mitral, and Ural (2007) are based on the poverty lines recommended by Deaton and Dreze (2002; henceforth, DD) and their approach for adjusting poverty estimates for a change in the questionnaire design of the 1999–2000 NSS household expenditure survey. However, as robustness checks, Hasan, Mitra, and Ural also use two additional sets of poverty measures: Government of India (GOI) estimates of poverty with an adjustment made for the new questionnaire adopted in 1999–2000 and a longer series (ten years of data for the 1990s and late 1980s) of state-level poverty rates created by Ozler, Datt, and Ravallion (1996; henceforth, ODR) using both the "thick" and "thin" rounds of the NSS in India.[2] Finally, while the "thick-round" analysis in Hasan, Mitra, and Ural is based on poverty estimates for three years—corresponding to the latest three available "thick" rounds of the NSS (i.e., 1987–88, 1993–94, and 1999–2000) for which protection data are available—Topalova's analysis is restricted to two thick rounds, those for 1987–88 and 1999–2000. Topalova justifies her approach based on the uncertainty regarding whether the 1993–94 poverty is driven by post- or prereform policies; by contrast, Hasan, Mitra, and Ural include 1993–94 in their thick-round analysis, since the state-level trade exposure measure is being used as a regressor.

Given the importance of understanding the effects of trade liberalization on poverty, this chapter updates and extends the study by Hasan, Mitra, and Ural (2007). For updating the study, we construct using household-level data from the latest available large-sample round of the National Sample Survey (NSS Round 61), the standard poverty measures both at the state and region levels. In terms of extending the analysis, we look at whether and how the gains in poverty reduction from trade liberalization vary depending on road connectivity and financial development. While roads will determine how changes in prices at the border translate into local prices, financial development determines how well the banking system responds to the changes in the needs of producers for credit in response to trade reforms. In the face of greater competition through trade liberalization, domestic producers might have to increase their scale of production or invest in more modern techniques, for which they need access to credit. We also try to see how the effects of trade liberalization on poverty vary by the degree of labor market flexibility in the various states; while this was also done in the earlier study, we experiment with alternative measures in the present study.

In this new study, we continue to rely on state- and NSS-region-specific poverty estimates based on the poverty lines developed by Deaton (2003a). However, since the latter only cover the years 1987–88, 1993–94, and 1999–2000 (referred to in Hasan, Mitra, and Ural 2007 as "Deaton and Dreze" or "the DD poverty measures"), we incorporate in our analysis poverty estimates for 2004–5 by using the poverty lines updated by Amoranto and Hasan (2010) for that year using the procedures of Deaton (2003a). In addition, we check the robustness of our results by using a second set of state- and NSS-region-specific poverty estimates, namely those from the government's Expert Group (Government of India 2009) for the years 1993–94 and 2004–5, with observations generated for 1987–88 by extrapolating the Expert Group's poverty lines for the year 1987–88 using Deaton's (2003a) Fischer prices indexes. All our poverty rate estimates are at the state and region levels and are calculated for the rural and urban sectors separately as well for the overall state or region.

The protection measures are the same as those used by Hasan, Mitra, and Ural (2007) but extended to the year 2003, which serves as the lagged protection for the year 2004–5 (NSSO Round 61). They are weighted by employment in different industries to create overall, rural, and urban protection measures (tariff, NTB, and a principal-components combination of the two) from the industry-level protection measures at the national level. Since we want to see whether the trade-poverty nexus is affected by labor market flexibility, we use the measure of labor market flexibility used by Hasan, Mitra, and Ural (2007) and by Hasan, Mitra, and Ramaswamy (2007), which partitions the set of major Indian states into the subset of flexible labor market states and rigid labor market states. Since there is disagreement on this partitioning, we use two alternative partitionings. Our results are robust to all three measures, indicating that the four common states in the flexible subset across the measures (relative to the six common states in the rigid subset) might be driving the results regarding the differential effects of trade on poverty in flexible versus rigid states.

These effects could also be different because the degree of transmission of international prices and protection can differ by state depending on road connectivity. We control for that in our regressions using road density by state. This also allows us to see how the effects of exposure to foreign trade on poverty could vary as road connectivity changes across states and over time. Another state characteristic that can lead to a differential effect is financial development. We use a survey-based measure capturing the proportion of firms facing difficulties in obtaining credit and, alternatively, a principal-components measure based on credit-deposit ratios in nationalized banks and the post office-to-population ratio, among other things, from Ghosh and De (2004). Finally, we also control for and analyze the impact of another component of globalization, namely foreign direct investment (FDI). We do this by using the ratio of foreign direct investment to the gross domestic product of a state.

We find that on average, for every percentage-point reduction in the weighted tariff rate there was a .57 percent reduction in poverty, which implies that a 38 percent reduction in poverty during 1987–2004 can be attributed to change in the exposure to foreign trade. An alternative interpretation is that a state that experienced a percentage-point higher reduction in employment-weighted tariff than another state experienced a .57 percent greater reduction in poverty. Since our regressions use time controls and poverty all across the country has been declining over time, we can infer that trade liberalization (and the greater exposure of the labor force to foreign competition) actually speeded up poverty reduction. Qualitatively similar but quantitatively much larger estimates result from the use of NTBs, possibly additionally capturing the effects of other correlated policy and institutional variables.

In the case of urban poverty, we find not only that have reductions in tariff rates been associated with reductions in urban poverty across India's states, but also that the extent of this poverty reduction has been larger in states with flexible labor regulations. In addition, we find that reductions in urban poverty induced by trade liberalization have been faster in states with higher road density and more advanced banking and financial systems. In the case of rural poverty, while the overall effect of protection on poverty is qualitatively similar, the evidence for differential effects based on labor-market flexibility, road density, and financial development is quite weak.

The remainder of this chapter is organized as follows. The next section reviews the literature on the relationships between trade, growth, and poverty. We then describe key elements of the Indian policy framework relating to trade, labor regulations, and the industrial licensing regime over the 1980s and 1990s. Next, we discuss data issues concerning poverty and measures relating to the policies described earlier. This is followed by the results of our empirical work and concluding remarks.

TRADE AND POVERTY: REVIEW OF RELATED LITERATURE

It has been argued by Bhagwati (2004) that trade, by fostering growth, leads to higher incomes and in turn a reduction in poverty. Therefore, we first review the literature on the effects of trade barriers on growth and income, which have been empirically studied since the early 1990s. Various cross-country macro studies, using different measures of openness, have showed positive effects of trade on growth (see, for instance, Dollar 1992, Sachs and Warner 1995, and Edwards 1998). However, these papers have been strongly criticized by Rodriguez and Rodrik (2001) for the problems with their openness and protection measures, their econometric techniques, and the difficulty in establishing the direction of causality. While the measure of openness used by Sachs and Warner (1995), as argued by Rodriguez and Rodrik (2001), captures many aspects of the macroeconomic environment in addition to trade policy, Baldwin (2003) has recently defended that approach on the grounds that the other policy reforms captured in the measure accompany most trade reforms. Therefore, the use of such a measure tells us the value of the entire package of trade and accompanying reforms. Wacziarg and Welch (2003) have updated the Sachs-Warner dataset and have again shown the positive growth effects of such reforms.

The more recent papers look at the effects of trade on income levels rather than growth rates. Frankel and Romer (1999), using gravity- and geography-based predicted trade flows as instruments, find positive effects of trade on income levels that are greater than the estimates produced by ordinary least squares. Irwin and Tervio (2002) demonstrate the robustness of these results, applying the same approach to cross-country data from various periods in the twentieth century.

Rodrik, Subramanian, and Trebbi (2002) have looked at the simultaneous effects of institutions, geography, and trade on per capita income levels. Using a measure of property rights and the rule of law to capture institutions and the trade–GDP ratio to capture openness in trade, and appropriately instrumenting them, they find that "the quality of institutions trumps everything else." However, trade and institutions have positive effects on each other, so trade does have indirect effects on income.

The literature on the direct determinants of poverty rates and changes (or rather reductions) in them is much smaller.[3] Dollar and

Kraay (2002), in a cross-country study of ninety-two countries over the last four decades, find that the growth rates of average incomes of people in the bottom quintile are no different from the growth rates of overall per capita incomes; growth in the former is always associated with growth in the latter. Also, policies that promote overall growth promote growth in the incomes of the poor. These policies include trade openness, macroeconomic stability, moderate government size, financial development, strong property rights, and the rule of law. In another paper, Dollar and Kraay (2004), based on data from the post-1980 "globalizing developing economies," argue that per capita income growth arising from expansion in trade in those countries has led to a sharp fall in absolute poverty in the past twenty years.

Similarly, Ravallion (2001) finds that an increase in the per capita income by 1 percent can reduce the proportion of people below the $1-a-day poverty line by about 2.5 percent on average. This varies across countries, depending how close the poor are to the poverty line. Research by Ravallion and Datt (1999) on the determinants of poverty reduction across India's major states between 1960 and 1994 also shows empirically the importance of initial conditions. They find that a 1 percent increase in nonagricultural state domestic product leads to a 1.2 percent decline in poverty rates in the states of Kerala and West Bengal versus only .3 percent decline in Bihar. The fact that growth of nonfarm output was also relatively meager in Bihar over the period under consideration exacerbated the poverty problem in Bihar. Ravallion and Datt find that more than half of the differential impact of nonfarm output on poverty rates is attributable to Kerala's much higher levels of initial literacy. Their results suggest that while the transition from (low-wage) agriculture to (higher-wage) nonfarm sectors may be key for the removal of poverty, making the transition is not easy or automatic for the poor. In other words, there are pecuniary costs as well as nonpecuniary ones associated with investments in minimum levels of education, nutrition, and health to be incurred on the part of a poor agricultural worker trying to make the transition.

Finally, Hasan, Quibria, and Kim (2003) argue, using cross-country evidence, that "policies and institutions that support economic freedom are critical for poverty reduction." Economic freedom indicators used by these authors include government size, price stability, freedom to trade with foreigners, absence of overregulation of markets, and civil liberties as reflected in property rights, rule of law, and so on.

We end this literature review with two cautionary notes. First, most of these studies are cross-country. Such studies, despite using numerous controls, cannot control for the institutional diversity across the world. Second, some of the poverty studies use a uniform $1-a-day definition of poverty. Although the conversion of local currencies into the US dollar is made using purchasing power parities, there are some well-known limitations of these for the purposes of comparing poverty across countries and even within them (Asian Development Bank 2008).

INDIAN POLICY FRAMEWORK

Trade Policy Reforms in India

From independence through the early 1980s, India pursued a development strategy of import substitution. While some liberalization began in the 1980s, by far the most decisive break with the trade policies of the past came in 1991 in response to a balance-of-payments crisis resulting from a rapid rise in the fiscal deficit-to-GDP ratio, in foreign commercial debt, and in the debt service ratio. These problems were further accentuated into a crisislike situation by the dramatic oil price rise originating from the Gulf War. The government approached the International Monetary Fund (IMF) for financial assistance, which came attached with the strong conditionality of major economic reforms. These reforms were initiated almost immediately. Given several earlier attempts to avoid IMF loans and the associated conditionalities, these reforms came as a surprise.

The main objectives of the reform program included simplification of rules, the removal over time of import and export barriers (including both price and quantity restrictions), and the eventual full convertibility of the Indian rupee for foreign exchange transactions. The maximum tariff was reduced from 400 percent to 150 percent in July 1991 and to roughly 45 percent by 1997–98. Mean tariffs, which were 128 percent before July 1991, had fallen to roughly 35 percent by 1997–98. The mean manufacturing tariff fell to under 15 percent by 2005. The reductions in mean tariffs were also accompanied by significant reductions in tariff dispersion. Nontariff barriers were also reduced. Prior to 1991, there were quantitative restrictions on 90 percent of the value added in the manufacturing sector. In April 1992, all twenty-six import-licensing lists were eliminated, along with the introduction of a "negative list" (from which most intermediate and capital goods were excluded) of prohibited import items. This eliminated many of the licensing procedures and discretionary aspects of the previous import regime. The reductions in tariffs and nontariff barriers to trade were also accompanied by significant devaluations of the Indian rupee in 1991 and 1992.

Labor Markets: Regulations and Rigidity

A comprehensive review of labor regulations in India is beyond the scope of this chapter.[4] However, two features of India's labor regulations are noteworthy. First, under the Indian constitution, both the central (federal) government and individual state governments have the authority to legislate on labor-related issues and even amend central legislations. Enforcement of all labor regulations is mainly performed by the state governments.

Second, there is considerable debate among observers of the Indian economy regarding the impact of labor market regulations on the various dimensions of economic performance. Consider Chapter VB of the Industrial Disputes Act (IDA), which makes it compulsory for employers with more than one hundred workers to seek the prior approval of the government before workers can be dismissed. In practice, governments have often been unwilling to grant permission to retrench (Datta-Chaudhuri 1996).[5] Therefore, critics of these labor laws argue that they have created both a strong disincentive to hire (additional) workers and a bias against hiring (abundant) labor relative to (scarce) capital, leading to weak employment growth. Similar arguments have been made for other elements of labor regulations, including specific provisions of the Industrial Employment (Standing Orders) Act and the Trade Union Act (TUA).[6]

Not all analysts agree with the above view. Their counterargument is that most of India's labor regulations have been either ignored (see Nagaraj 2002) or circumvented through the increased usage of temporary or contract labor (see, in particular, Datta 2003 and Ramaswamy 2003). Ultimately, whether India's labor laws have created significant rigidities in labor markets or not is therefore an empirical question.

DATA

Poverty

Our main measure of (absolute consumption) poverty is the headcount index, or poverty rate. This measures the proportion of the population with consumption expenditures below a given threshold, or poverty line. We also consider an alternative measure of poverty, the poverty gap index (PGI). The PGI, unlike the poverty rate, gives a sense of how poor the poor are. It is equivalent to the shortfall of consumption below the poverty line per head of the total population, and is expressed as a percentage of the poverty line.[7]

In principle, the official poverty lines of the government of India and the large-scale or quinquennial-round consumer expenditure surveys carried out by the National Sample Survey Organisation (henceforth referred to as NSS surveys) approximately every five years provide an excellent basis for estimating measures of rural and urban poverty at the national, state, and NSS region level[8] over 1987–2004, the period of interest to us in this chapter. In practice, however, there has been considerable controversy about the estimates of poverty that these data yield. There are two main points of contention.[9] First, the information on food expenditures obtained by the NSS survey carried out in 1999–2000 has been deemed by many researchers to be incomparable with expenditure data from other large-scale NSS surveys carried out before *and* since then. Given the large share of food in total expenditures—almost two-thirds of total expenditures on average even for households in the fifth decile of the distribution of per capita expenditures in 2004–5—any incomparability in the food expenditures data would translate into incomparability of poverty estimates.[10]

Second, and more generally, many researchers have raised concerns about the official poverty lines used to generate official estimates of poverty. To understand these concerns, it is useful to briefly describe the official methodology for estimating poverty lines and poverty used currently (but under review as of the writing of this chapter). The current procedures, developed by the 1993 Expert Group (Government of India 1993) and adopted since March 1997 by India's Planning Commission, take as their starting point separate "all-India" poverty lines of Rs. 49.09 per person per month in rural India and Rs. 56.64 in urban India at 1973–74 prices. These poverty lines, developed originally by a specially constituted task force (Government of

India 1979), represent the monthly per capita consumption expenditures required on average to satisfy food consumption corresponding to specified calorie norms (2,400 kcal per capita per day in rural areas and 2,100 kcal per capita per day in urban areas) and some minimum of nonfood requirements (such as clothing, shelter, etc.). Crucially, the computation of these poverty lines is based on the observed expenditure patterns of households as captured by the NSS consumer expenditure survey of 1973–74. These all-India rural and urban poverty lines are then adjusted in two ways. First, state- and sector-specific price indexes for 1973–74 are used to come up with state- and sector-specific poverty lines to capture interstate price differentials (as they existed in 1973–74). Second, the state-specific poverty lines are updated for later years using price indexes based on the state-specific CPI of Agricultural Laborers (CPI-AL) in rural areas and CPI of Industrial Workers (CPI-IW) for urban areas to capture changes in the cost of living over time.[11] These poverty lines are then used against the NSS surveys to identify the poor as those whose monthly per capita expenditures fall below the poverty lines appropriate to their state and sector.

There are three main concerns with these procedures. First, 1973–74 consumption patterns are likely to have at best a weak relationship with consumption patterns of the poor today in both rural and urban areas. Second, as argued by Deaton (2003a), the CPIs used to adjust the state-specific rural and urban poverty lines over time yield implausible estimates of poverty. For example, the official urban poverty lines of Andhra Pradesh and Karnataka have been around *70 percent* higher than the corresponding rural lines in recent years and resulted in official estimates of urban poverty being much higher than rural poverty in these states, a situation deemed by many to be unreasonable. Indeed, the rural-urban price differentials implicit in the poverty lines have gone from an average of a little under 15 percent in 1973–74 to between 35 and 40 percent during 1987–1999. According to Deaton, such large price differentials reflect not so much real differences in the cost of living across rural and urban areas as the use of defective price indexes (which themselves arise on account of either defective price data and/or the use of outdated weights in aggregating prices) and a failure to consider changes in patterns of consumption across states over long periods of time. Finally, on the assumption that health care and education would be adequately provided by the state, the price indexes used to update the official poverty lines take no account of the price of obtaining health and educational services—a serious omission, given the increasing private expenditures on health and education over time (Government of India 2009).

We deal with the criticisms of the official poverty lines by using for our analysis poverty estimates based on two alternative sets of poverty lines. The first set of poverty lines are those developed by Deaton (2003a) covering the years 1987–88, 1993–94, and 1999–2000 and updated by Amoranto and Hasan (2010) for 2004–5 using the procedures of Deaton (2003a). In particular, Amoranto and Hasan extend to 2004–5 the Deaton poverty lines, which are specific to each state and rural/urban sector and anchored to the official all-India rural poverty line of 1987–88 (Rs. 115.70), using Törnqvist temporal and spatial price indexes calculated and used exactly along the lines of Deaton (2003a).[12]

In order to deal with the potential contamination of expenditure data caused by the use of seven- and thirty-day recall periods in the 1999–2000 NSS survey, we use the adjustments of Deaton (2003a) and Deaton (2003b) applied to data at the state and NSS region level, respectively, as in Hasan, Mitra, and Ural (2007).[13] This adjustment is designed to make the 1999–2000 expenditure information comparable with other large sample NSS rounds.[14]

As for the second set of state- and sector-specific poverty lines, we use the poverty lines (or poverty rates when available for the year or level of aggregation used in our analysis) developed by the 2009

Expert Group (Government of India 2009) for the years 1993–94 and 2004–5. Given the controversy surrounding the NSS survey for 1999–2000, we drop this year from our analysis entirely when using the Expert Group's poverty lines and poverty estimates. However, this still leaves us with the task of estimating poverty in 1987–88 using poverty lines that would be at least roughly consistent with the Expert Group's poverty lines for 1993–94. To do so, we use Deaton's (2003a) Fischer price indexes for 1993–94 relative to 1987–88 to translate the Expert Group's state- and sector-specific poverty lines for 1993–94 to come up with their corresponding 1987–88 values. (The 2009 Expert Group relied on the Fischer price index for their temporal and spatial price indexes.) We then use these poverty lines against the expenditure data reported in the 1987–88 NSS survey to estimate poverty rates in that year. In doing so, we are careful to follow the procedures of the Expert Group so that, rather than use household expenditures reported on a uniform thirty-day basis for our computations, we use "mixed reference period" expenditures, whereby the thirty-day expenditures for high-frequency consumption items (food, fuels, etc.) are combined with 365-day expenditures for low-frequency consumption items (clothing, footwear, and durables) duly prorated to thirty days.[15]

Admittedly, our approach for extending the Expert Group poverty lines back to 1987–88 is imperfect, as the Deaton (2003a) temporal price indexes are based on unit values of food, fuel, and intoxicants, while the Expert Group's price indexes also include information from unit values for clothing, bedding, and footwear based on the NSS surveys. The Expert Group's price indexes also incorporate information on the costs of education and health care expenditures, among others. Nevertheless, the common use of unit values for food and fuel items—a large part of the budget share of many Indian households—and an approach to controlling for temporal and spatial variations in prices that are similar in spirit across Deaton (2003a) and the approach of the 2009 Expert Group suggests that this exercise is defensible. Consider, for example, the use of much cruder national-level CPIs used to update international poverty lines (such as the $1.25-a-day poverty line in 2005 PPPs) over time and used routinely in cross-country analyses of poverty (for example, Chen and Ravallion 2008).

In summary, our estimates of poverty are based not on the Government of India's official poverty lines but, rather, the poverty lines of Deaton (2003a) and the 2009 Expert Group (Government of India 2009) adjusted to cover 2004–5 in the case of the former and 1987–88 in the case of the latter. Both sets of poverty estimates are available for rural and urban areas separately by state.[16] In addition, it may be noted that some of our analysis entails estimating the relationship between poverty and trade liberalization at the NSS region level. For this, we rely on state- and sector-specific poverty lines to estimate poverty for the corresponding regions. In addition, we employ the adjustment outlined in Deaton (2003a and 2003b) to deal with problems associated with the 1999–2000 NSS survey when using poverty estimates based on the Deaton poverty lines. Finally, some of our analysis is carried out by combining rural and urban areas. Combined rural and urban poverty estimates for any given state are simple averages of the corresponding rural and urban poverty estimates, each weighted by the sector's share in the combined population (as derived from NSS data). The time plots of the various estimates of poverty by state are described in Figures 4.1 and 4.2.

Protection

We follow Hasan, Mitra, and Ural (2007) for constructing state-level measures of trade protection at three levels of aggregation—the state as a whole, and urban and rural sectors within states. In particular, industry-level tariff rates and NTB coverage rates for agricultural, mining, and manufacturing industries are weighted by state- and sector-specific employment shares as follows:[17]

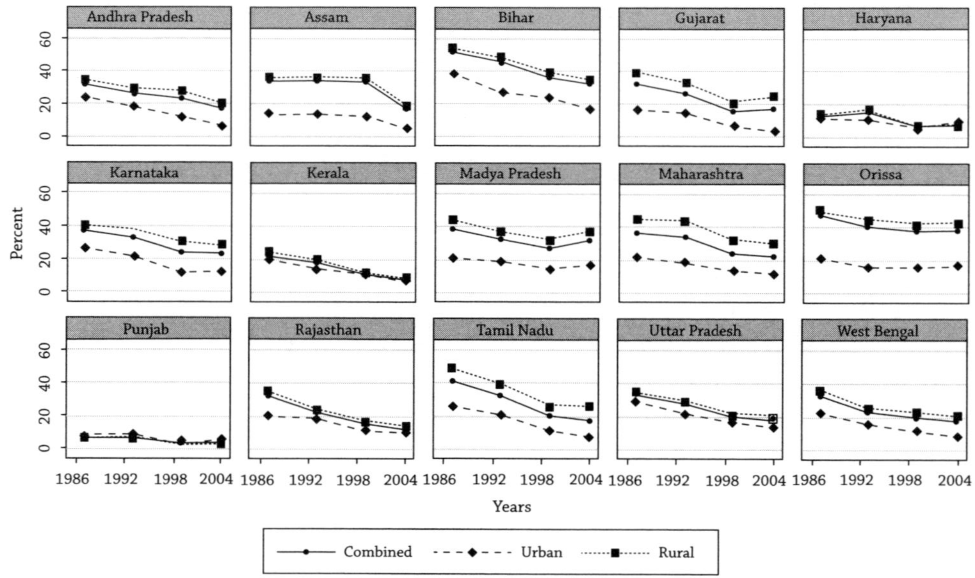

Figure 4.1. Poverty Rates by State (Deaton Poverty Lines)

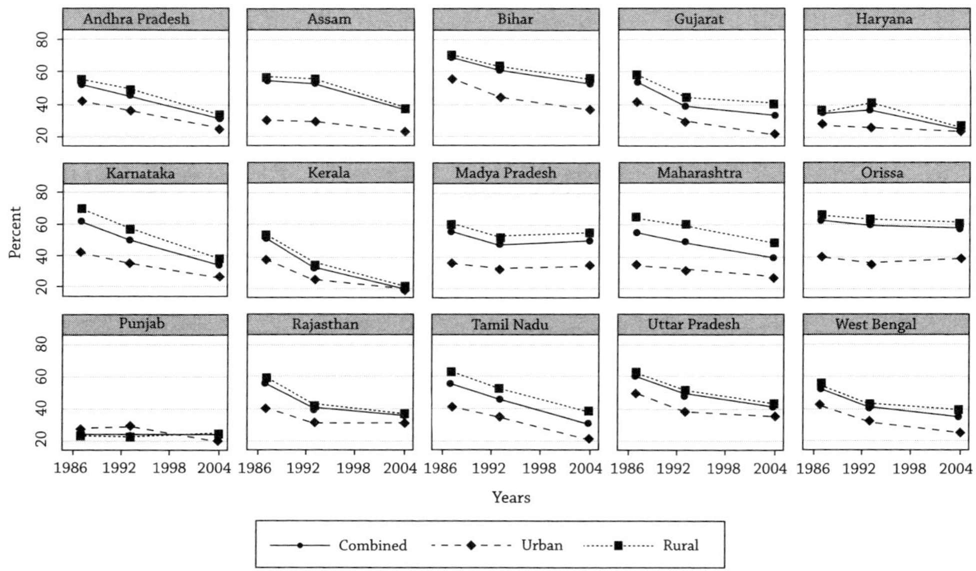

Figure 4.2. Poverty Rates by State (2009 Expert Group Poverty Lines)

where $\gamma^{j}_{ik,1993}$ is the employment share of industry k in broad sector j of state i derived from the 1993 employment-unemployment sur-

$$Tariff^{j}_{it} = \sum_{k} \gamma^{j}_{ik,1993} * Ind\_Tariff_{kt} \qquad (2)$$

$$NTB^{j}_{it} = \sum_{k} \gamma^{j}_{ik,1993} * Ind\_NTB_{kt} \qquad (3)$$

vey.[18] Ind_Tariff_{kt} and Ind_NTB_{kt} are industry-specific tariff rates and nontariff coverage rates that are measured at the two-digit industry level for each year t. $\sum_{k_m} \gamma^{j}_{ik,1993} = 1$ where k represents tradable two-digit industries (comprising agricultural, mining, and manufacturing industries). Nontradable industries were excluded from the calculations.[19]

A multicollinearity problem arises when tariffs and nontariff barriers are simultaneously used on the right-hand side of our regressions. This is due to the strong correlation between the two protection measures, and it prevents the precise estimation of their individual effects. To get around this problem, a combined measure of tariffs and NTBs is calculated using principal component analysis (PCA). PCA is commonly used to reduce the dimension of a matrix of correlated variables by combining them into a smaller set of variables that contains most of the variation in the data. In our case, the first principal component contains approximately 90 percent of the variation in the protection data for all industry groups, and hence is used as a combined measure. Figures 4.3 and 4.4 show the plots of tariff rates and NTB coverage ratios by state for the combined rural and urban sectors.

Labor Market Flexibility

As noted earlier, India's states can be expected to vary in terms of the flexibility of their labor markets, and this may have implications for the relationship between trade liberalization and poverty reduction.

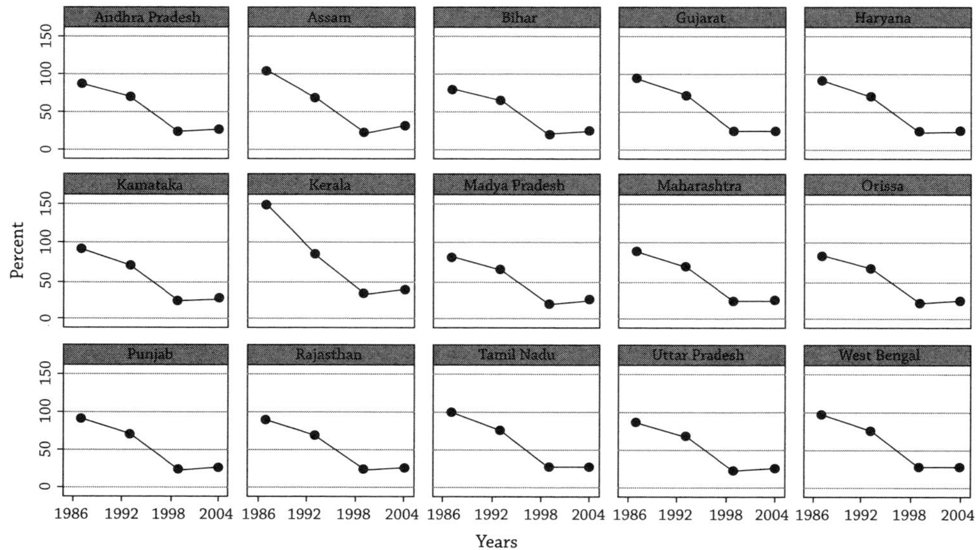

Figure 4.3. Tariff Rates (Lagged) by State

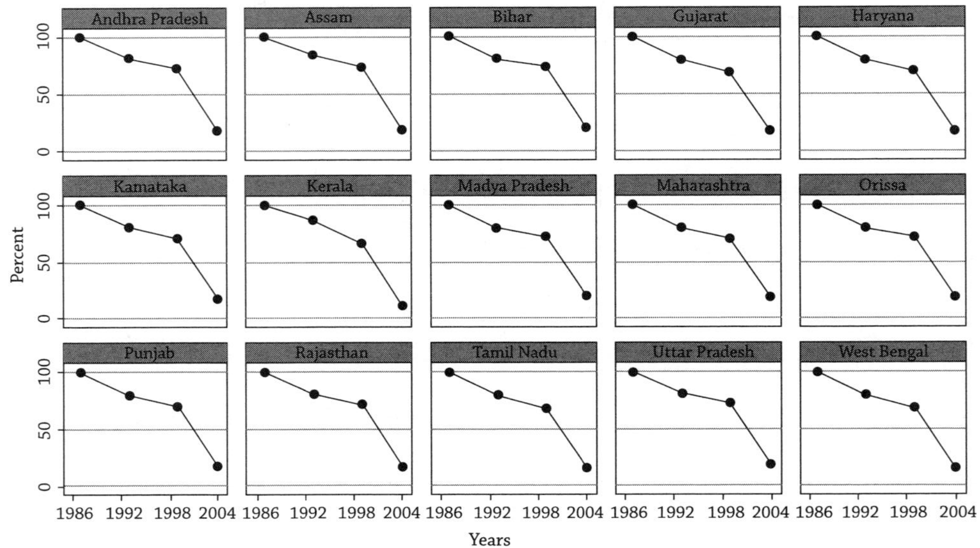

Figure 4.4. NTB Coverage Ratios (Lagged) by State

We use two approaches to partition states in terms of whether or not they have flexible labor markets. A first approach starts with Besley and Burgess's (2004) coding of amendments to the Industrial Disputes Act (IDA) from 1958 to 1992 as pro-employee, antiemployee, or neutral, and extends it to 2004.[20] Five states are found to have had antiemployee amendments (in net year terms, as defined in Besley and Burgess 2004): Andhra Pradesh, Karnataka, Kerala, Rajasthan, and Tamil Nadu.[21] Since antiemployee amendments are likely to give rise to flexible labor markets, a natural partition of states would be to treat these five states as having flexible labor markets.[22] These states are termed FLEX1 states in our empirical analysis. For these states the variable FLEX1 equals 1; for others it equals 0.

This partition has some puzzling features, however. Maharashtra and Gujarat, two of India's most industrialized states, are categorized as having inflexible labor markets on account of having passed pro-employee amendments to the IDA. However, businesses in India typically perceive these states to be good locations for setting up manufacturing plants. It is questionable whether businesses in India would consider Maharashtra and Gujarat to be especially good destinations for their capital if their labor markets were very rigid. Conversely, Kerala is categorized as having a flexible labor market despite an industrial record that is patchy compared with that of Maharashtra and Gujarat. Moreover, few businesses in India would consider it a prime location for setting up manufacturing activity.

An alternative partition of states arises by including Maharashtra and Gujarat in the list of states with flexible labor markets while dropping Kerala. A World Bank research project on the investment climate faced by manufacturing firms across ten Indian states lends strong support to such a switch (see Dollar, Iarossi, and Mengistae 2002 and World Bank 2003).[23] First, based on rankings by managers of surveyed firms, Maharashtra and Gujarat were the two states categorized as "Best Investment Climate" states; Kerala was one of the three "Poor Investment Climate" states. Second, the study reports that small and medium-sized enterprises receive twice as many factory inspections a year in poor-climate states (of which Kerala is a member) as in the two best-climate states, Maharashtra and Gujarat. This suggests that even if IDA amendments have been pro-employee in Maharashtra and Gujarat, their enforcement may be weak. Finally, a question on firms' perceptions about "overmanning"—that is, how the optimal level of employment would differ from current employment given the current level of output—indicate that while overmanning is present in all states, it is lowest on average in Maharashtra and Gujarat.[24] Thus, we consider a modified partition in which Maharashtra and Gujarat are treated as states with flexible labor markets, while Kerala is treated as a state with inflexible labor markets. The six states with flexible labor markets as per this modification are termed FLEX2 states (Andhra Pradesh, Gujarat Karnataka, Maharashtra, Rajasthan, and Tamil Nadu). For these states, the variable FLEX2 equals 1; for others it equals 0.

We also consider a final alternative partition of states that has recently been used by Gupta, Hasan, and Kumar (2009). This partition is based on combining information from Besley and Burgess (2004), Bhattacharjea (2008), and OECD (2007).[25] Bhattacharjea focuses his attention on characterizing state-level differences in Chapter VB of the IDA (which relates specifically to the requirement for firms to seek government permission for layoffs, retrenchments, and closures). However, Bhattacharjea considers not only the content of legislative amendments, but also judicial interpretations to Chapter VB in assessing the stance of states vis-à-vis labor regulation. He also carries out his own assessment of legislative amendments rather than relying on that of Besley and Burgess. The OECD study uses a very different approach and relies on a survey of key informants to identify the areas in which states have made specific changes to the implementation and administration of labor laws (including not only the IDA but other regulations as well). The OECD study aggregates the responses on each individual item across the various regulatory and administrative areas into an index that reflects the extent to which procedural changes have reduced transaction costs vis-à-vis labor issues. Gupta et al. take each of the three studies, partition states into those with flexible, neutral, or inflexible labor regulations, and then finally come up with a composite labor market regulation indicator variable using a simple majority rule across the different partitions. Based on their work, we define FLEX3, which takes a value of 1 for five states deemed to have flexible labor regulations (Andhra Pradesh, Karnataka, Rajasthan, Tamil Nadu, and Uttar Pradesh) and 0 for the remaining states.[26]

Other Variables

In addition to labor regulations, there may be other characteristics of states that influence the effects of trade liberalization in poverty. Two important characteristics pertain to the quality of the transportation infrastructure and financial system across states. The transmission of changes in protection rates to domestic prices may vary across states for a variety of reasons; one important factor is the quality of the transportation infrastructure. To allow for this possibility, we use information on road density by state (total kilometers of surfaced road divided by total state area in kilometers) to construct a proxy for transportation costs. Data on total kilometers of surfaced road is taken from the official website of the Ministry of Road Transport and Highways.[27] Data is available for the years 1987, 1993, and 1998 to 2002. As noted below, we introduce measures of protection and state characteristics (such as road density) with a one-year lag in our poverty regressions. Since the years for which we have poverty measures are 1987, 1993, 1999, and 2004, we use simple linear interpolation and extrapolation to generate values for road density for the years 1986, 1992, and 2003 (1998 not being available).

Similarly, it has been argued that the welfare effects of trade liberalization can depend crucially on the ability of households and enterprises to access credit, which in turn will depend on how well developed the financial system is at the state level (see Sundaram 2010 for details). Accordingly, we use an index of states' financial development created by Ghosh and De (2004) using information from 1981 to 1997 on credit-to-deposit ratios in nationalized banks, share of state tax revenue in net state domestic product, and the number of post offices per 10,000 of the population. Since the Ghosh and De index is available for 1981, 1991, and 1997, we again use simple linear interpolation and extrapolation to generate values for the financial development index for the years 1986, 1992, 1998, and 2003. Interestingly, this measure is highly correlated with an interpolated and extrapolated measure of states' financial development proposed by Hasan, Jandoc, and Khor (2010). This measure uses information from the NSS survey of unregistered enterprises carried out in 2000 and 2005. In particular, it uses the responses from a question on whether a firm was facing difficulties obtaining capital or not and uses these to compute at the state level the proportion of firms complaining about difficulties obtaining capital. States in which this proportion is relatively low are deemed to have a better-developed financial system than others. The two measures are generally highly correlated. Pairwise correlations range from −.40 to −.75, while Spearman rank correlations range from −.42 to −.75. The negative correlations make perfect sense, since states with high values on the financial development index can be expected to be states where a smaller share of firms would be expected to deem capital to be a problem and vice versa. This gives us confidence that our two measures, despite relying on interpolation and extrapolations, are capturing something very real regarding financial development.

We also introduce state GDP per capita and state-level per capita development expenditures as controls in our econometric analysis.

State GDP and population data are obtained from the official website of the Ministry of Statistics and Programme Implementation,[28] while state development expenditures are obtained from the official website of Reserve Bank of India.[29]

Finally, we consider the relationship between poverty and another aspect of globalization, namely foreign direct investment (FDI). We do this by introducing the share of state-specific FDI in states' gross domestic product in place of protection in our regression analysis. Since we only have state-specific FDI data from 1994 to 2002, we extrapolated the value for FDI at the state level back to 1991 using the growth rate between 1994 and 1997. We then introduce the share of FDI to GDP at the state level lagged by two years to analyze its effect on poverty from 1993 to 2004.

Table 4.1 provides some summary statistics for our measures of poverty and protection by state for the initial and final years we work with. To save space, we only report combined rural and urban figures. As can be seen, there is considerable variation in poverty rates across states and over time. This is true for poverty rates based on both the Deaton poverty lines and the 2009 Expert Group poverty lines. Interestingly, while the two sets of poverty rates look quite different—those of the Expert Group are considerably higher—they are highly correlated. Qualitatively speaking, states with very high (low) poverty tend to be the same across the two measures.[30] (Pearson correlation coefficients are .95 in both the initial and final years. Spearman rank correlations are also high: .94 and .93 in 1987 and 2004, respectively.) Interestingly, the extent of poverty reduction is similar according to both the Deaton and 2009 Expert Group poverty lines. As will be seen later, the correlation coefficient between reductions in the two sets of poverty rates over 1987 and 2004 is .82.

Table 4.2 provides by state the values taken by the three different measures of labor market flexibility we consider and measures of the quality of the transportation infrastructure and financial system. For

Table 4.1 SUMMARY STATISTICS

	Poverty (combined rural and urban, %)				*Protection*			
	Deaton		Expert Group		Tariff (%)		NTB (%)	
State	1987	2004	1987	2004	1987	2004	1987	2004
Andhra Pradesh	32.0	16.2	51.8	29.9	88.3	26.6	100.0	17.9
Assam	33.7	17.0	53.9	34.4	104.6	31.9	100.0	18.5
Bihar	52.5	32.5	68.9	52.2	79.9	25.6	100.0	20.3
Gujarat	31.7	16.6	52.9	31.8	95.1	25.2	100.0	17.8
Haryana	13.2	7.3	33.4	24.1	91.6	25.3	100.0	17.2
Karna-taka	36.3	22.5	61.5	33.4	92.9	27.4	100.0	17.5
Kerala	23.1	7.9	50.5	19.7	149.6	39.1	100.0	10.7
Madhya Pradesh	38.6	31.4	55.3	48.8	81.6	25.7	100.0	19.9
Maha-rashtra	35.6	21.2	54.5	38.1	89.1	25.7	100.0	18.3
Orissa	46.6	37.6	62.7	57.2	84.5	25.5	100.0	19.0
Punjab	6.6	4.0	22.5	20.9	91.3	25.1	100.0	17.4
Rajast-han	31.9	12.8	54.7	34.4	89.2	25.4	100.0	16.7

(*continued*)

Table 4.1 (*continued*)

	Poverty (combined rural and urban, %)					*Protection*		
Tamil Nadu	41.3	17.2	54.2	28.9	99.6	26.5	100.0	15.6
Uttar Pradesh	33.8	17.8	59.8	40.5	85.8	25.7	100.0	18.8
West Bengal	32.5	17.1	51.8	34.3	97.5	27.0	100.0	15.9

the last three variables, which are time-variant, we show only the values of first and last years used in our econometric analysis (1986 and 2003, respectively, given that these are variables are introduced with one-year lags, as noted below).

ESTIMATION STRATEGY

We estimate variants of the following basic specification for the various measures of poverty, trade protection, labor market flexibility, transportation infrastructure, and financial development, with and without controls:

$$\begin{aligned} y_{it}^{j} &= \alpha + \beta_1 protection_{it-1}^{j} + \beta_2 * X_{it-1} * protection_{it-1}^{j} \\ &\quad + \beta_3 * X_{it-1} + \beta_4 * Z_{it} + \delta_i + \mu_t + \varepsilon_{it} \end{aligned} \tag{4}$$

where y^{j}_{it} is the logarithm of poverty in state i and sector j (overall, urban, and rural), $protection^{j}_{it-1}$ refers to one of our three measures of

Table 4.2 STATE-SPECIFIC CHARACTERISTICS

	*Labor Regulations**			*Transportation Infrastructure (total surfaced road divided by total state area, in kms.)*		*Financial Development*			
	Besley and Burgess	*Hasan, Mitra, and Ramaswamy*	*Gupta, Hasan, and Kumar*			*KPROB*		*FINDEV*	
State	(FLEX1)	(FLEX2)	(FLEX3)	1986	2003	1986	2003	1986	2003
Andhra Pradesh	1	1	1	245.2	438.3	0.712	0.305	6.39	6.23
Assam	0	0	0	119.6	164.1	0.761	0.709	2.69	3.50
Bihar	0	0	0	170.2	180.8	1.000	0.692	3.37	3.76
Gujarat	0	1	0	310.1	636.5	0.985	0.296	5.67	5.32
Haryana	0	0	0	511.0	599.9	0.419	0.426	6.09	5.23
Karnataka	1	1	1	394.9	532.5	0.285	0.278	7.04	6.83
Kerala	1	0	0	676.0	1,301.7	0.596	0.431	6.66	6.11

Madhya Pradesh	0	0	0	150.9	173.2	0.410	0.596	5.09	4.90
Maharashtra	0	1	0	369.2	702.2	0.495	0.394	6.42	6.26
Orissa	0	0	0	39.7	338.1	1.000	0.693	4.49	3.43
Punjab	0	0	0	781.1	1,047.4	0.313	0.546	4.65	4.86
Rajasthan	1	1	1	138.8	215.0	0.306	0.550	4.97	4.52
Tamil Nadu	1	1	1	757.7	987.2	0.588	0.291	7.78	8.84
Uttar Pradesh	0	0	1	259.0	573.8	0.708	0.605	4.10	3.25
West Bengal	0	0	0	289.8	571.1	0.979	0.757	4.91	5.59

Note: * For labor regulations: 1 = proemployer; 0 = proemployee.

trade protection lagged once,[31] X_{it} is a measure of a state characteristic, possibly time-invariant, that may influence how reductions in protection affect poverty (for example, labor regulations, the quality of transportation infrastructure, or the financial system), Z_{it} denotes a time-varying state-level control variable (for example, per capita development expenditures), δ_i represents fixed state effects, μ_t represents year dummies, and ϵ_{it} is an error term assumed to satisfy the usual properties. In some of our analysis we work with measures of poverty and protection at the NSS region level.

While our specification is fairly standard, a couple of points need to be noted on the inferences that can be drawn from our estimated coefficients, especially as they concern the impact of trade liberalization on poverty. First, the inclusion of year dummies means that the effects of any factor that changes over time but is common across states will be subsumed in the estimated coefficients on the year dummies. Crucially, and borrowing the terminology of Topalova (2005), this includes the "level" effects of trade liberalization on poverty. Thus, with year dummies included in our estimation, the coefficient on the trade liberalization term will capture the differential impact of liberalization on poverty across geographical areas depending on how open they are to trade and on how the degree of openness changed differentially across states and regions. While the effects of trade liberalization on poverty that are common across the country will get subsumed in the coefficient on the year dummies, these year dummies will also control for the effects of macroeconomic shocks.

Second, the interaction terms involving trade liberalization are used to capture the possibility that the effects of trade liberalization are contingent on state-level characteristics. Consider, for example, a case where the state characteristic being considered is labor regulations and the estimate of β_2 is positive (and statistically significant at conventional levels). This implies that a reduction in protection is associated with bigger reductions (or smaller increases) in poverty rates in states with more flexible labor regulations. A negative estimate of β_2 can be interpreted as a reduction in protection to be associated with smaller reductions (or larger increases) in poverty rates in states with more flexible labor regulations.

RESULTS

Main Results

Table 4.3 describes pairwise correlations involving reductions in the two sets of poverty estimates (i.e., those based on the Deaton [2003a] and the 2009 Expert Group poverty lines)[32] and our two main protection measures (i.e., tariff rates and NTB coverage rates) over 1987 and 2004. The correlation coefficient involving reductions in the two sets of poverty rates is .82. The correlations between reductions in poverty and reductions in protection are also high and fairly similar for the two sets of poverty estimates: around half to almost two-thirds in the case of tariffs, and around three-fourths in the case of nontariff barriers. These correlations are consistent with the notion that trade liberalization has been beneficial for poverty reduction. Of course, these correlations may simply reflect the fact that India's economy has opened up considerably to trade over the last two decades and that poverty has been declining for reasons that have little to do with trade liberalization. We therefore turn to our econometric analysis, which allows us to carry out a more nuanced assessment of the links between trade liberalization and poverty reduction.

To conserve space, we describe results based mainly on Deaton poverty lines/rates. (A complete set of results based on the Expert

Table 4.3 PAIRWISE CORRELATIONS: REDUCTIONS IN POVERTY AND LAGGED PROTECTION, 1987 AND 2004

	Reductions in Poverty		*Reductions in Lagged Tariffs*
	Deaton	*Expert Group*	
Reductions in Expert Group poverty	0.8179*** (0.00)		
Reductions in tariffs	0.6216** (0.01)	0.4940* (0.06)	
Reductions in NTB	0.7536*** (0.00)	0.7530*** (0.00)	0.7357*** (0.00)

Note: Actual significance levels in parentheses.
* significant at 10%; ** significant at 5%; *** significant at 1%

Group poverty rates is available from us upon request.) Table 4.4 presents results for a simple version of equation (4). The right-hand variables include state-level protection measures, state and year fixed effects, and state-level per capita development expenditures. As noted earlier, the state-level protection measures used are tariffs and NTB coverage rates weighted by state- and industry-specific employment shares across the different tradable sectors, as well as a principal-components combination of the two. Columns 1–3 pertain to the overall (i.e., urban and rural combined) state-level poverty rates, while columns 4–6 and 7–9 pertain to the urban and rural state-level poverty rates, respectively.

Focusing first on results for the overall poverty rates, the positive and statistically significant coefficients on each of the three protection

Table 4.4 DEPENDENT VARIABLE: LOG OF DEATON POVERTY RATES, STATE LEVEL

	Combined Rural + Urban			*Urban*			*Rural*		
	NRP	NTB	FPC	NRP	NTB	FPC	NRP	NTB	FPC
Regressors	(1)	(2)	(3)	(4)	(5)	(6)	(7)	(8)	(9)
L. Protection	0.0057	0.0395	0.3142	0.0125	0.0175	0.7051	0.0047	0.0359	0.2436
	[2.26]**	[2.77]***	[3.08]***	[1.66]	[1.46]	[2.19]**	[1.72]*	[2.74]***	[2.43]**
L. Log DEVEXP PC	–0.0919	0.0209	–0.069	0.1321	0.136	0.1644	–0.1771	–0.0973	–0.1675
	[0.44]	[0.12]	[0.33]	[0.56]	[0.55]	[0.71]	[0.83]	[0.49]	[0.78]
Constant	3.4606	1.94	3.9978	0.4664	0.3341	2.4924	4.2378	2.9898	4.7188
	[2.39]**	[1.44]	[2.66]**	[0.24]	[0.15]	[1.51]	[2.89]***	[1.95]*	[3.06]***
R^2	0.80	0.83	0.81	0.79	0.78	0.80	0.72	0.75	0.73

Notes: Robust *t* statistics in brackets. Also included as regressors but not shown are year and state dummy variables. Number of observations: 60; number of states: 15.
* significant at 10%; ** significant at 5%; *** significant at 1%

terms suggests that, controlling for time, trade liberalization has contributed to poverty reduction. A more conservative interpretation is that states experiencing bigger reductions in the employment-weighted protection experienced faster reductions in poverty. The estimates of column 1 imply that, controlling for time, for every percentage point reduction in the weighted tariff rate, there was a .57 percent reduction in poverty. During the period 1987–2004, the average value across states of the weighted tariff rate (lagged) went down by about 68 percentage points, which implies the actual tariff reduction that took place would have been associated with a 38 percent reduction in poverty during this period. An alternative interpretation is that a state that experienced a percentage-point higher reduction in employment-weighted tariff than another state experienced .57 percent greater reduction in poverty. Since our regressions use time controls and poverty all across the country has been declining over time, we can infer that trade liberalization (and the greater exposure of the labor force to foreign competition) actually speeded up poverty reduction.

The estimates of column 2 are qualitatively similar. Controlling for time, they imply that there is a 4 percent reduction in poverty corresponding to every percentage-point reduction in the NTB coverage ratio. The impact of trade liberalization on poverty indicated by these estimates is probably an overestimate, as several other factors, correlated with trade reforms, could be driving poverty. Moreover, the estimates of columns 1–3 may be masking important differences in the way trade liberalization has affected poverty in urban and rural areas. An examination of the remaining columns strongly suggests that this is the case. For example, comparing the coefficients on the tariff terms across columns 4 and 7, we see that though tariff reductions can have large effects on poverty, these are imprecisely estimated. On the other hand, the effects of tariffs on poverty are lower in rural areas, but they are precisely estimated. These results suggest that it is important to consider separately the effects of trade liberalization on urban and rural sectors. They also suggest that there may be considerable variation in how trade liberalization has affected poverty across states, especially in the urban sector. Accordingly, in what follows we introduce interactions involving protection and various state-level characteristics. We also carry out our analysis separately for the urban and rural sectors.

Table 4.5 presents the results for equation (4) using urban sector poverty rates as the dependent variable. In addition to the various controls, the protection measures are introduced both directly and in interaction with various state-level characteristics. Columns 1–3 of the top panel reveal that both the direct and interaction terms involving tariff rates are positive and statistically significant. In other words, not only have states experiencing bigger reductions in weighted tariff rates been associated with bigger reductions in urban poverty, but the extent of this poverty reduction has been larger in states with flexible labor regulations. This result holds no matter which of the three measures of flexibility we use. Somewhat similarly, columns 4–6 suggest that poverty reductions induced by trade liberalization have been faster in states with better transport infrastructure and more developed financial systems. The last relationship follows from the finding that states with *fewer* complaints about difficulties in obtaining capital by unregistered enterprises experience a larger reduction in poverty for a given reduction in tariff rates, as captured by the negative sign of the interaction between tariff and KPROB (column 5). The positive sign on the interaction between tariff and FINDEV (where a higher value of FINDEV represents a state with a relatively well-developed financial system) leads to qualitatively the same conclusion (column 6). In addition, the sign of the coefficients of the level terms in

Table 4.5 DEPENDENT VARIABLE: LOG OF DEATON POVERTY RATES, STATE LEVEL (URBAN)

	State Characteristics					
Regressors	FLEX1	FLEX2	FLEX3	ROAD	KPROB	FINDEV
Tariff	(1)	(2)	(3)	(4)	(5)	(6)
L. Protection	0.0145 [1.97]*	0.0125 [1.96]*	0.0186 [2.63]**	0.0082 [0.94]	0.0148 [2.07]**	0.0044 [0.52]
L. Protection interaction	0.0029 [2.63]**	0.0031 [2.63]**	0.0033 [3.02]***	0.0014 [1.88]*	−0.0067 [2.35]**	0.0008 [2.22]**
L. State characteristic				−0.079 [0.74]	1.2602 [2.75]***	−0.2621 [3.11]***
L. Log of DEVEXP per capita	0.1613 [0.76]	0.1283 [0.59]	0.1825 [0.80]	0.2156 [0.93]	0.1008 [0.43]	0.0072 [0.03]
Constant	−0.1203 [0.07]	0.3301 [0.18]	−0.8133 [0.43]	0.5101 [0.26]	0.1293 [0.07]	3.1616 [1.41]
R^2	0.81	0.82	0.81	0.80	0.82	0.83

(*continued*)

Table 4.5 (*continued*)

	State Characteristics					
Nontariff barriers	(7)	(8)	(9)	(10)	(11)	(12)
L. Protection	0.0164	0.0182	0.0187	0.0133	0.0243	0.0073
	[1.37]	[1.54]	[1.49]	[0.99]	[1.91]*	[0.62]
L. Protection interaction	0.0028	0.0037	0.0023	0.0013	−0.0083	0.0009
	[1.64]	[2.05]**	[1.28]	[1.30]	[1.88]*	[1.79]*
L. State characteristic				−0.1364	1.2709	−0.244
				[1.21]	[2.63]**	[3.15]***
L. Log of DEVEXP per capita	0.1453	0.1344	0.2094	0.2028	0.1488	−0.0307
	[0.64]	[0.59]	[0.84]	[0.77]	[0.63]	[0.13]
Constant	0.2827	0.1271	−0.3543	0.307	−0.712	3.3039
	[0.13]	[0.06]	[0.15]	[0.12]	[0.32]	[1.43]
R^2	0.80	0.81	0.79	0.80	0.82	0.82

(*continued*)

Table 4.5 (*continued*)

	State Characteristics					
First principal component	(13)	(14)	(15)	(16)	(17)	(18)
L. Protection	0.8614 [3.00]***	0.7298 [2.58]**	1.0061 [3.43]***	0.527 [1.59]	0.8336 [2.43]**	0.4176 [1.29]
L. Protection interaction	0.0909 [2.80]***	0.0862 [2.44]**	0.097 [2.81]***	0.0328 [1.60]	−0.2042 [2.40]**	0.0208 [2.02]*
L. State characteristic				0.0056 [0.04]	0.729 [2.34]**	−0.1702 [1.86]*
L. Log of DEVEXP per capita	0.1997 [0.98]	0.163 [0.76]	0.2855 [1.29]	0.2173 [0.92]	0.1562 [0.69]	0.0296 [0.13]
Constant	2.6447 [1.92]*	2.6325 [1.85]*	2.343 [1.58]	1.735 [1.09]	2.2396 [1.35]	3.9733 [2.32]**
R^2	0.83	0.83	0.82	0.81	0.83	0.83

Notes: Robust *t* statistics in brackets. Also included as regressors but not shown are year and state dummy variables. Number of observations: 60; number of states: 15.
* significant at 10%; ** significant at 5%; *** significant at 1%

these variables, namely roads, KPROB, and FINDEV (labeled as state characteristic), in combination with their estimated interaction coefficient multiplied by the actual protection rate, clearly shows that states experiencing greater financial development saw bigger reductions in poverty.

The results based on NTBs as our measure of protection are not quite as strong (middle panel of Table 4.5). In particular, the interaction terms involving NTBs and FLEX1, FLEX3, and Roads fail to be significant at the 10 percent level. However, the interaction terms involving NTBs and FLEX2 and both measures of the financial system remain statistically significant and have the same signs as those of tariff rates. Critically, these results, as well as those of the first principal-components measure of protection, show no indication that trade liberalization has had an adverse impact on urban poverty in Indian states (bottom panel of Tables 4.5). In fact, they suggest a *beneficial* impact of trade liberalization on urban poverty in the right institutional setting. Also, financial development has a poverty-reducing effect both by itself and in interaction with poverty. There is also some weak evidence that greater road density leads to bigger gains from trade in terms of poverty reduction.

Table 4.6 presents the rural analog of Table 4.5. While a number of the direct-protection terms are positive and statistically significant at the 10 percent level or lower, none of the interactions with the labor market flexibility variables are significant. There are only a couple of interaction terms that are statistically significant. Both have the same sign as in the previous table. The first of these is the term involving tariff rates and roads. It is positively signed, thus in states with better transportation, trade liberalization has been associated with reduction in rural poverty. In addition, the negative sign of the interaction between tariff and KPROB shows that relatively financially developed states saw bigger reductions in rural poverty.

Tables 4.7 and 4.8 present results based on estimating specifications that are nearly identical to those of Tables 4.5 and 4.6, respectively. The main difference is that the various versions of equation (4) are now estimated at the region level. That is, the dependent

Table 4.6 DEPENDENT VARIABLE: LOG OF DEATON POVERTY RATES, STATE LEVEL (RURAL)

	State Characteristics					
Regressors	FLEX1	FLEX2	FLEX3	ROAD	KPROB	FINDEV
Tariff	(1)	(2)	(3)	(4)	(5)	(6)
L. Protection	0.0015	0.0048	0.0049	0.0023	0.0091	0.0004
	[0.37]	[1.74]*	[1.77]*	[0.70]	[2.77]***	[0.08]
L. Protection	0.002	0.0006	0.0009	0.0023	−0.0074	0.0006
interaction	[1.12]	[0.38]	[0.60]	[2.05]**	[1.72]*	[1.05]
L. State				−0.0365	0.4045	−0.0184
characteristic				[0.37]	[1.03]	[0.25]
L. Log of	−0.1546	−0.1785	−0.781	−0.0723	−0.1948	−0.1251
DEVEXP per capita	[0.74]	[0.83]	[0.83]	[0.36]	[0.90]	[0.57]
Constant	4.3094	4.2125	4.1989	3.8248	4.1173	4.0993
	[3.00]***	[2.86]***	[2.85]***	[2.88]***	[2.92]***	[2.43]**
R^2	0.72	0.72	0.72	0.75	0.74	0.72

(*continued*)

Table 4.6 (*continued*)

	State Characteristics					
Nontariff barriers	(7)	(8)	(9)	(10)	(11)	(12)
L. Protection	0.0277	0.0361	0.0359	0.0368	0.0367	0.0355
	[2.20]**	[2.68]**	[2.68]**	[2.30]**	[2.79]***	[2.41]**
L. Protection interaction	0.0018 [1.37]	0.0005 [0.39]	0.0011 [0.93]	0.0001 [0.10]	−0.0025 [0.73]	0.0001 [0.12]
L. State characteristic				0.0199 [0.22]	0.0899 [0.25]	0.0136 [0.19]
L. Log of DEVEXP per capita	−0.1046 [0.49]	−0.0978 [0.48]	−0.0614 [0.30]	−0.1066 [0.54]	−0.0947 [0.46]	−0.0832 [0.38]
Constant	3.1858	2.9877	2.7213	3.0352	2.9336	2.8184
	[1.89]*	[1.90]*	[1.69]*	[1.93]*	[1.87]*	[1.47]
R^2	0.75	0.75	0.75	0.75	0.75	0.75

(*continued*)

Table 4.6 (*continued*)

	State Characteristics					
First principal component	(13)	(14)	(15)	(16)	(17)	(18)
L. Protection	0.1308	0.249	0.2511	0.2167	0.2952	0.1972
	[1.12]	[2.43]**	[2.44]**	[1.60]	[2.88]***	[1.38]
L. Protection interaction	0.0428	0.0126	0.0236	0.0215	−0.0955	0.005
	[1.39]	[0.48]	[0.93]	[0.97]	[1.23]	[0.50]
L. State characteristic				0.0837	−0.0583	0.0114
				[0.94]	[0.24]	[0.13]
L. Log of DEVEXP per capita	−0.1531	−0.1687	−0.1447	−0.1604	−0.1679	−0.1505
	[0.72]	[0.77]	[0.66]	[0.78]	[0.76]	[0.69]
Constant	4.3905	4.7513	4.5877	4.5949	4.7596	4.4905
	[2.89]***	[3.00]***	[2.93]***	[3.13]***	[3.02]***	[2.57]**
R^2	0.74	0.73	0.73	0.74	0.74	0.73

Notes: Robust *t* statistics in brackets. Also included as regressors but not shown are year and state dummy variables. Number of observations: 60; number of states: 15.
* significant at 10%; ** significant at 5%; *** significant at 1%

variables are urban and rural poverty across the various *regions* of the fifteen major states we work with. Similarly, our measures of protection are tariffs and NTB coverage rates weighted by *region* and industry-specific employment shares across the different tradable sectors, as well as a principal-components combination of the two. The remaining right-hand variables are as before—that is, they are state-specific.

Table 4.7 DEPENDENT VARIABLE: LOG OF DEATON POVERTY RATES, REGION LEVEL (URBAN)

	State Characteristics						
Regressors	Own Term	FLEX1	FLEX2	FLEX3	ROAD	KPROB	FINDEV
Tariff	(1)	(2)	(3)	(4)	(5)	(6)	(7)
L. Protection	0.0074	0.0068	0.0044	0.0079	0.0061	0.0106	0.0006
	[1.76]*	[1.68]*	[1.09]	[1.88]*	[1.46]	[2.17]**	[0.14]
L. Protection interaction		0.0037	0.0038	0.0025	0.0018	−0.0087	0.0011
		[2.72]***	[3.33]***	[1.87]*	[2.94]***	[2.75]***	[2.34]**
L. State characteristic					−0.1165	1.4468	−0.254
					[1.21]	[3.57]***	[2.93]***
L. Log of DEVEXP per capita	−0.1224	−0.1032	−0.1311	−0.0892	−0.0356	−0.1714	−0.2274
	[0.54]	[0.47]	[0.59]	[0.39]	[0.15]	[0.74]	[1.04]
Constant	2.8866	2.7301	2.9809	2.6081	2.3093	2.5517	5.0229
	[1.72]*	[1.68]*	[1.81]*	[1.55]	[1.37]	[1.52]	[2.87]***
R^2	0.52	0.55	0.55	0.53	0.54	0.55	0.55

(*continued*)

Table 4.7 (*continued*)

	State Characteristics						
Nontariff barrier	(8)	(9)	(10)	(11)	(12)	(13)	(14)
L. Protection	0.0093	−0.0102	0.005	0.0056	0.0042	0.0109	0.0024
	[0.34]	[0.38]	[0.18]	[0.20]	[0.15]	[0.39]	[0.09]
L. Protection interaction		0.0047	0.0042	0.003	0.0016	−0.0074	0.0007
		[2.36]**	[2.33]**	[1.48]	[1.67]*	[1.37]	[0.99]
L. State characteristic					−0.1651	1.2221	−0.2543
					[1.57]	[2.47]**	[2.78]***
L. Log of DEVEXP per capita	−0.0995	−0.1422	−0.1478	−0.0016	−0.0982	−0.0986	−0.3159
	[0.42]	[0.61]	[0.62]	[0.01]	[0.41]	[0.42]	[1.34]
Constant	2.741	4.8335	3.2926	2.3594	4.0815	2.2732	6.3604
	[0.82]	[1.48]	[0.95]	[0.67]	[1.24]	[0.68]	[1.72]*
R^2	0.51	0.53	0.53	0.52	0.53	0.54	0.53

First principal component	(15)	(16)	(17)	(18)	(19)	(20)	(21)
L. Protection	0.3949	0.3102	0.2794	0.4131	0.2657	0.3764	0.2147
	[1.59]	[1.33]	[1.14]	[1.62]	[1.06]	[1.40]	[0.91]
L. Protection interaction		0.0887	0.0922	0.0665	0.0379	–0.1885	0.019
		[2.25]**	[2.77]***	[1.68]*	[2.07]**	[1.92]*	[1.44]
L. State characteristic					0.0045	0.7104	–0.1829
					[0.04]	[2.69]***	[1.92]*
L. Log of DEVEXP per capita	–0.0955	–0.0932	–0.1326	–0.0062	–0.0622	–0.12	–0.657
	[0.42]	[0.41]	[0.58]	[0.03]	[0.27]	[0.51]	[1.18]
Constant	3.8344	3.6797	3.9303	3.2845	3.3115	3.3894	5.8527
	[2.23]**	[2.17]**	[2.28]**	[1.91]*	[1.86]*	[1.90]*	[3.37]***
R^2	0.52	0.54	0.54	0.53	0.54	0.55	0.54

Notes: Robust *t* statistics in brackets. Also included as regressors but not shown are year and region dummy variables. Number of observations: 232; number of regions: 58.

* significant at 10%; ** significant at 5%; *** significant at 1%

Table 4.8 DEPENDENT VARIABLE: LOG OF DEATON POVERTY RATES, REGION LEVEL (RURAL)

	State Characteristics						
Regressors	Own Term	FLEX1	FLEX2	FLEX3	ROAD	KPROB	FINDEV
Tariff	(1)	(2)	(3)	(4)	(5)	(6)	(7)
L. Protection	0.0057	0.0012	0.0054	0.0054	0.0029	0.0116	0.0009
	[1.79]*	[0.32]	[1.70]*	[1.72]*	[0.87]	[3.18]***	[0.22]
L. Protection interaction		0.003	0.0024	0.0022	0.0026	−0.0109	0.0009
		[1.92]*	[1.70]*	[1.51]	[3.21]***	[2.67]***	[2.04]**
L. State characteristic					−0.0478	0.7854	−0.0115
					[0.66]	[2.16]**	[0.17]
L. Log of DEVEXP per capita	−0.2863	−0.277	−0.29	−0.2817	−0.2213	−0.3384	−0.2269
	[1.70]*	[1.68]*	[1.74]*	[1.70]*	[1.32]	[2.02]**	[1.23]
Constant	4.9426	4.9561	4.9484	4.8976	4.5482	4.8751	4.6281
	[4.24]***	[4.33]***	[4.27]***	[4.26]***	[3.96]***	[4.25]***	[3.15]***
R^2	0.46	0.47	0.47	0.47	0.49	0.48	0.47

Nontariff barrier	(8)	(9)	(10)	(11)	(12)	(13)	(14)
L. Protection	0.0248	0.0168	0.0236	0.0232	0.0215	0.0253	0.0256
	[1.53]	[1.00]	[1.42]	[1.42]	[1.23]	[1.53]	[1.55]
L. Protection interaction		0.0019	0.0012	0.0012	0.0004	−0.0022	0
		[1.32]	[0.88]	[0.90]	[0.53]	[0.57]	[0.10]
L. State characteristic					−0.0419	0.2152	0.018
					[0.54]	[0.53]	[0.26]
L. Log of DEVEXP per capita	−0.2365	−0.2539	−0.2499	−0.1953	−0.2353	−0.2412	−0.2211
	[1.45]	[1.52]	[1.49]	[1.13]	[1.42]	[1.45]	[1.20]
Constant	2.6349	3.4888	2.7874	2.4743	2.9494	2.6145	2.3789
	[1.29]	[1.64]	[1.33]	[1.16]	[1.39]	[1.26]	[1.00]
R^2	0.46	0.47	0.47	0.47	0.46	0.46	0.46

(*continued*)

Table 4.8 (*continued*)

				State Characteristics			
First principal component	(15)	(16)	(17)	(18)	(19)	(20)	(21)
L. Protection	0.2427	0.1222	0.2315	0.2308	0.1767	0.2916	0.1883
	[2.01]**	[0.90]	[1.89]*	[1.88]*	[1.26]	[2.31]**	[1.35]
L. Protection interaction		0.0477	0.0341	0.0337	0.025	−0.1185	0.0063
		[1.58]	[1.31]	[1.26]	[1.65]	[1.50]	[0.70]
L. State characteristic					0.0562	0.1025	0.0272
					[0.70]	[0.45]	[0.35]
L. Log of DEVEXP per capita	−0.2696	−0.2749	−0.2815	−0.2316	−0.2619	−0.2923	−0.2537
	[1.62]	[1.65]	[1.66]*	[1.37]	[1.55]	[1.72]*	[1.38]
Constant	5.5351	5.3319	5.6329	5.2588	5.3284	5.6272	5.2271
	[4.39]***	[4.20]***	[4.39]***	[4.15]***	[4.05]***	[4.35]***	[3.28]***
R^2	0.46	0.47	0.47	0.47	0.47	0.47	0.46

Notes: Robust *t* statistics in brackets. Also included as regressors but not shown are year and region dummy variables. Number of observations: 232; number of regions: 58.

* significant at 10%; ** significant at 5%; *** significant at 1%

The overall flavor of the results is similar. As Table 4.7 shows, states with bigger reductions in employment-weighted tariff rates are associated with larger reductions in urban poverty (top panel). Moreover, states with more flexible labor regulations, better transportation infrastructure, and more developed financial systems experience larger reductions in urban poverty as a result of tariff reductions. Results for NTB coverage rates the first principal component are weaker in that none of the own terms are significant (middle panel). However, even here, the evidence suggests that states with more flexible labor regulations as measured by FLEX1 and FLEX2 and states with better road connectivity see larger reductions in urban poverty on account of trade liberalization.

Interestingly, the results of Table 4.8, pertaining to rural poverty at the region level, lend more support to a beneficial impact of trade liberalization on rural poverty than the results of Table 4.6: where *tariff* reductions are concerned, the results are consistent with trade liberalization reducing rural poverty in states with flexible labor regulations (in terms of the FLEX1 and FLEX2 measures), better transportation infrastructure, and a more developed financial system. In addition, and unlike previous results, we see in several specifications that increases in per capita development expenditures at the state level are associated with statistically significant reductions in rural poverty at the region level.

What happens if we combine all of our state characteristics? Tables 4.9 and 4.10 describe the results at the state level for the urban and rural sectors, respectively. Estimates of the direct protection measures are always positive and significant in five cases (all of them are with the first principal component), so trade liberalization is associated with reductions in poverty in the specifications. As for the statistically significant interaction terms involving our various protection measures, the results generally indicate that trade liberalization has been associated with reductions in poverty in urban sectors of states

Table 4.9 DEPENDENT VARIABLE: LOG OF DEATON POVERTY RATES, STATE LEVEL (URBAN)

	FLEX1		*FLEX2*		*FLEX3*	
Regressors	KPROB	FINDEV	KPROB	FINDEV	KPROB	FINDEV
Tariff	(1)	(2)	(3)	(4)	(5)	(6)
L. Protection	0.0101	0.0076	0.0047	0.0087	0.0119	0.0101
	[1.20]	[0.80]	[0.51]	[1.06]	[1.49]	[1.11]
L. Protection	0.0019	0.0018	0.0027	0.0038	0.0026	0.0026
* FLEX	[1.50]	[1.26]	[1.51]	[2.19]**	[2.20]**	[2.50]**
L. Protection	0.0011	0.0004	0.0016	0.0013	0.0013	0.0005
* ROAD	[1.07]	[0.38]	[1.59]	[1.35]	[1.32]	[0.51]
L. Protection	−0.0015	0.0002	0.0016	−0.0006	−0.0008	0.0002
* KPROB/ FINDEV	[0.33]	[0.33]	[0.27]	[0.79]	[0.18]	[0.42]
L. Road	−0.0168	−0.0839	−0.0833	−0.1806	−0.0511	−0.1159
(own term)	[0.19]	[0.80]	[0.82]	[1.48]	[0.57]	[1.07]
L. KPROB/	0.7417	−0.2288	0.2394	−0.1727	0.6676	−0.2304
FINDEV (own term)	[1.13]	[2.47]**	[0.28]	[1.96]*	[1.03]	[2.44]**
L. Log of	0.1891	0.0286	0.2302	0.0279	0.2367	0.0673
DEVEXP per capita	[0.82]	[0.12]	[0.96]	[0.12]	[0.95]	[0.29]
Constant	0.0266	2.9077	0.4588	2.7883	−0.5745	2.1428
	[0.01]	[1.45]	[0.24]	[1.27]	[0.30]	[0.93]
R^2	0.84	0.84	0.84	0.85	0.84	0.84

(*continued*)

Table 4.9 (*continued*)

	FLEX1		*FLEX2*		*FLEX3*	
Nontariff barriers	(7)	(8)	(9)	(10)	(11)	(12)
L. Protection	0.0149	0.0099	0.0072	0.0147	0.0153	0.0115
	[0.89]	[0.74]	[0.40]	[1.19]	[0.93]	[0.88]
L. Protection * FLEX	0.0017	0.0020	0.0039	0.0056	0.0024	0.0025
	[0.86]	[0.90]	[1.61]	[2.41]**	[1.42]	[1.44]
L. Protection * ROAD	0.0010	0.0006	0.0018	0.0018	0.0013	0.0008
	[0.70]	[0.50]	[1.20]	[1.61]	[0.90]	[0.68]
L. Protection * KPROB/ FINDEV	−0.0025	0.0000	0.0045	−0.0014	−0.0017	0.0000
	[0.36]	[0.05]	[0.51]	[1.43]	[0.24]	[0.04]
L. Road (own term)	−0.0818	−0.1588	−0.1160	−0.2360	−0.1154	−0.1948
	[0.88]	[1.33]	[1.21]	[2.10]**	[1.25]	[1.66]
L. KPROB/ FINDEV (own term)	0.7939	−0.2209	0.0443	−0.1532	0.7295	−0.2210
	[1.11]	[2.70]**	[0.05]	[1.89]*	[1.02]	[2.73]***
L. Log of DEVEXP per capita	0.1880	0.0211	0.1879	0.0270	0.2736	0.1117
	[0.73]	[0.08]	[0.71]	[0.11]	[1.01]	[0.42]
Constant	−0.1475	2.9473	0.5813	2.6417	−0.7914	2.1561
	[0.05]	[1.15]	[0.20]	[1.03]	[0.27]	[0.83]
R^2	0.83	0.83	0.84	0.85	0.83	0.83

(*continued*)

Table 4.9 (*continued*)

	FLEX1		*FLEX2*		*FLEX3*	
First principal component	(13)	(14)	(15)	(16)	(17)	(18)
L. Protection	0.7252	0.6085	0.4553	0.5086	0.7960	0.6826
	[1.84]*	[1.76]*	[1.00]	[1.74]*	[2.08]**	[2.05]**
L. Protection * FLEX	0.0638	0.0723	0.0723	0.1162	0.0806	0.0841
	[1.58]	[1.53]	[1.36]	[2.43]**	[2.18]**	[2.42]**
L. Protection * ROAD	0.0167	0.0106	0.0354	0.0374	0.0236	0.0147
	[0.52]	[0.38]	[1.12]	[1.53]	[0.78]	[0.57]
L. Protection * KPROB/ FINDEV	−0.0719	−0.0016	0.0225	−0.0233	−0.0587	0.0009
	[0.51]	[0.09]	[0.12]	[1.15]	[0.43]	[0.06]
L. Road (own term)	0.0278	−0.0631	0.0232	−0.0834	−0.0020	−0.0997
	[0.25]	[0.45]	[0.22]	[0.67]	[0.02]	[0.72]
L. KPROB/ FINDEV (own term)	0.6054	−0.1849	0.3593	−0.2050	0.5918	−0.1826
	[1.75]*	[1.99]*	[0.85]	[2.21]**	[1.75]*	[1.96]*
L. Log of DEVEXP per capita	0.2005	0.0677	0.2117	0.0522	0.3018	0.1727
	[0.89]	[0.29]	[0.88]	[0.22]	[1.22]	[0.70]
Constant	1.9359	4.0131	1.5216	3.8370	1.4025	3.4518
	[1.29]	[2.41]**	[0.97]	[2.42]**	[0.87]	[2.12]**
R^2	0.85	0.84	0.85	0.86	0.85	0.85

Notes: Robust *t* statistics in brackets. Also included as regressors but not shown are year and state dummy variables. Number of observations: 60; number of states: 15.
* significant at 10%; ** significant at 5%; *** significant at 1%

Table 4.10 DEPENDENT VARIABLE: LOG OF DEATON POVERTY RATES, STATE LEVEL (RURAL)

	FLEX1		*FLEX2*		*FLEX3*	
Regressors	KPROB	FINDEV	KPROB	FINDEV	KPROB	FINDEV
Tariff	(1)	(2)	(3)	(4)	(5)	(6)
L. Protection	0.0028	0.0046	0.0052	0.0078	0.0043	0.0059
	[0.42]	[0.84]	[0.90]	[0.93]	[0.84]	[1.04]
L. Protection * FLEX	0.0006	0.0027	−0.0007	0.0015	0.0001	0.0011
	[0.27]	[1.10]	[0.29]	[0.61]	[0.05]	[0.69]
L. Protection * ROAD	0.0019	0.0032	0.0017	0.0032	0.0019	0.0030
	[1.30]	[1.78]*	[1.18]	[1.72]*	[1.29]	[1.73]*
L. Protection * KPROB/ FINDEV	−0.0021	−0.0011	−0.0047	−0.0008	−0.0030	−0.0006
	[0.36]	[1.03]	[0.61]	[0.68]	[0.54]	[0.67]
L. Road (own term)	−0.0441	−0.0612	−0.0400	−0.0580	−0.0445	−0.0500
	[0.45]	[0.60]	[0.41]	[0.55]	[0.45]	[0.49]
L. KPROB/ FINDEV (own term)	0.0617	0.0945	0.2730	0.0924	0.1228	0.0732
	[0.12]	[1.10]	[0.37]	[0.96]	[0.25]	[0.89]
L. Log of DEVEXP per capita	−0.0824	−0.0432	−0.1007	−0.0518	−0.0921	−0.0465
	[0.36]	[0.22]	[0.45]	[0.26]	[0.41]	[0.23]
Constant	3.8865	3.3484	3.8440	3.0695	3.8421	3.1875
	[2.78]***	[2.21]**	[2.76]***	[2.00]*	[2.75]***	[2.06]**
R^2	0.75	0.76	0.75	0.75	0.75	0.75

(*continued*)

Table 4.10 (*continued*)

	FLEX1		*FLEX2*		*FLEX3*	
Nontariff barriers	(7)	(8)	(9)	(10)	(11)	(12)
L. Protection	0.0288	0.0276	0.0399	0.0384	0.0380	0.0372
	[1.64]	[1.90]*	[2.17]**	[2.15]**	[2.19]**	[2.27]**
L. Protection * FLEX	0.0019	0.0030	−0.0002	0.0008	0.0007	0.0013
	[1.25]	[1.85]*	[0.11]	[0.42]	[0.58]	[1.03]
L. Protection * ROAD	−0.0001	0.0003	−0.0002	0.0003	−0.0001	0.0003
	[0.10]	[0.29]	[0.20]	[0.21]	[0.09]	[0.24]
L. Protection * KPROB/ FINDEV	0.0001	−0.0007	−0.0037	−0.0002	−0.0019	−0.0002
	[0.03]	[0.93]	[0.52]	[0.21]	[0.42]	[0.31]
L. Road (own term)	0.0107	−0.0156	0.0270	0.0153	0.0135	0.0009
	[0.11]	[0.15]	[0.26]	[0.14]	[0.13]	[0.01]
L. KPROB/ FINDEV (own term)	−0.1211	0.0502	0.2079	0.0352	0.0526	0.0328
	[0.30]	[0.67]	[0.30]	[0.41]	[0.13]	[0.43]
L. Log of DEVEXP per capita	−0.1077	−0.0939	−0.0979	−0.0873	−0.0744	−0.0398
	[0.51]	[0.42]	[0.48]	[0.39]	[0.34]	[0.17]
Constant	3.2447	2.9065	2.8438	2.6932	2.7688	2.3851
	[1.89]*	[1.48]	[1.68]	[1.32]	[1.63]	[1.14]
R^2	0.76	0.76	0.75	0.75	0.75	0.75

(*continued*)

Table 4.10 (*continued*)

	FLEX1		*FLEX2*		*FLEX3*	
First principal component	(13)	(14)	(15)	(16)	(17)	(18)
L. Protection	0.1385	0.1516	0.2689	0.3040	0.2510	0.2690
	[0.70]	[0.93]	[1.63]	[1.38]	[1.60]	[1.59]
L. Protection * FLEX	0.0329	0.0677	−0.0031	0.0286	0.0135	0.0297
	[0.87]	[1.68]	[0.07]	[0.65]	[0.50]	[1.06]
L. Protection * ROAD	0.0155	0.0322	0.0127	0.0320	0.0151	0.0295
	[0.58]	[1.03]	[0.44]	[0.93]	[0.55]	[0.93]
L. Protection * KPROB/ FINDEV	−0.0103	−0.0187	−0.0720	−0.0114	−0.0435	−0.0080
	[0.10]	[1.02]	[0.48]	[0.49]	[0.42]	[0.48]
L. Road (own term)	0.0488	0.0666	0.0540	0.1031	0.0541	0.0883
	[0.47]	[0.61]	[0.54]	[1.03]	[0.55]	[0.90]
L. KPROB/ FINDEV (own term)	−0.0984	0.0147	−0.0490	0.0301	−0.0758	0.0277
	[0.39]	[0.17]	[0.14]	[0.34]	[0.29]	[0.31]
L. Log of DEVEXP per capita	−0.1466	−0.1187	−0.1656	−0.1393	−0.1477	−0.1033
	[0.67]	[0.57]	[0.75]	[0.65]	[0.66]	[0.48]
Constant	4.3864	3.9076	4.6941	4.3743	4.5845	4.0849
	[2.74]***	[2.37]**	[2.94]***	[2.62]**	[2.86]***	[2.48]**
R^2	0.74	0.75	0.74	0.74	0.74	0.74

Notes: Robust *t* statistics in brackets. Also included as regressors but not shown are year and state dummy variables. Number of observations: 60; number of states: 15.
* significant at 10%; ** significant at 5%; *** significant at 1%

with flexible labor regulations as measured by FLEX2 and FLEX3. The results are weaker in the rural sector: here the only interaction terms that are sometimes significant are those involving roads. Conducting this analysis at the region level yields similar results (though fewer terms are statistically significant). The main difference is that the interaction term involving protection and financial development is significant in a couple of cases for the urban sector. Hence there is some evidence that financial development and trade liberalization are complements in reducing poverty.

Taken together, the results lend no support to the notion that trade liberalization has been inimical to poverty reduction. On the contrary, they suggest that trade liberalization has been good for poverty reduction, especially in institutional environments characterized by more flexible labor regulations, better transportation infrastructure, and more developed financial systems.

Robustness Checks

In what follows, we explore the robustness of these results in three ways. First, we examine whether our results are robust to dropping data from 1999–2000 from the analysis. As may be recalled from our earlier discussion, there are concerns about the comparability of poverty estimates based on the 1999–2000 NSS survey of household expenditures with those of other rounds. Although our poverty estimates incorporate adjustments due to Deaton (2003a and 2003b), it is useful to determine whether the 1999–2000 numbers are somehow driving our key results. Second, we consider whether our results hold up if we use an alternative set of poverty estimates, namely those proposed by the 2009 Expert Group. Finally, we consider an alternative measure of poverty. In particular, we substitute the poverty rate (or headcount index) with the poverty gap index.

Carrying out the first robustness check reveals that our results do not depend on the inclusion of 1999–2000. These results can be obtained from us on request. Tables 4.11 and 4.12 describe results from the second robustness check, whereby state-level urban and rural poverty rates based on the Expert Group poverty lines (backcast to 1987–88 by us as described earlier, and without 1999–2000) are used in place of the Deaton poverty rates. Once again, results match up fairly well with our previous ones. Interestingly, if anything the effects of trade liberalization on rural poverty appear stronger.[33] Finally, Tables 4.13 and 4.14 describe the results from regressing the state-level poverty gap index based on Deaton poverty lines on our protection measures, directly and in interaction with state characteristics, and our various controls. The results are qualitatively similar to those based on poverty rates.

We end this subsection with Table 4.15, where we present our results with state-specific foreign direct investment (FDI) as a share of state GDP as our openness variable. The own-level term here often has the correct sign but is significant only in one case, and in this case the interaction term is also significant. There is weak evidence here that states that received greater amounts of foreign investment relative to the size of their GDP have been able to reduce urban poverty faster. Also, the positive and significant interaction between the FDI variable with KPROB in case of urban poverty suggests that the poverty-reducing association of FDI is stronger in states that are financially more developed. None of the terms are significant in the case of the rural sector.

Exploring the Possible Channels through Which the Trade-Poverty Relationship Operates

As noted by Bhagwati (2004), "The scientific analysis of the effect of trade on poverty . . . has centered on a two-step argument: that trade enhances growth, and that growth reduces poverty." In this subsection

Table 4.11 DEPENDENT VARIABLE: LOG OF 2009 EXPERT GROUP POVERTY RATES, STATE LEVEL (URBAN)

	State Characteristics						
Regressors	Own Term	FLEX1	FLEX2	FLEX3	ROAD	KPROB	FINDEV
Tariff	(1)	(2)	(3)	(4)	(5)	(6)	(7)
L. Protection	0.00784	0.0103	0.00759	0.01229	0.00389	0.00838	0.00191
	[1.80]*	[2.94]***	[2.01]*	[2.94]***	[0.85]	[1.92]*	[0.43]
L. Protection interaction		0.00281	0.0018	0.00263	0.00069	−0.00348	0.00066
		[3.54]***	[2.01]*	[2.56]**	[0.90]	[1.34]	[2.83]***
L. State characteristic					−0.1306	0.79606	−0.17437
					[1.68]	[2.85]***	[3.56]***
L. Log of DEVEXP per capita	−0.00516	0.02476	−0.0033	0.172	0.08529	0.00971	−0.17751
	[0.03]	[0.16]	[0.02]	[1.08]	[0.49]	[0.06]	[0.93]
Constant	2.62551	1.98148	2.55128	0.75711	2.5257	2.24037	5.0107
	[1.78]*	[1.75]*	[2.00]*	[0.57]	[2.08]**	[1.83]*	[3.08]***
R^2	0.74	0.83	0.78	0.80	0.78	0.81	0.83

Nontariff barriers	(8)	(9)	(10)	(11)	(12)	(13)	(14)
L. Protection	0.00749	0.00525	0.00894	0.00788	0.00001	0.01333	–0.00178
	[0.65]	[0.48]	[0.74]	[0.67]	[0.00]	[1.03]	[0.17]
L. Protection interaction		0.00237	0.00213	0.00164	0.00084	–0.00482	0.00078
		[2.25]**	[1.98]*	[1.36]	[1.02]	[1.70]	[3.20]***
L. State characteristic					–0.13772	0.86659	–0.16945
					[1.56]	[3.81]***	[3.79]***
L. Log of DEVEXP per capita	–0.0201	0.0035	–0.03292	0.075	0.09585	–0.00631	–0.19092
	[0.09]	[0.02]	[0.20]	[0.36]	[0.53]	[0.04]	[1.10]
Constant	3.00588	2.99496	2.86076	2.28304	2.96323	2.08495	5.5529
	[1.79]*	[2.30]**	[2.00]*	[1.36]	[2.30]**	[1.46]	[3.52]***
R^2	0.72	0.77	0.76	0.74	0.78	0.81	0.82

(*continued*)

Table 4.11 (*continued*)

	State Characteristics						
First principal component	(15)	(16)	(17)	(18)	(19)	(20)	(21)
L. Protection	0.39048 [1.83]*	0.49008 [2.77]**	0.4115 [2.44]**	0.55808 [2.95]***	0.17155 [0.75]	0.42642 [2.15]**	0.16129 [0.80]
L. Protection interaction		0.06624 [3.18]***	0.04859 [2.19]**	0.00865 [2.41]**	0.0678 [0.91]	−0.10428 [1.65]	0.01691 [2.98]***
L. State characteristic					−0.07441 [0.59]	0.54157 [3.79]***	−0.11283 [1.97]*
L. Log of DEVEXP per capita	−0.03236 [0.16]	−0.01582 [0.12]	−0.03872 [0.25]	0.10947 [0.68]	0.07011 [0.40]	−0.00935 [0.07]	−0.18498 [1.04]
Constant	3.08397 [2.23]**	2.74023 [2.86]***	3.04826 [2.80]***	1.78639 [1.58]	2.80795 [2.53]**	2.64578 [2.61]**	4.96377 [3.25]***
R^2	0.74	0.82	0.79	0.79	0.78	0.82	0.83

Notes: Robust *t* statistics in brackets. Also included as regressors but not shown are year and state dummy variables. Number of observations: 45; number of states: 15.
* significant at 10%; ** significant at 5%; *** significant at 1%.

Table 4.12 DEPENDENT VARIABLE: LOG OF 2009 EXPERT GROUP POVERTY RATES, STATE LEVEL (RURAL)

		State Characteristics					
Regressors	Own Term	FLEX1	FLEX2	FLEX3	ROAD	KPROB	FINDEV
Tariff	(1)	(2)	(3)	(4)	(5)	(6)	(7)
L. Protection	0.00969 [3.80]***	0.00259 [1.10]	0.01021 [3.47]***	0.00998 [3.34]***	0.00938 [2.77]**	0.01396 [4.20]***	0.00248 [0.61]
L. Protection interaction		0.00456 [3.97]***	0.00284 [2.32]**	0.00336 [2.84]***	0.00018 [0.13]	−0.0078 [2.15]**	0.00094 [2.20]**
L. State characteristic					−0.01051 [0.11]	0.69804 [2.07]**	−0.04648 [0.83]
L. Log of DEVEXP per capita	−0.13242 [0.77]	−0.03204 [0.17]	−0.13728 [0.72]	−0.0065 [0.03]	−0.1189 [0.65]	−0.07629 [0.41]	−0.05181 [0.22]
Constant	4.00102 [3.58]***	3.8249 [3.11]***	3.88776 [3.17]***	3.04478 [2.51]**	3.94115 [3.43]***	3.24788 [2.76]**	3.90684 [2.27]**
R^2	0.77	0.84	0.80	0.81	0.77	0.80	0.80

(continued)

Table 4.12 (*continued*)

				State Characteristics			
Nontariff barriers	(8)	(9)	(10)	(11)	(12)	(13)	(14)
L. Protection	0.03132 [1.89]*	0.01282 [0.87]	0.03206 [1.83]*	0.03092 [1.78]*	0.02762 [1.37]	0.03222 [1.97]*	0.02184 [1.30]
L. Protection interaction		0.00342 [3.06]***	0.00177 [1.85]*	0.00212 [2.17]**	−0.0001 [0.09]	−0.00595 [2.35]**	0.00075 [1.92]*
L. State characteristic					−0.06634 [0.51]	0.68582 [2.46]**	−0.01516 [0.25]
L. Log of DEVEXP per capita	−0.02615 [0.21]	0.00459 [0.03]	−0.03391 [0.22]	0.0835 [0.60]	−0.00168 [0.01]	−0.01161 [0.07]	0.03846 [0.17]
Constant	1.03966 [0.57]	2.63378 [1.35]	0.94669 [0.47]	0.28416 [0.15]	1.21426 [0.59]	0.64252 [0.33]	1.24131 [0.50]
R^2	0.74	0.81	0.76	0.77	0.74	0.78	0.77

First principal component	(15)	(16)	(17)	(18)	(19)	(20)	(21)
L. Protection	0.42893	0.25199	0.44913	0.43645	0.49516	0.46818	0.30645
	[7.98]***	[4.77]***	[7.54]***	[7.23]***	[4.30]***	[8.95]***	[3.61]***
L. Protection interaction		0.05843	0.04323	0.04905	0.0001	−0.112	0.01209
		[3.39]***	[2.48]**	[2.84]***	[0.01]	[2.14]**	[1.79]*
L. State characteristic					0.07346	0.22757	0.00872
					[0.72]	[1.20]	[0.14]
L. Log of DEVEXP per capita	−0.14113	−0.07541	−0.15199	−0.01998	−0.18943	−0.0932	−0.09505
	[0.89]	[0.43]	[0.83]	[0.12]	[1.06]	[0.53]	[0.43]
Constant	4.18406	4.01932	4.191974	3.34204	4.42031	3.77796	3.93194
	[3.98]***	[3.47]***	[3.51]***	[2.97]***	[3.87]***	[3.25]***	[2.41]**
R^2	0.81	0.85	0.84	0.84	0.81	0.84	0.83

Notes: Robust *t* statistics in brackets. Also included as regressors but not shown are year and state dummy variables. Number of observations: 45; number of states: 15.
* significant at 10%; ** significant at 5%; *** significant at 1%.

Table 4.13 DEPENDENT VARIABLE: LOG OF DEATON POVERTY GAP INDEX, STATE LEVEL (URBAN)

		State Characteristics					
Regressors	Own Term	FLEX1	FLEX2	FLEX3	ROAD	KPROB	FINDEV
Tariff	(1)	(2)	(3)	(4)	(5)	(6)	(7)
L. Protection	0.0114 [1.27]	0.0147 [1.66]	0.0114 [1.47]	0.0219 [2.57]**	0.0043 [0.42]	0.0165 [1.79]*	−0.0002 [0.02]
L. Protection interaction		0.0048 [3.01]***	0.0048 [3.17]***	0.0056 [3.58]***	0.0021 [2.11]**	−0.009 [2.15]**	0.0012 [2.01]*
L. State characteristic					−0.1485 [1.08]	1.2627 [2.00]*	−0.3759 [3.36]***
L. Log of DEVEXP per capita	−0.1654 [0.42]	−0.1181 [0.33]	−0.1713 [0.47]	−0.0795 [0.22]	−0.0259 [0.07]	−0.2074 [0.53]	−0.3434 [0.98]
Constant	0.9601 [0.33]	0.0108 [0.00]	0.7477 [0.27]	−1.2225 [0.42]	1.021 [0.35]	0.5251 [0.18]	4.8209 [1.63]
R^2	0.79	0.83	0.83	0.83	0.82	0.81	0.84

Nontariff barriers	(8)	(9)	(10)	(11)	(12)	(13)	(14)
L. Protection	0.0078 [0.48]	0.0061 [0.39]	0.0088 [0.55]	0.0098 [0.59]	0.0011 [0.06]	0.0178 [1.00]	−0.008 [0.53]
L. Protection interaction		0.0045 [2.14]**	0.0051 [2.35]**	0.0037 [1.60]	0.0025 [1.87]*	−0.0114 [1.86]*	0.0013 [1.92]*
L. State characteristic					−0.1615 [1.32]	1.2856 [2.04]**	−0.3748 [3.54]***
L. Log of DEVEXP per capita	−0.1771 [0.42]	−0.1624 [0.42]	−0.1794 [0.46]	−0.0624 [0.15]	−0.1009 [0.24]	−0.1632 [0.41]	−0.4325 [1.17]
Constant	1.7585 [0.50]	1.6766 [0.51]	1.4756 [0.44]	0.682 [0.19]	2.1877 [0.57]	0.5781 [0.17]	6.3151 [1.99]*
R^2	0.79	0.81	0.81	0.80	0.81	0.81	0.83

(*continued*)

Table 4.13 (*continued*)

	State Characteristics						
First principal component	(15)	(16)	(17)	(18)	(19)	(20)	(21)
L. Protection	0.5043 [1.05]	0.7291 [1.67]	0.5398 [1.27]	0.9286 [2.01]*	0.1915 [0.38]	0.7406 [1.43]	0.0554 [0.12]
L. Protection interaction		0.1308 [3.15]***	0.1242 [2.88]***	0.1368 [2.96]***	0.0578 [2.11]**	−0.2703 [2.22]**	0.0319 [2.06]**
L. State characteristic					0.0116 [0.08]	0.5726 [1.36]	−0.2719 [2.22]**
L. Log of DEVEXP per capita	−0.1481 [0.37]	−0.0973 [0.27]	−0.1501 [0.41]	0.0227 [0.06]	−0.0555 [0.14]	−0.1573 [0.40]	−0.3648 [1.00]
Constant	2.5241 [0.87]	2.7433 [1.08]	2.726 [1.05]	2.3135 [0.86]	1.1971 [0.44]	2.5213 [0.89]	4.9069 [1.79]*
R^2	0.79	0.82	0.83	0.82	0.82	0.82	0.83

Notes: Robust *t* statistics in brackets. Also included as regressors but not shown are year and state dummy variables. Number of observations: 60; number of states: 15.
* significant at 10%; ** significant at 5%; *** significant at 1%

Table 4.14 DEPENDENT VARIABLE: LOG OF DEATON POVERTY GAP INDEX, STATE LEVEL (RURAL)

	State Characteristics						
Regressors	Own Term	FLEX1	FLEX2	FLEX3	ROAD	KPROB	FINDEV
Tariff	(1)	(2)	(3)	(4)	(5)	(6)	(7)
L. Protection	0.0013	−0.0084	0.0022	0.0024	−0.006	0.0121	−0.0098
	[0.36]	[1.35]	[0.60]	[0.66]	[0.12]	[3.12]***	[1.14]
L. Protection interaction		0.006	0.0034	0.0049	0.0036	−0.0178	0.0015
		[2.09]**	[1.41]	[2.03]**	[1.98]*	[2.79]***	[1.59]
L. State characteristic					0.0365	0.9298	−0.0348
					[0.26]	[1.70]*	[0.28]
L. Log of DEVEXP per capita	0.0245	0.0926	0.0166	0.0194	0.1335	−0.0188	0.1724
	[0.07]	[0.28]	[0.05]	[0.06]	[0.43]	[0.06]	[0.48]
Constant	1.7142	1.9304	1.5656	1.5052	1.302	1.4509	1.2029
	[0.70]	[0.87]	[0.65]	[0.65]	[0.62]	[0.67]	[0.45]
R^2	0.76	0.79	0.77	0.78	0.79	0.81	0.78

(continued)

Table 4.14 (*continued*)

	State Characteristics						
Nontariff barriers	(8)	(9)	(10)	(11)	(12)	(13)	(14)
L. Protection	0.026 [2.53]**	0.008 [0.58]	0.0266 [2.56]**	0.026 [2.57]**	0.0299 [1.72]*	0.028 [2.58]**	0.019 [1.32]
L. Protection interaction		0.004 [2.26]**	0.0021 [1.25]	0.0041 [2.59]**	0.0007 [0.57]	−0.0059 [1.24]	0.0007 [0.98]
L. State characteristic					0.105 [0.78]	0.1365 [0.28]	0.0026 [0.02]
L. Log of DEVEXP per capita	0.076 [0.22]	0.0601 [0.16]	0.0738 [0.20]	0.2073 [0.56]	0.0238 [0.07]	0.0817 [0.22]	0.106 [0.28]
Constant	0.1844 [0.07]	0.6114 [0.22]	0.175 [0.06]	−0.797 [0.29]	0.4565 [0.17]	0.0928 [0.03]	0.0198 [0.01]
R^2	0.77	0.78	0.77	0.79	0.77	0.78	0.77

First principal component	(15)	(16)	(17)	(18)	(19)	(20)	(21)
L. Protection	0.108	–0.1864	0.1319	0.1372	0.1039	0.235	–0.092
	[0.99]	[1.01]	[1.18]	[1.20]	[0.47]	[2.20]**	[0.45]
L. Protection interaction		0.1117	0.0552	0.0919	0.0397	–0.2329	0.0217
		[2.45]**	[1.47]	[2.64]**	[1.51]	[2.06]**	[1.41]
L. State characteristic					0.2116	–0.1681	0.0524
					[1.38]	[0.50]	[0.40]
L. Log of DEVEXP per capita	0.0264	0.0639	0.0213	0.1155	0.0103	0.025	0.1023
	[0.07]	[0.18]	[0.06]	[0.32]	[0.03]	[0.07]	[0.28]
Constant	1.272	0.4154	1.4146	0.7603	1.341	1.3894	0.2494
	[0.49]	[0.17]	[0.54]	[0.30]	[0.55]	[0.55]	[0.09]
R^2	0.76	0.79	0.77	0.78	0.78	0.79	0.77

Notes: Robust *t* statistics in brackets. Also included as regressors but not shown are year and state dummy variables. Number of observations: 60; number of states: 15.
* significant at 10%; ** significant at 5%; *** significant at 1%

Table 4.15 DEPENDENT VARIABLE: LOG OF DEATON POVERTY RATES, STATE LEVEL

	State Characteristics						
Regressors	Own Term	FLEX1	FLEX2	FLEX3	ROAD	KPROB	FINDEV
Urban	(1)	(2)	(3)	(4)	(5)	(6)	(7)
L2. FDI share to GDP	−0.0056 [0.44]	−0.0052 [0.41]	−0.0052 [0.43]	−0.0052 [0.41]	0.0008 [0.06]	−0.0734 [2.22]**	0.0354 [1.29]
L2. FDI share interaction		−0.0166 [0.69]	−0.0264 [1.02]	−0.016 [0.66]	0.0026 [0.17]	0.0709 [1.86]*	−0.0097 [1.44]
L2. State characteristics					−0.2123 [1.23]	0.4326 [0.59]	−0.2856 [2.51]**
L. Log of DEVEXP per capita	0.3988 [1.46]	0.3762 [1.36]	0.3757 [1.36]	0.3745 [1.35]	0.4324 [1.43]	0.3005 [1.17]	0.1116 [0.39]
Constant	0.0783 [0.04]	0.2324 [0.12]	0.2364 [0.12]	0.2441 [0.13]	−0.1935 [0.09]	0.1888 [0.10]	3.4631 [1.51]
R^2	0.68	0.68	0.69	0.68	0.69	0.71	0.74

Rural	(8)	(9)	(10)	(11)	(12)	(13)	(14)
L2. FDI share to GDP	0.0019	0.0015	0.0018	0.0015	0.0038	−0.0245	0.0078
	[0.25]	[0.18]	[0.22]	[0.18]	[0.40]	[0.72]	[0.34]
L2. FDI share		0.0179	0.0085	0.0188	−0.0146	0.0289	0.0014
interaction		[0.94]	[0.39]	[0.96]	[0.87]	[0.87]	[0.24]
L2. State					−0.0734	−0.2031	−0.0304
characteristics					[0.38]	[0.50]	[0.29]
L. Log of DEVEXP	−0.0627	−0.0382	−0.0552	−0.0341	−0.0333	−0.0796	−0.0944
per capita	[0.27]	[0.17]	[0.24]	[0.15]	[0.14]	[0.36]	[0.35]
Constant	3.764	3.5972	3.7129	3.5692	3.5488	3.7089	4.1321
	[2.40]**	[2.29]**	[2.34]**	[2.28]**	[2.16]**	[2.44]**	[1.89]*
R^2	0.57	0.57	0.57	0.58	0.58	0.58	0.57

Notes: Robust *t* statistics in brackets. Also included as regressors but not shown are year and state dummy variables. Number of observations: 45; number of states: 15.
* significant at 10%; ** significant at 5%; *** significant at 1%

Table 4.16 DEPENDENT VARIABLE: LOG OF STATE GDP PER CAPITA (COMBINED URBAN AND RURAL)

	State Characteristics						
	Own Term	FLEX1	FLEX2	FLEX3	ROAD	KPROB	FINDEV
Regressors	(1)	(2)	(3)	(4)	(5)	(6)	(7)
L. Tariff	−0.0051 [2.32]**	0.0017 [0.72]	−0.0058 [3.46]***	−0.0057 [2.81]***	0.0024 [0.79]	0.0046 [2.40]**	0.0008 [0.63]
L. Tariff interaction		−0.0023 [3.51]***	−0.0028 [6.09]***	−0.0013 [1.84]*	−0.0006 [1.22]	0.0047 [2.80]***	−0.0012 [8.15]***
L. State characteristic					0.0727 [1.04]	−0.7997 [4.09]***	0.0133 [0.35]
L. Log of DEVEXP per capita	0.219 [1.02]	0.1955 [1.13]	0.2235 [1.43]	0.2051 [0.96]	0.1572 [0.88]	0.245 [1.34]	0.0566 [0.60]
Constant	7.8543 [5.21]***	7.7843 [6.34]***	8.0423 [7.31]***	8.0571 [5.46]***	8.0094 [6.10]***	7.7469 [6.02]***	9.1432 [12.73]***
R^2	0.88	0.91	0.94	0.89	0.89	0.91	0.95

Notes: Robust *t* statistics in brackets. Also included as regressors but not shown are year and state dummy variables. Number of observations: 60; number of states: 15.
* significant at 10%; ** significant at 5%; *** significant at 1%

we first examine the evidence for the two-step argument using our measures of poverty, trade liberalization, and state per capita incomes (state GDP per capita).

Table 4.16 presents results from regressions of state per capita incomes on state-level employment-weighted tariffs and their interactions with state characteristics such as labor market flexibility, road density, and our two measures of financial development. Clearly trade protection has a negative effect on per capita incomes. In other words, trade openness increases per capita incomes. Alternatively, we can interpret our results as follows: states whose workers were more exposed to foreign competition (states in which employment was concentrated in the relatively less protected sectors) and saw greater reduction in their employment-weighted average tariff grew faster than others. Using our various alternative measures of labor market flexibility, we find this effect of trade openness to be stronger for states with relatively more flexible labor markets. Also, using both our measures of financial development, we find very strong evidence that this effect is stronger in the financially more developed states. Thus, the first step in Bhagwati's two step argument certainly works very well. We next empirically investigate the second step of this argument.

Did higher state economic growth help reduce poverty faster? If yes, then after accounting for this effect, did trade have an additional role in poverty reduction, possibly through its redistributive effect in favor of workers? Table 4.17 describes results for regressions of state (overall) poverty on state per capita incomes and then additionally on employment-weighted tariffs. Clearly columns 1 and 2 indicate that states that have been growing faster are also the ones that have reduced their poverty faster. For a 1 percent increase in per capita income, we get a .42 percent reduction in poverty. When we additionally control for protection in column 3, this effect falls to .35, and the significance

Table 4.17 DEPENDENT VARIABLE: LOG OF DEATON POVERTY RATES, STATE LEVEL (COMBINED URBAN AND RURAL)

	Trade Protection			*State Characteristics*					
	Own Term			*FLEX1*	*FLEX2*	*FLEX3*	*ROAD*	*KPROB*	*FINDEV*
Regressors	(1)	(2)	(3)	(4)	(5)	(6)	(7)	(8)	(9)
L. Log of GSDP per capita	−0.41911 [2.03]**	−0.42162 [2.15]**	−0.35228 [1.66]	−0.24913 [1.21]	−0.30054 [1.05]	−0.29729 [1.38]	−0.22257 [1.06]	−0.17814 [0.73]	−0.18621 [0.65]
L. Tariff			0.0039 [1.54]	0.00204 [0.62]	0.00425 [1.47]	0.00446 [1.70]*	0.00084 [0.28]	0.00801 [2.25]**	0.00038 [0.06]
L. Tariff interaction				0.00146 [1.07]	0.0005 [0.31]	0.00097 [0.81]	0.00218 [2.39]**	−0.00601 [1.47]	0.00053 [0.77]
L. State characteristic (own term)							−0.05316 [0.65]	0.40758 [1.04]	−0.07937 [1.14]

L. Log of DEVEXP per capita		0.01132	−0.00954	−0.02077	−0.02255	−0.02219	0.06414	−0.06699	−0.05475
		[0.06]	[0.05]	[0.11]	[0.12]	[0.12]	[0.36]	[0.35]	[0.27]
Constant	6.71356	6.65462	6.18867	5.47933	5.76704	5.70505	4.90167	4.74695	5.51223
	[3.45]***	[2.64]**	[2.36]**	[2.09]**	[1.81]*	[2.11]**	[1.93]*	[1.64]	[1.70]*
R^2	0.80	0.80	0.81	0.81	0.81	0.81	0.84	0.82	0.82

Notes: Robust *t* statistics in brackets. Also included as regressors but not shown are year and state dummy variables. Number of observations: 60; number of states: 15.
* significant at 10%; ** significant at 5%; *** significant at 1%

of the log of GSDP per capita falls somewhat. In addition, tariff still enters with a positive sign, even though it is only very marginally significant. This indicates the possibility that trade, in addition to reducing poverty by increasing average incomes, also works to reduce poverty by redistributing income. From column 7, it is clear that this effect is stronger in states with better road connectivity, possibly due to better transmission of trade policies and border prices in such states.

The regression results examined in this subsection identify possible channels through which this evident trade-poverty nexus works. The results suggest that, through their positive impact on per capita income, reductions in trade protection may have contributed to reducing poverty. For trade liberalization to generate economic growth and at the same time reduce poverty, it is essential that reductions in trade protection do not significantly worsen income distribution. In fact, we find that trade liberalization has an additional beneficial effect on poverty reduction, over and above its growth-enhancing effect.

CONCLUSIONS

Our empirical investigation of the impact of trade liberalization shows that there is a fair amount of evidence in support of its poverty-reducing effects. The most conservative interpretation of our results is that poverty reduction was greater in states and NSS regions that were more open by virtue of the exposure of their labor force to foreign competition, measured by the employment-weighted average tariff at the state or region level. There is also some weak evidence that states that received more FDI relative to their domestic output fared better with poverty reduction.

We find that the beneficial effects of openness are typically larger in states with more flexible labor market institutions (especially in the urban sectors of such states), better connectivity through transportation, and more developed financial systems. Compared to a state with rigid labor market institutions, we find that a state that had flexible labor market institutions and also experienced a percentage-point higher reduction in employment-weighted tariff would have experienced a 1.5 percent greater reduction in urban poverty. Similarly, we find that a state with a greater degree of financial development would have experienced greater reduction in urban poverty as a result of trade liberalization. The results are qualitatively similar with road connectivity. These results help to underscore the importance of improving physical mobility within India by upgrading the transportation infrastructure and improving banking and financial infrastructure to fully reap the benefits of globalization. By "globalization," we do not mean simply trade liberalization; we have also considered FDI. There too, we find that the gains from FDI are best exploited in the presence of better-developed financial institutions.

APPENDIX

Appendix Table 4.A1 DEATON POVERTY LINES (BY RUPEES)

	43rd Round		*50th Round*		*55th Round*		*61st Round*	
	(1987–88)		(1993–94)		(1999–2000)		(2004–5)	
Sector/State	Rural	Urban	Rural	Urban	Rural	Urban	Rural	Urban
Andhra Pradesh	108.8	120.4	192.4	212.6	309.6	344.8	342.3	379.1
Assam	123.5	133.3	214.8	239.7	339.9	379.0	372.5	411.5
Bihar	121.0	130.8	192.8	216.9	296.9	321.6	331.5	370.3
Gujarat	127.8	134.8	228.9	240.8	337.3	369.4	383.4	424.3
Haryana	114.4	128.3	203.0	234.7	310.8	358.4	360.2	413.9
Karnataka	114.9	126.4	203.4	224.9	322.6	367.2	349.5	399.2
Kerala	121.4	125.6	221.5	230.8	373.9	386.2	381.8	399.7
Madhya Pradesh	109.0	123.2	185.1	214.3	288.9	321.3	321.4	378.4

Maharashtra	120.1	137.0	207.7	245.5	319.9	385.4	360.5	429.4
Orissa	111.8	123.2	182.4	201.5	300.3	312.3	309.2	340.3
Punjab	109.0	123.4	206.3	235.6	316.5	350.5	371.8	414.0
Rajasthan	120.2	128.3	207.3	230.7	323.9	353.2	349.7	389.0
Tamil Nadu	122.1	133.0	210.3	230.6	336.5	366.1	365.5	405.0
Uttar Pradesh	105.7	124.9	180.4	210.2	280.5	320.4	317.0	374.9
West Bengal	114.8	129.4	189.9	223.0	306.8	343.5	347.9	394.0

Source: Deaton (2003a) for rounds 43–55; Amoranto and Hasan (2010) for round 61.

Appendix Table 4.A2 DEATON POVERTY RATES (BY PERCENTAGE)

	43rd Round (1987–88)		*50th Round* (1993–94)		*55th Round* (1999–2000)		*61st Round* (2004–5)	
Sector/State	Rural	Urban	Rural	Urban	Rural	Urban	Rural	Urban
Andhra Pradesh	35.0	23.4	29.2	17.8	27.9	11.3	19.9	6.4
Assam	36.1	13.6	35.4	13.0	35.7	12.1	18.9	5.0
Bihar	54.6	38.1	48.6	26.7	39.3	23.5	34.9	16.9
Gujarat	39.4	16.4	32.5	14.7	20.4	6.6	24.6	3.9
Haryana	13.6	11.8	17.0	10.6	6.5	5.1	6.7	8.7
Karnataka	40.8	26.0	37.9	21.4	30.3	11.5	28.2	12.1
Kerala	23.8	21.0	19.5	13.9	11.6	10.5	8.2	7.2
Madhya Pradesh	43.7	20.7	36.7	18.5	31.2	14.1	36.5	16.3

Maharashtra	44.3	21.2	42.9	18.2	30.8	13.0	29.1	11.2
Orissa	50.4	20.8	43.5	15.2	41.3	15.6	41.7	15.7
Punjab	6.6	6.6	6.2	7.8	2.8	4.0	5.0	2.2
Rajasthan	35.3	19.8	23.0	18.3	16.2	10.6	13.7	9.7
Tamil Nadu	49.0	26.2	38.5	20.9	25.6	11.1	26.2	7.5
Uttar Pradesh	34.9	29.3	28.7	21.7	20.8	16.5	18.9	14.0
West Bengal	36.3	22.3	25.1	15.5	22.7	11.4	20.6	8.0

Source: Rounds 43–55 are from Deaton (2003a); round 61 was estimated using NSS unit-level data based on poverty lines from Amoranto and Hasan (2010).

Appendix Table 4.A3 EXPERT GROUP POVERTY LINES (BY RUPEES)

Sector/State	*43rd Round* (1987–88)		*50th Round* (1993–94)		*61st Round* (2004–5)	
	Rural	Urban	Rural	Urban	Rural	Urban
Andhra Pradesh	138.9	159.2	244.1	282.0	433.4	563.2
Assam	153.4	172.7	266.3	306.8	478.0	600.0
Bihar*	147.8	161.7	236.1	266.9	433.4	526.2
Gujarat	163.8	193.9	279.4	320.7	501.6	659.2
Haryana	168.7	175.7	294.1	312.1	529.4	626.4
Karnataka	152.4	166.6	266.9	294.8	417.8	588.1
Kerala	166.5	166.9	286.5	289.2	537.3	584.7
Madhya Pradesh*	135.3	160.7	232.5	274.5	408.4	532.3

Maharashtra	155.5	181.9	268.6	329.0	484.9	632.9
Orissa	136.1	166.4	224.2	279.3	407.8	497.3
Punjab	150.5	183.0	286.9	342.3	543.5	642.5
Rajasthan	163.0	174.9	271.9	300.5	478.0	568.2
Tamil Nadu	150.7	169.2	252.6	288.2	441.7	559.8
Uttar Pradesh*	145.5	170.1	244.3	281.3	435.1	532.1
West Bengal	141.4	173.0	235.5	295.2	445.4	572.5

Note: *Bihar poverty lines for 61st round are population-weighted averages of Bihar and Jharkand poverty lines; Madhya Pradesh poverty lines are population-weighted averages of Madhya Pradesh and Chattisgarh poverty lines; and Uttar Pradesh poverty lines are population-weighted averages of Uttar Pradesh and Uttaranchal poverty lines.

Source: Amoranto and Hasan (2010) for 43rd round; Government of India (2009) for 50th and 61st rounds.

Appendix Table 4.A4 EXPERT GROUP POVERTY RATES (BY PERCENTAGE)

	43rd Round (1987–88)		*50th Round* (1993–94)		*61st Round* (2004–5)	
Sector/State	Rural	Urban	Rural	Urban	Rural	Urban
Andhra Pradesh	54.7	41.3	48.1	35.2	32.3	23.4
Assam	56.2	28.9	54.9	27.7	36.4	21.8
Bihar	70.8	55.3	63.1	43.5	54.8	35.5
Gujarat	57.8	40.1	43.1	28.0	39.1	20.1
Haryana	35.3	26.2	40.0	24.2	24.8	22.4
Karnataka	69.5	41.9	56.6	34.2	37.5	25.9
Kerala	53.1	37.1	33.9	23.9	20.2	18.4
Madhya Pradesh	60.2	34.6	51.1	31.1	54.0	33.7

Maharashtra	64.6	34.0	59.3	30.3	47.9	25.6
Orissa	65.8	38.6	63.0	34.5	60.8	37.6
Punjab	21.5	25.0	20.3	27.2	22.1	18.7
Rajasthan	58.7	39.4	40.8	29.9	35.8	29.7
Tamil Nadu	62.2	39.6	51.0	33.7	37.5	19.7
Uttar Pradesh	62.2	49.3	50.3	37.3	42.4	33.6
West Bengal	55.1	41.8	42.5	31.2	38.2	24.4

Source: Calculated from NSS unit-level data using poverty lines from Amoranto and Hasan (2010) for 43rd round; Government of India (2009) for 50th and 61st rounds, except for Bihar, Madhya Pradesh, and Uttar Pradesh, which were calculated from unit-level data using poverty lines provided in Appendix Table 4.A3.

NOTES

This chapter represents the views of the authors and does not necessarily represent those of the Asian Development Bank, its executive directors, or the countries that they represent.

1. The NSSO sampling methodology is not constructed with the aim of making the sample within a district random. In addition, it is extremely difficult, if not impossible, to keep controlling for the changes in district boundaries that happen every so often.
2. While in theory the DD measure is superior to both the GOI and the ODR measures, in practice in a world with imperfect data it is possible that it is not so. This could be due to the high demands placed on the wide variety of data required to compute the DD measure. Also, the ODR offers a much longer series.
3. For an excellent, comprehensive survey of the evidence on the globalization-poverty linkage, see Harrison (2006).
4. See Anant et al. (2006) for a detailed discussion of India's labor market regulations.
5. The term "layoff" refers to a temporary or seasonal dismissal of a group of workers due to slackness of current demand. "Retrenchment," on the other hand, denotes the permanent dismissal of a group of workers. Both terms may be distinguished from "termination," which refers to the separation of an individual from his or her job.
6. As per the Standing Orders Act, worker consent is required to modify job descriptions or move workers from one plant to another. While the goal of promoting worker consent is certainly important, Anant (2000) argues that rigidities can creep in based on how one defines or establishes worker consent. Given that the Trade Union Act allows multiple unions within the same establishment and rivalries are common across unions, a requirement of worker consent for enacting changes "can become one of consensus amongst all unions and groups, a virtual impossibility" (ibid., 251).
7. The PGI can be expressed as:

$$PGI = \left(1/n\right)\sum_{i=1}^{m}\frac{z-y_i}{n}$$

where y_i represents consumption of the *i*th poor person, *z* is the poverty line, *n* the total population, and *m* the number of poor. The poverty rate, or headcount index, is of course simply m/n.

8. NSS regions are geographically contiguous areas *within* states sharing common agro-climatic conditions.

9. There are other points of contention. For example, Bhalla's (2003) comparisons of consumption expenditure totals from the NSS surveys with their national accounts analogs has led him to argue that the NSS surveys understate consumption expenditures in India. Moreover, he argues that this understatement also takes place for poorer households and thereby results in an overstatement of poverty in India.
10. Since the 1950s NSS consumption expenditure surveys have used a thirty-day recall period in canvassing information on households' food expenditures. The 55th round of the survey, undertaken in 1999–2000, adopted two recall periods for food, one based on a seven-day recall and the other on the standard thirty-day recall. Since the question on the seven-day recall came before the thirty-day recall (columns for the two recalls appear side by side against each consumption item in the questionnaire), most researchers agree that the consumption expenditures recorded are driven by the seven-day recall (i.e., the thirty-day recall is essentially a prorated version of the seven-day recall). Pilot surveys have strongly suggested that the shorter recall period yields, on average, higher consumption expenditures (on a prorated basis, of course), quite possibly due to a tendency for respondents to forget some items of consumption when the recall period is longer. A comprehensive discussion of this and related issues in the context of the NSS consumption expenditure surveys is provided by the papers in Deaton and Kozel (2005).
11. These price indexes reweight the components of the CPI-AL and CPI-IW to reflect the expenditure shares of the consumption basket of the poor in 1973–74 at the all-India level.
12. The steps taken by Amoranto and Hasan (2010) include identifying food and fuel items which are common across the NSS surveys of 1999–2000 and 2004–5 and for which unit values (i.e., expenditures divided by quantities purchased as a proxy for prices) satisfy various consistency checks, and using median unit values and average budget shares (weighted by population or household weights as appropriate) to estimate three sets of price indexes: a price index for 2004–5 relative to 1999–2000 for rural India; sector-specific price indexes for states relative to all of rural India for 2004–5; and price indexes for urban relative to rural sectors by state for 2004–5. Armed with these price indexes and taking as their starting point Deaton's all-India rural poverty line for 1999–2000 of Rs.303.52, Amoranto and Hasan derive state- and sector-specific poverty lines for 2004–5 as follows. First, they scale up the 1999–2000 all-India rural poverty line reported in Deaton (2003a) by the Tornqvist price index for the 61st round relative to the 55th round (rural sector) to get an all-India rural poverty line for the 61st round (Rs.340.8). Next, they obtain rural poverty lines for each state by multiplying the all-India rural poverty line by the rural price indexes for each state relative to all of India. Finally, they derive urban poverty lines for each state from the state-specific rural poverty lines by using states' urban relative to rural price indexes.

13. Poverty estimates based on the Deaton (2003a) poverty lines were referred to as the Deaton-Dreze (or DD) poverty estimates in Hasan, Mitra, and Ural (2007). Deaton (2003a) reports adjusted estimates of poverty only at the state level. In order to work with the region level, we also need region-specific estimates of poverty for 1999–2000. We obtain these using the state- and sector-specific poverty lines of Deaton (2003a) and applying a simplified parametric version of the methods of Deaton (2003a) to adjust for the changes in the 1999–2000 NSS questionnaire. Deaton (2003b) describes this simplified parametric version and also reports the corresponding poverty estimates at the region level.
14. The adjustment exploits the fact that the 1999–2000 expenditure survey used a 30-day recall period exclusively for a number of items, including fuel and light, noninstitutional medical care, and various miscellaneous goods and services. Deaton and Dreze (2002) find that the expenditure on these items turns out to be highly correlated with total expenditures and therefore use these to estimate total expenditures comparable with those of previous thick-sample rounds.
15. The Expert Group's procedures for estimating poverty in 1993–94 and 2004–5 rely on monthly per capita expenditures based on a "mixed reference period" of 365 days for "low-frequency" items of consumption (prorated to thirty days and covering clothing, footwear, durables, and expenditures on education and health [institutional]) and thirty days for the remaining items, including food. The NSS survey for 1987–88 collected expenditures on a 365-day basis for three of the low-frequency groups (i.e., clothing, footwear, and durables); education and health expenditures were only collected on a thirty-day basis. However, this is unlikely to raise serious comparability issues vis-à-vis the other two rounds, since the weight of these items in total consumption expenditures is not very high.
16. Appendix Tables 4.A1 and 4.A2 provide the Deaton poverty lines and poverty estimates at the state and sector level, respectively, from 1987–2004, while Appendix Tables 4.A3 and 4.A4 provide the 2009 Expert Group poverty lines and poverty estimates at the state and sector level, respectively, for 1987–93 and 2004–5.
17. The information on industry-level tariff rates and NTB coverage rate are from Pandey (1999) and Das (2008). Pandey reports these for various years over 1988 to 1998. Das updates these for various years up to 2003 using the methodology of Pandey. Simple linear interpolation is used to account for the years from 1988 to 2003, for which there is no information on trade protection. As explained, the estimation strategy requires protection-related data for 1986. This is estimated by assuming that tariff and NTB coverage rates grew at the same annual rate from 1986 to 1988 as they did from 1988 to 1989. The NTB coverage rates estimated for 1986 are bounded at 100 percent.
18. The year 1993–94 is one of the middle years in the data and is thus treated as the base (reference) year in the construction of state-level openness index. As

in the case of any good index, the weights are not allowed to change from one year to another.

19. Similar employment-weighted protection measures have been used in other recent studies. One such example is Edmonds, Pavcnik, and Topalova (2008). The idea is that there is an interaction between the industry-level tariff vector and the employment vector in determining various outcomes.
20. Besley and Burgess (2004) consider each state-level amendment to the IDA from 1958 to 1992 and code it as a 1, −1, or 0 depending on whether the amendment in question is deemed to be proemployee, antiemployee, or neutral. The scores are then cumulated over time; for any years with multiple amendments, the scores are coded to give the general direction of change. See Besley and Burgess (2004) for details. (The Besley and Burgess coding is available at econ.lse.ac.uk/staff/rburgess/#wp.)
21. With the exception of Karnataka, these antiemployee amendments took place in 1980 or earlier. For Karnataka the antiemployee amendments took place in 1988.
22. An alternative measure of labor market flexibility and/or rigidity would have been to use the cumulative scores on amendments. This is the approach of Besley and Burgess (2004). Using these scores in place of our labor market flexibility dummy variable leaves our results qualitatively unchanged.
23. Over one thousand firms were surveyed across ten states. Over nine hundred belong to the manufacturing sector.
24. A supplement to the original World Bank survey carried out in two good-investment-climate states and one poor-investment-climate state was aimed at determining the reasons behind overmanning. The results indicated that overmanning was partially the result of labor hoarding in anticipation of higher growth in the future in the good-investment-climate states, but hardly so in the poor-investment-climate state. In fact, labor regulations were noted as a major reason for overmanning in the poor investment climate state. This lends indirect support to the notion that given Maharashtra and Gujarat's ranking as best-investment-climate states, labor regulations have in effect been less binding on firms than the amendments to the IDA may suggest.
25. See also Bhattacharjea (2006) for a critique of the Besley-Burgess coding system.
26. While, as is obvious from our discussion above, we believe that Gujarat and Maharashtra are the states most likely to have relatively flexible labor markets and labor laws, ongoing debates on coding of some states include these two. We therefore use the third measure to show the robustness of our results to using all existing measures, allowing the reader to pick the preferred measure.
27. http://morth.nic.in
28. www.mospi.gov.in
29. www.rbi.org.in

30. There is more disagreement in the middle, but with the exception of Uttar Pradesh, that does not seem to be too serious.
31. We experimented with using contemporaneous protection on the right-hand side in our previous article. The overall message remained unchanged: trade liberalization reduces poverty on average and at times, more so in flexible labor market states. We therefore decided to work exclusively with lagged protection measures here.
32. The Deaton (2003a, 2003b) adjustment to expenditure data for 1999–2000 is always used in conjunction with the Deaton poverty lines.
33. Bigger differences, however, appear when we consider the results based on region-level analysis. While the main flavor of the results remains the same—in that to the extent that trade liberalization has a statistically significant effect on poverty, it works to reduce it—a number of the interaction terms, especially those pertaining to flexibility of labor regulations, fail to be statistically significant. Of course, when they are significant, they work in the same way as found earlier.

REFERENCES

Aghion, Philippe, Robin Burgess, Stephen J. Redding, and Fabrizio Zilibotti (2008). "The Unequal Effects of Liberalization: Evidence from Dismantling the License Raj in India." *American Economic Review* 98(4), 1397–1412.

Amoranto, Glenita, and Rana Hasan (2010). "A Note on Updating Poverty Lines over Time: An Application to India." Mimeo, Economics and Research Department, Asian Development Bank.

Anant, T. C. A. (2000). "Reforming the Labour Market." In S. Gangopadhyay and W. Wadhwa, eds., *Economic Reforms for the Poor*. Delhi: Konark.

Anant, T. C. A., Rana Hasan, Prabhu Mohapatra, Rayaprolu Nagaraj, and S. K. Sasikumar (2006). "Labor Markets in India: Issues and Perspectives." In Jesus Felipe and Rana Hasan, eds., *Labor Markets in Asia: Issues and Perspectives*. New York: Palgrave Macmillan.

Asian Development Bank (2008). "Comparing Poverty across Countries: The Role of Purchasing Power Parities." Key Indicators 2008. Asian Development Bank.

Baldwin, Robert (2003). "Openness and Growth: What Is the Empirical Relationship?" NBER Working Paper no. 9578.

Besley, Timothy J., and Robin Burgess (2004). "Can Labor Regulation Hinder Economic Performance? Evidence from India." *Quarterly Journal of Economics* 19(1), 91–134.

Bhagwati, Jagdish (2004). *In Defense of Globalization*. New York: Oxford University Press.

Bhalla, Surjit S. (2003). "Recounting the Poor: Poverty in India, 1983–99." *Economic and Political Weekly* 38(4), January 25, 338–49.

Bhattacharjea, Aditya (2006). "Labour Market Regulation and Industrial Performance in India: A Critical Review of Empirical Evidence." *Indian Journal of Labour Economics* 49(2), 211–32.

——— (2008). "How Do Indian Firms Respond to Employment Protection Legislation?" Mimeo.

Chen, Shaohua, and Martin Ravallion (2008). "The Developing World Is Poorer Than We Thought, but No Less Successful in the Fight against Poverty." World Bank Policy Research Paper 4703.

Das, D. (2008). "Trade Barriers Measurement: A Methodological Overview." Mimeo.

Datta, Ramesh (2003). "Labor Market, Social Institutions, Economic Reforms, and Social Costs." In S. Uchikawa, ed., *Labour Market and Institution in India, 1990s and Beyond*. New Delhi: Manohar.

Datta-Chaudhuri, Mirnal (1996). "Labor Markets as Social Institutions in India." IRIS-India Working Paper no. 10, University of Maryland at College Park.

Deaton, Angus (2003a). "Prices and Poverty in India, 1987–2000." *Economic and Political Weekly* 38(4), January 25, 362–68.

——— (2003b). "Regional Poverty Estimates for India, 1999–2000." Research Program in Development Studies, Princeton University, August 22.

Deaton, Angus, and Jean Dreze (2002). "Poverty and Inequality in India: A Reexamination." *Economic and Political Weekly* 37(7), September 7, 3729–48.

Deaton, Angus, and Valerie Kozel (2005). "Data and Dogma: The Great Indian Poverty Debate." New Delhi: Macmillan India.

Dollar, David (1992). "Outward-Oriented Developing Economies Really Do Grow More Rapidly: Evidence from 95 LDCs, 1976–1985." *Economic Development and Cultural Change* 40(3), 523–44.

Dollar, David, Giuseppe Iarossi, and Taye Mengistae (2002). "Investment Climate and Economic Performance: Some Firm Level Evidence from India." Mimeo, World Bank.

Dollar, David, and Aart Kraay (2002). "Growth Is Good for the Poor." *Journal of Economic Growth* 7(3), 195–225.

——— (2004). "Trade, Growth, and Poverty." *Economic Journal* 114(493), F22–F49.

Edmonds, Eric V., Nina Pavcnik, and Petia Topalova (2008). "Trade Adjustment and Human Capital Investments: Evidence from Indian Tariff Reform." NBER Working Paper no. 12884.

Edwards, Sebastian (1998). "Openness, Productivity and Growth: What Do We Really Know?" *Economic Journal* 108(447), 383–98.

Frankel, Jeffrey, and David Romer (1999). "Does Trade Cause Growth?" *American Economic Review* 89(3), 379–99.

Ghosh, Buddhadeb, and Prabir De (2004). "How Do Different Categories of Infrastructure Affect Development? Evidence from Indian States." *Economic and Political Weekly* 39(42), October 16, 4645–57.

Government of India (1979). Report of the Task Force on Projections of Minimum Needs and Effective Consumption Demand. Perspective Planning Division, Planning Commission.

——— (1993). Report of the Expert Group on Estimation of Proportion and Number of Poor. Perspective Planning Division, Planning Commission.

——— (2009). Report of the Expert Group to Review the Methodology for Estimation of Poverty. Planning Commission.

Gupta, Poonam, Rana Hasan, and Utsav Kumar (2009). "Big Reforms but Small Payoffs: Explaining the Weak Record of Growth in Indian Manufacturing." *India Policy Forum* 5.

Harrison, Ann (2006). "Globalization and Poverty." Mimeo, University of California, Berkeley.

Hasan, Rana, Karl R. Jandoc, and Niny Khor (2010). "Do Constraints to Growth Vary by Firm Size? Evidence from India over a Period of Trade Liberalization." Mimeo, Economics and Research Department, Asian Development Bank.

Hasan, Rana, Devashish Mitra, and K. V. Ramaswamy (2007). "Trade Reforms, Labor Regulations, and Labor Demand Elasticities: Empirical Evidence from India." *Review of Economics and Statistics* 89(3), 466–81.

Hasan, Rana, Devashish Mitra, and Beyza P. Ural (2007). "Trade Liberalization, Labor Market Institutions, and Poverty Reduction: Evidence from Indian States." *India Policy Forum, 2006–7.*

Hasan, Rana, M. G. Quibria, and Yangseon Kim (2003). "Poverty and Economic Freedom: Evidence from Cross-Country Data." East-West Center Working Paper.

Irwin, Douglas A., and J. Marko Tervio (2002). "Does Trade Raise Income? Evidence from the Twentieth Century." *Journal of International Economics* 58, 1–18.

Nagaraj, Rayaprolu (2002). "Trade and Labour Market Linkages in India: Evidence and Issues." Economic Series Working Paper no. 50, East-West Center.

Pandey, Mihir (1999). *NCAER Report on Trade Protection in India.* New Delhi: National Council of Applied Economic Research.

OECD (2007). "India." *OECD Economics Surveys* 2007(14).

Ozler, Berk, Gaurav Datt, and Martin Ravallion (1996). *A Database on Poverty and Growth in India.* Washington, DC: World Bank.

Ramaswamy, K. V. (2003). "Liberalization, Outsourcing, and Industrial Labor Markets in India: Some Preliminary Results." In S. Uchikawa, ed., *Labour Market and Institution in India, 1990s and Beyond.* New Delhi: Manohar.

Ravallion, Martin (2001). "Growth, Inequality, and Poverty: Looking beyond Averages." *World Development* 29(11), 1803–15.

Ravallion, Martin, and Gaurav Datt (1999). "How Important to India's Poor Is the Sectoral Composition of Economic Growth?" *World Bank Economic Review* (10)1, 1–25.

Rodriguez, Francisco, and Dani Rodrik (2001). "Trade Policy and Economics Growth: A Skeptic's Guide to the Cross-National Evidence." In B. Bernanke and K. S. Rogoff, eds., *Macroeconomics Annual 2000*. Cambridge, MA: MIT Press for NBER.

Rodrik, Dani, Arvind Subramanian, and Francesco Trebbi (2002). "Institutions Rule: The Primacy of Institutions over Geography and Integration in Economic Development." NBER Working Paper no. 9305.

Sachs, Jeffrey D., and Andrew Warner (1995). "Economic Reform and the Process of Global Integration." *Brookings Papers on Economic Activity* 1995(1), 1–118.

Sundaram, Asha (2010). "The Impact of Trade Liberalization on Micro Enterprises: Evidence from Indian Manufacturing." Mimeo, Syracuse University.

Topalova, Petia (2005). "Trade Liberalization, Poverty and Inequality: Evidence from Indian Districts." NBER Working Paper no. 11614.

Wacziarg, Romain, and Karen Horn Welch (2003). "Trade Liberalization and Growth: New Evidence." NBER Working Paper no. 10152.

World Bank (2003). *Improving the Investment Climate in India*. Washington, DC: World Bank.

Chapter 5

Growth, Openness, and the Socially Disadvantaged

MEGHA MUKIM AND ARVIND PANAGARIYA*

There is now broad agreement that declining levels of poverty have accompanied sustained rapid growth in India during the last three decades. Recent econometric work by Hasan, Mitra, and Ural (2006–7) and Cain, Hasan, and Mitra (2010) has also shown that openness and labor market flexibility have contributed positively to poverty alleviation. Contrary to the prior findings of Topalova (2007), these authors find no evidence that states and regions that were more exposed to trade liberalization on account of greater employment in import-competing sectors experienced a slower reduction or an increase in poverty. On the contrary, to the extent that a statistically significant relationship between poverty and trade liberalization can be found, the evidence points to greater exposure to trade leading to larger reductions in poverty.

There remains deep skepticism on the part of the nongovernmental organizations (NGOs) and journalists, however, about growth and openness having done much to alleviate poverty among the socially disadvantaged groups referred to as the Scheduled Castes (SC), Scheduled Tribes (ST), and Other Backward Castes (OBC).[1] For example, a submission by the National Campaign on Dalit Human Rights to the House of Commons of the UK Parliament published on

January 14, 2011, states, "In spite of high economic growth rates the poverty rate among excluded communities in India has increased, coupled with the insecurity of livelihoods." In the same vein, writing in the *Financial Chronicle* (December 29, 2010), journalist Praful Bidwai asserts, "Rising inequalities highlight what is wrong with India's growth trajectory, driven as it is by elite consumption and sectoral imbalances, *which exclude disadvantaged groups from the benefit of rising GDP*, while aggravating income disparities" (emphasis added).[2]

Even though the concerns in these statements are couched in terms of equity, it is clear that at a deeper level they relate to the impact of growth on poverty among the disadvantaged groups. Unfortunately, the scholarly literature analyzing the impact of reforms and accelerated growth on poverty among the traditionally disadvantaged groups remains sparse. The focus of the literature devoted to studying the changes in the fortunes of the socially disadvantaged groups during the postreform era has been on intergroup inequality rather than poverty. For example, Kijima (2006) studies whether the gap between the average consumption levels of the SC and ST households, on the one hand, and Non-Scheduled (NS) households, on the other, declined between 1983 and 1999–2000 and, if so, whether this decline could be attributed to reduced discrimination. She answers the former question in the positive but the latter in the negative. Hnatkovska, Lahiri, and Paul (2010) offer a much more comprehensive analysis of intergroup inequality, asking whether the wages, education levels, and occupational structure between the SC and ST as a group and the NS have converged. They answer forcefully in the affirmative on each count and attribute it to "the rapid structural changes in the Indian economy over the past 25 years" (p. 42).[3]

To our knowledge, the only study that comes close to addressing the evolution of poverty as opposed to inequality in the postreform era is Sundaram and Tendulkar (2003). These authors study the change in poverty levels of the SC, ST, and NS households, distinguished according to the means of livelihood, in rural and urban India at the national level between 1993–94 and 1999–2000.[4] They find that during these years, the ST in rural areas experienced the lowest decline in poverty, while those in urban areas saw a rise in poverty. In contrast, the SC households, whether in rural or in urban areas and whether agricultural laborers or in other occupations, experienced poverty reduction matching that experienced by the rural population on average. The authors conclude (p. 5275), "This fact holds the important message that the benefits of growth have indeed been accessed by the socially and economically disadvantaged groups of India. It highlights the fact that a growth-centered strategy for poverty reduction in India can and must be followed."

In this chapter, we undertake a comprehensive analysis of poverty among various social groups and its relationship to growth and openness. Our main results may be summarized as follows. First, whereas the distribution of the SC between rural and urban areas and across states is broadly similar to that of the general population, ST individuals are distributed differently. Based on the 61st National Sample Survey (NSS) round, conducted in 2004–5, only 8 percent of ST individuals compared with 20 percent of SC individuals live in urban areas. Likewise, the top five states ranked by their proportion of SC population mirror the five most populous states. But only one state among the top five ranked by their proportion of ST population is among the five most populous states. In other words, the distribution of the SC follows that of the general population, while that of the ST is very different from it.

Second and more importantly, nationally, every successive sample survey we analyze—that is, the 38th, 43rd, 50th, and 61st rounds, conducted in 1983, 1987–88, 1993–94, and 2004–5, respectively—shows a declining rate of poverty for every social group in every region (rural, urban, and overall). In aggregate, the poverty rate fell by twenty percentage points for the SC and by eighteen percentage points for each of the ST and the NS between 1983 and 2004–5. Therefore, data forcefully refute any claims that higher growth in recent decades has not been associated with any benefits for disadvantaged social groups. What can be justifiably argued is that since the overall poverty rates were much higher for the ST and SC than for the NS in 1983 and that since the percentage-point reductions have been broadly equal across the groups, the proportionate differences in the poverty rates for the SC and ST on the one hand and the NS on the other have risen.

Third, our econometric analysis offers strong evidence of rising incomes leading to declining rates of poverty for the ST, NS, and all groups taken together. Our results for the SC are weaker: while the coefficient of per capita income has the correct sign, it is not statistically significant. These results are based on regressions of poverty on per capita income with appropriate control variables based on pooled data for the eighteen largest states that account for 98 percent of the national population over our four survey years.

Finally, we test for the effect of trade openness on poverty among various social groups. Our results show that for no social group did poverty fall less in states that were exposed to greater openness following trade liberalization. To the extent we find statistically significant effects, they show greater reductions in poverty in the states that were more exposed to openness. Specifically, one or more measures of protection shows a negative and statistically significant effect of openness on poverty for the SC and NS in urban, rural and urban and rural areas combined. For the ST, we find statistically significant effects in urban areas only.

This chapter is organized as follows. In the next section, we describe the size and the location of the socially disadvantaged groups. In the third section, we report the estimates of poverty at the national level for the three major groups in various regions (rural, urban, and combined) for the four surveys that we analyze. In the fourth section, we describe poverty trends based on estimates for the top ten states by SC and ST populations. At this stage we also estimate the relationship between poverty and per capita incomes. In the fifth section, we test the relationship between openness and poverty alleviation. In the sixth section we perform some sensitivity analysis and in the final section we conclude and discuss the implications of our findings.

THE SOCIALLY DISADVANTAGED: HOW MANY AND WHERE?

Demographic data on the SC and ST come from two sources: the Census Commission and the National Sample Survey Office (NSSO). The counts from these sources do not match and they also relate to different years. Because virtually all of our quantitative analysis relies on unit-level data from the NSSO, we report the indicators based predominantly on this source. But where relevant, we do point out the differences with the census data.

Though the NSSO conducts a smaller, "thin" expenditure survey each year, it conducts a larger, "thick" survey approximately every five years only. Our analysis is based on these quinquennial thick surveys beginning with the one conducted in 1983. We consider five NSSO surveys in all relating to the years 1983, 1987–88, 1993–94, 1999–2000, and 2004–5 and labeled rounds 38, 43, 50, 55, and 61, respectively.[5] Of these, the expenditure data generated by the 55th round, relating to the year 1999–2000, are not directly comparable to those in other rounds due to the application of a different sample design (see Panagariya 2008, pp. 136–41, for details). Therefore, we do not consider the 55th round except for the purpose of reporting the population shares of various social groups, which are not influenced by the difference in the sample design. The bulk of our analysis is focused on rounds 38, 43, 50, and 61.

How Many?

The first three of the latest five thick rounds identify only the SC and ST households as separate social groups. The last two rounds identify additionally the Other Backward Castes (OBC). Accordingly, in Table 5.1, we report the proportions of the SC and ST in the total population in all five rounds and those of the OBC in the last two rounds. The residual group is labeled Forward Castes (FC), with the Non-Scheduled (NS) category defining the total population minus the SC and ST or, equivalently, the OBC and the FC. Unless otherwise stated, all our indicators drawn from the NSSO expenditure surveys are based on the eighteen largest states (counting Delhi as a state) for the first three surveys and on the twenty-one largest states for the last two. The latter include the states of Chhattisgarh, Jharkhand, and Uttarakhand, carved out of Madhya Pradesh, Bihar, and Uttar Pradesh, respectively, in 2000. We exclude the six smallest northeastern states, Sikkim, and all union territories (UTs) except Delhi.[6] For comparison, we also report the data from the 2001 census, which are based on all states and UTs.

Table 5.1 gives rise to four observations. First, the share of the SC in the population could be anywhere between 16 and 20 percent. If we go by the census and the two earlier NSS rounds, the proportion is closer to 16 percent, but if we rely on the three latest NSS rounds, it is closer to 20 percent. We do not take a position between these two numbers, letting the reader make this choice. Second, the share of the ST is between 8 and 9 percent. Thankfully, there is strong agreement among the five surveys and between them and the census in this regard. Third, the OBC are likely to be somewhere between 36

Table 5.1 SHARES OF VARIOUS SOCIAL GROUPS IN THE POPULATION

Survey/Census Year	*SC*	*ST*	*OBC*	*FC*	*NS*	*Total Population (million)*
1983	16.7	8.3			74.9	660.4
1987–88	16.6	9.2			74.1	648.7
1993–94	19.4	8.5			72	767.3
1999–2000	19	8.3	36.1	36.6	72.7	904.5
2004–5	19.7	8.1	41.2	30.9	72.1	968
Census 2001	16.2	8.2			75.6	1029

Source: Authors' calculations using the unit-level data of the relevant NSS expenditure surveys and Table T00-005 from the Census of India website at http://www.censusindia.gov.in/Tables_Published/A-Series/A-Series_links/t_00_005.aspx (accessed February 9, 2011)

and 41 percent of the total population. This is a wide range, and we must await the results of the 66th NSS round and the 2011 Caste Census for some resolution of whether the true share is nearer the lower or upper limit or some figure outside this range. Finally, as a word of caution, we note that there is wide discrepancy in the total population figures generated by the NSSO and the census. It is generally recognized that while the NSSO generates good estimates of various proportions, the census produces more accurate absolute totals. Therefore, for example, when the Planning Commission calculates the absolute number of poor, it multiplies the estimated poor from NSS data by a factor equaling the census-based total population divided by the NSS-based total population.

Where: The Rural-Urban Split

Next, we turn to the rural-urban split of shares of various social groups. For this purpose, we rely exclusively on the 2004–5 NSSO survey, which is the latest available survey that explicitly identifies the share of the OBC. Table 5.2 summarizes the information.

Four features of this table are worthy of note. First, at .7 percent, the share of the ST residing in the urban areas in the total population of the twenty-one largest states is tiny. Seen another way, as much as 92 percent of the total ST population in the country lives in the rural areas. In this sense, any targeted programs to improve the fortunes of

Table 5.2 RURAL-URBAN CATEGORIZATION ACROSS SOCIAL GROUPS, 2004–5

Region	*SC*	*ST*	*OBC*	*FC*	*NS*	*Total*
SHARES IN THE TOTAL POPULATION						
Rural	15.7	7.5	32.2	19.3	51.5	74.7
Urban	4	0.7	9	11.6	20.6	25.3
Rural + Urban	19.7	8.1	41.2	30.9	72.1	100
RURAL-URBAN SPLIT WITHIN EACH CASTE CATEGORY						
Rural	79.8	91.9	78.1	62.4	71.4	74.7
Urban	20.2	8.1	21.9	37.6	28.6	25.3
Rural + Urban	100	100	100	100	100	100

Source: Authors' calculations from the 61st round of the NSSO expenditure survey

the ST require focus on rural areas though care must be taken to ensure that these programs do not impede migration to urban or other rural areas.[7] Second, though the OBC are more numerous than the SC, their rural-urban composition is almost the same as that of the latter. Third, together the SC, ST, and OBC account for as much as 74 percent of the rural population. This means that any policy that lowers rural poverty is almost sure to help one or more of these groups. Finally, the FC as a group is significantly more urbanized than the remaining social groups. It accounts for almost 46 percent of the urban population, even though its share in the total population is just 30.5 percent.

Where: The Statewise Distribution of Various Groups

Turning to the geographical distribution of various social groups, we rely once again on the 61st round, conducted in 2004–5, since it is the latest survey providing data on the OBC. We consider two sets of shares: the share of each state in any given social group and the share of each group in any given state. These are shown in Tables 5.3 and 5.4, respectively. For reasons outlined above, we limit ourselves to the twenty-one largest states (counting Delhi as a state) in each table. These states account for more than 98 percent of the total population of the country. The excluded entities include six northeastern states other than Assam, Sikkim and Goa, and the six Union Territories (UTs). We arrange the states in Tables 5.3 and 5.4 in the descending order of their total population shares within the twenty-one included states. Thus Uttar Pradesh, the most populous state, appears at the top of the list, and Himachal Pradesh, the least populous state, appears at the bottom.

Several observations follow from Table 5.3. First, the five largest states also have the highest shares of the SC population, although the individual rankings differ somewhat. These states—Uttar Pradesh,

Table 5.3 SHARES OF STATES IN SOCIAL GROUPS

*State**	*SC*	*ST*	*OBC*	*FC*	*NS*	*All*
Uttar Pradesh	20	1	21.8	13	18.1	17
Maharashtra	7.6	11	7.2	13.6	9.9	9.5
West Bengal	11.1	6.5	1.3	15.9	7.5	8.2
Bihar	8.4	0.5	11	4.4	8.2	7.6
Andhra Pradesh	7	6.5	8.6	6.8	7.8	7.5
Madhya Pradesh	5.5	16.2	5.9	4.4	5.3	6.2
Tamil Nadu	6.5	0.4	10.1	0.9	6.2	5.8
Rajasthan	6.1	9.2	6.2	4	5.2	5.7
Karnataka	4.6	4.1	4.8	6	5.3	5.1
Gujarat	2.6	8.8	4.6	5.6	5.1	4.9
Orissa	3.3	11	3.6	2.7	3.2	3.8
Kerala	1.7	0.6	4.6	2.9	3.9	3.2
Assam	1.3	5.7	1.1	4.6	2.6	2.6
Jharkhand	1.6	8.2	2.7	1.3	2.1	2.5
Punjab	4.4	0.1	1.2	3.3	2.1	2.4
Haryana	2.9	0.1	1.6	3.2	2.3	2.2
Chhattisgarh	1.6	8.8	2.4	0.7	1.6	2.2

(*continued*)

Table 5.3 (*continued*)

*State**	*SC*	*ST*	*OBC*	*FC*	*NS*	*All*
Delhi	1.6	0.2	0.4	2.6	1.3	1.3
Uttarakhand	0.9	0.5	0.4	1.6	0.9	0.9
Jammu and Kashmir	0.5	0.1	0.2	1.7	0.8	0.7
Himachal Pradesh	0.8	0.4	0.2	1.1	0.6	0.6
All twenty-one states	190.9	78.9	398.9	299.3	698.2	968
(Population in million)						

*States are listed in the descending order of size according to total population.
Source: Authors' calculations from the 61st round of the NSSO expenditure survey

Maharashtra, West Bengal, Bihar, and Andhra Pradesh—account for 50 percent of the total population and 54 percent of the SC population within the twenty-one largest states. Going further down the list, we see that the nine largest states continue to account for the top nine shares in the SC population. The shares of these nine states in the total and SC populations are 73 and 77 percent, respectively. It is only when we get to the tenth state that the pattern is broken, since Punjab, which is the fifteenth largest state, happens to have the tenth largest SC population. As we will see below, the SC account for an unusually large proportion of the total population in Punjab.

Second, the distribution of the ST differs significantly across states. The five largest states, accounting for 50 percent of the total population, account for only 25.5 percent of the ST population in the twenty-one states. The state with the highest share in the ST population of the

Table 5.4 SHARES OF GROUPS WITHIN EACH STATE

*State**	*SC*	*ST*	*OBC*	*FC*	*NS*	*Population (millions)*
Uttar Pradesh	23.1	0.5	52.8	23.6	76.4	165
Maharashtra	15.8	9.4	30.9	43.9	74.8	92.3
West Bengal	26.8	6.5	6.5	60.3	66.7	78.9
Bihar	21.9	0.6	59.7	17.8	77.5	73.6
Andhra Pradesh	18.3	7	46.9	27.8	74.7	72.9
Madhya Pradesh	17.4	21.2	39.4	22	61.4	60.1
Tamil Nadu	22.2	0.6	72.2	5	77.2	56.1
Rajasthan	20.9	13.1	44.6	21.4	66	55.3
Karnataka	17.9	6.6	39	36.4	75.4	49.3
Gujarat	10.5	14.8	39.2	35.5	74.8	47.2
Orissa	17	23.4	38.2	21.4	59.6	37.2
Kerala	10.5	1.6	60.2	27.7	87.9	30.8
Assam	9.9	17.8	17.6	54.6	72.2	25.2
Jharkhand	12.9	26.6	45	15.5	60.5	24.3
Punjab	35.9	0.4	20.4	43.3	63.6	23.2

(*continued*)

Table 5.4 (*continued*)

*State**	*SC*	*ST*	*OBC*	*FC*	*NS*	*Population (millions)*
Haryana	25.5	0.3	30.3	44	74.2	21.6
Chhattisgarh	14.2	32.4	44.1	9.3	53.4	21.5
Delhi	24.6	1.6	11.4	62.5	73.9	12.4
Uttarakhand	21.4	4.8	18	55.8	73.8	8.3
Jammu and Kashmir	12.7	0.6	12.5	74.2	86.7	6.8
Himachal Pradesh	26.2	4.9	14.9	54.1	68.9	6.1
All twenty-one states	19.7	8.1	41.2	30.9	72.1	968

*States are listed in the descending order of size according to total population.
Source: Authors' calculations from the 61st round of the NSSO expenditure survey

twenty-one states, Madhya Pradesh, is not among the five largest states by total population. Nevertheless, the degree of concentration of the ST is almost as high across states as of the SC population. The top five and top nine ST states account for 56 and 86 percent of the ST population in the twenty-one states, respectively. The top five ST states are Madhya Pradesh, Maharashtra, Orissa, Rajasthan, and Gujarat, in that order, with Chhattisgarh a close sixth. Only Maharashtra appears on both the top five SC and ST lists. Remarkably, none of the seven northeastern states, traditionally identified as those with high concentrations of the ST populations, appear on this list. These states do have very high proportions of the ST in their overall populations but being small in size, they house only a small proportion of the country's total

ST population. Assam, the largest northeastern state, accounts for only 6 percent of the ST population in the largest twenty-one states.

Third, the distribution of the OBC across states follows more closely the distribution of the SC. Nine states on the top ten SC and OBC lists are common. The top five and top nine OBC states account for 59 and 80 percent of the total OBC population in the twenty-one states, respectively. This close correspondence between distributions of the SC and OBC perhaps has a bearing on the political economy of reservations in jobs and education: living side by side with the SC populations, which enjoyed the benefits of reservations since the adoption of the Constitution in 1950, the OBC populations may have become sensitized to these advantages and perhaps actively sought similar reservations for themselves.

Finally, the distribution of the FC resembles to some degree that of the SC and OBC, though with greater concentration at the top and more even distribution over the remaining states. The top three FC states, which are also the three most populous states (Uttar Pradesh, Maharashtra, and West Bengal), account for 43 percent of the FC population in the twenty-one states, in comparison to 39 percent for the SC, 40 percent for the OBC, and 28 percent for the ST. There is a steep decline as we move from the third-largest FC state (Uttar Pradesh) to the fourth-largest (Andhra Pradesh): from 13 to 7 percent.

Some insight into the dispersion of various social groups across states can be gained with the help of the Theil index of inequality. This index belongs to the family of generalized entropy inequality measures. The value varies between 0 and ∞, with zero representing an equal distribution and higher values representing higher levels of inequality. The index allows us to identify separately the contribution of various entities to the overall concentration.

Using the demographic data from the 61st NSS round, conducted in 2004–5, the value of the index for the total population is 3.63, which provides a benchmark for the distribution of the population across different states in India. The values of the index for the SC and NS turn out to be close to this value: 4.46 and 3.85, respectively. But consistent with the observations above, the value of the index for the ST turns out to be much higher at 6.3.

The Theil index allows us to calculate the contributions of individual states to the final value of the index—states that host a large proportion of the population of any given social group make a larger contribution to the index. The maps in Figure 5.1 provide a visual depiction of each state's contribution to the Theil index by social group. While the contribution of states to the index for the NS is very similar to that of the general population ("All"), those of the SC and the ST diverge from the latter. The ST are more heavily concentrated in states such as Madhya Pradesh, Maharashtra, and Orissa, while the SC are more concentrated in Uttar Pradesh, West Bengal, and Bihar. In other words, even after controlling for the average dispersion across states, the ST individuals are strongly concentrated, and the SC individuals moderately concentrated, across states.

Where: The Groupwise Distribution of Population within States

Table 5.4 shows the shares of various social groups in the population of each of the twenty-one largest states. Several observations follow.

First, Chhattisgarh, Orissa, Jharkhand, and Madhya Pradesh, in that order, stand out in terms of having large numbers of both the SC and ST in their populations. The SC and ST also account for a significant proportion of the population in Rajasthan. Second, in the remaining states, it is either the SC or the ST that has a major presence, but not both. The SC account for 20 percent or more of the population in as many as ten states. Finally, and somewhat surprisingly, the OBC constitute the largest single social group in eleven out

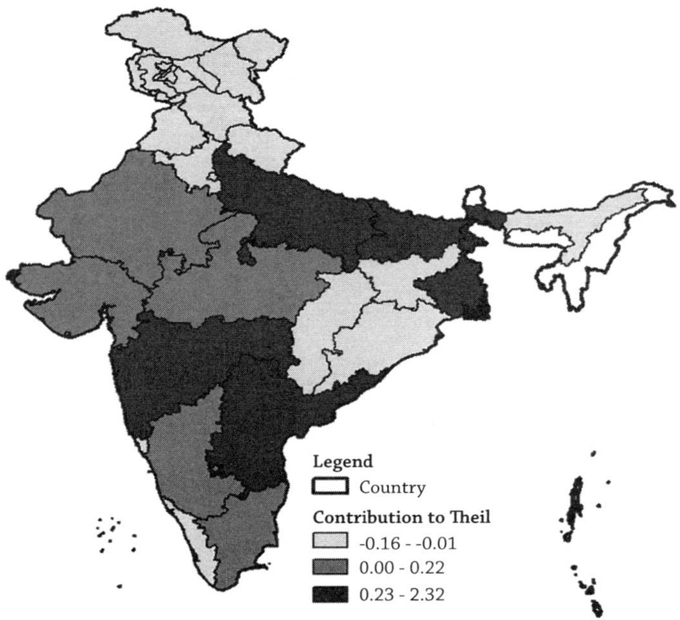

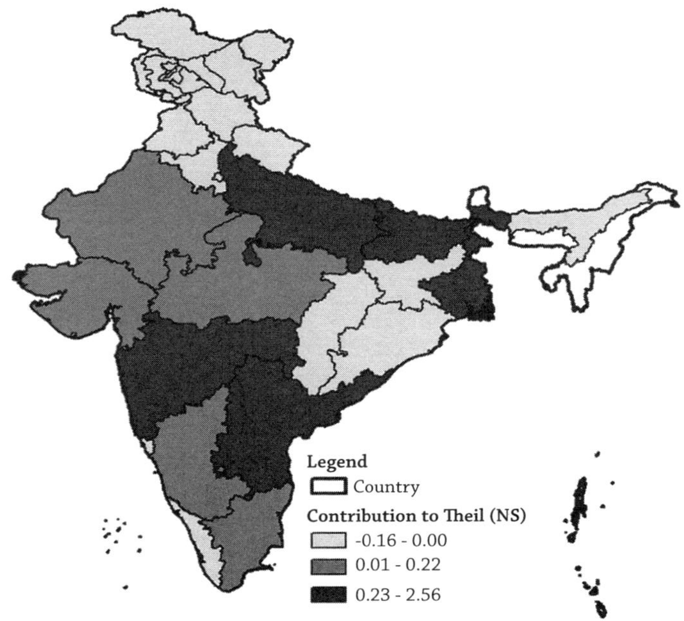

Figure 5.1. State Contributions to the Theil Index (All and NS)

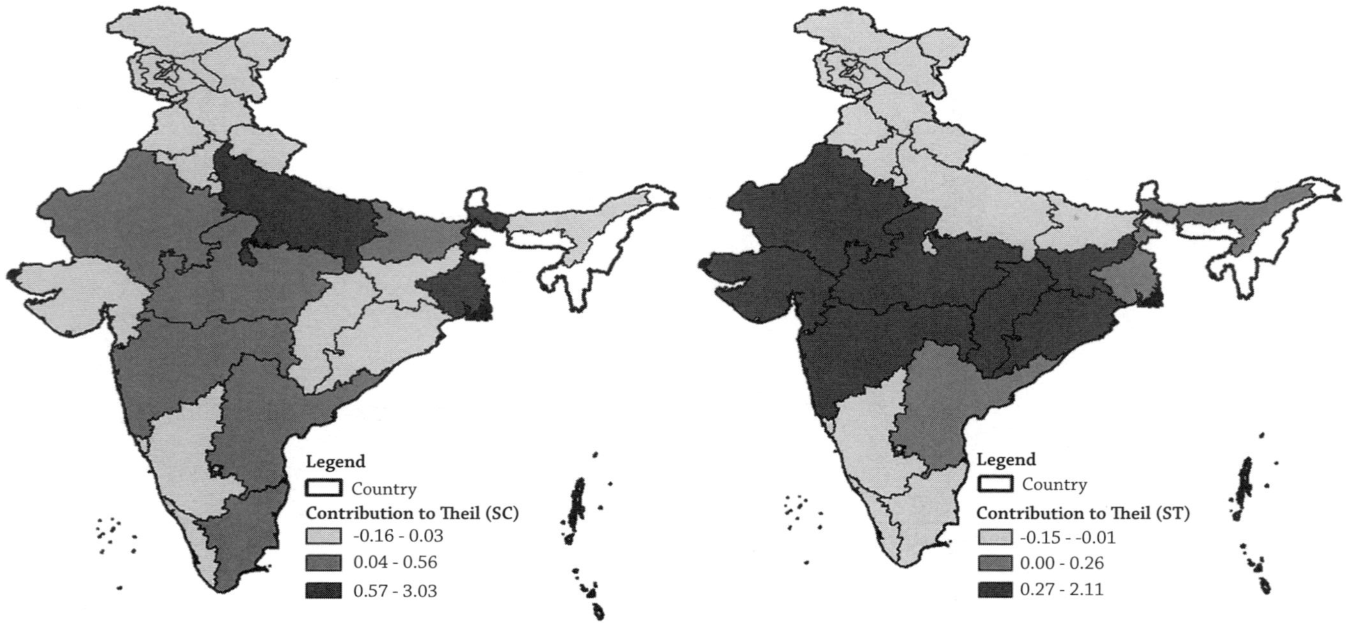

Figure 5.1. (continued) State Contributions to the Theil Index (SC and ST)

of the fourteen most populous states. The FC constitute the largest single group in nine out of the twenty-one states, but only two among them, Maharashtra and West Bengal, make it to the list of the twelve largest states.

COUNTING THE POOR BY SOCIAL GROUPS

We now turn to counting the poor by social group. As previously noted, Meenakshi, Ray, and Gupta (2000) have calculated the poverty rates for the SC and ST for 1993–94 at both national and state levels. Sundaram and Tendulkar (2003) have done the same at the national level, on a comparable basis, for 1993–94 and 1999–2000, showing declining poverty levels across the surveys. In this chapter, we offer estimates for the SC, ST, and NS (Non-Scheduled, consisting of the OBC and the FC) for 1983, 1987–88, 1993–94, and 2004–5 and for the OBC and FC separately for the year 2004–5. We choose to skip the year 1999–2000 because of noncomparability of the survey design that year to the surveys in other years. For comparability with the overall official poverty estimates published by the Planning Commission, we base all our estimates on the official poverty lines.

Poverty Rates across Groups Nationally and Statewise

We first present the poverty rates in 2004–5 across various social groups in rural and urban regions aggregated over the twenty-one largest states (counting Delhi as a state). Several observations follow from Table 5.5 with respect to the latest poverty picture. First, the poverty rates are the highest among the ST followed by the SC, the OBC, and then the FC in that order. The only exception is the urban poverty rate for the ST, which is a hair's breadth below the corresponding rate

Table 5.5 POVERTY RATES BY SOCIAL GROUPS IN THE TWENTY-ONE LARGEST STATES, 2004–5

Region	*SC*	*ST*	*OBC*	*FC*	*NS*	*All Groups*
Rural	37.2	47	25.9	17.5	22.8	28.2
Urban	41.1	39	31.3	16.2	22.8	26.1
All (rural + urban)	38	46.3	27.1	17	22.8	27.7

Source: Authors' calculations using the unit-level expenditure data from the 61st round

for the SC. But even this exception has limited relevance, since only 8 percent of the ST population lives in the urban areas. Second, the SC and ST poverty rates are an order of magnitude higher than either the average for all groups or the OBC and FC. Finally, for both the SC and OBC, the urban poverty rates are higher than the corresponding rural poverty rates, and for both groups the urban and rural poverty rates are substantially higher than the corresponding rates for the FC. It is possible that with the existence of antipoverty programs that concentrate mainly in rural areas and with rural-to-urban migration predicted to accelerate in coming years, urban poverty rates for the SC and OBC would remain higher than the corresponding rural poverty rates in the short to medium run.

We also find it useful to present the poverty picture by states in 2004–5 using maps. In Figure 5.2, we show the poverty rates for the general population and for the NS, SC, and ST social groups across states. Before describing the maps, we note one important limitation of some of our poverty estimates for the ST at the state level. In several states, the NSS survey ends up with only a small number of

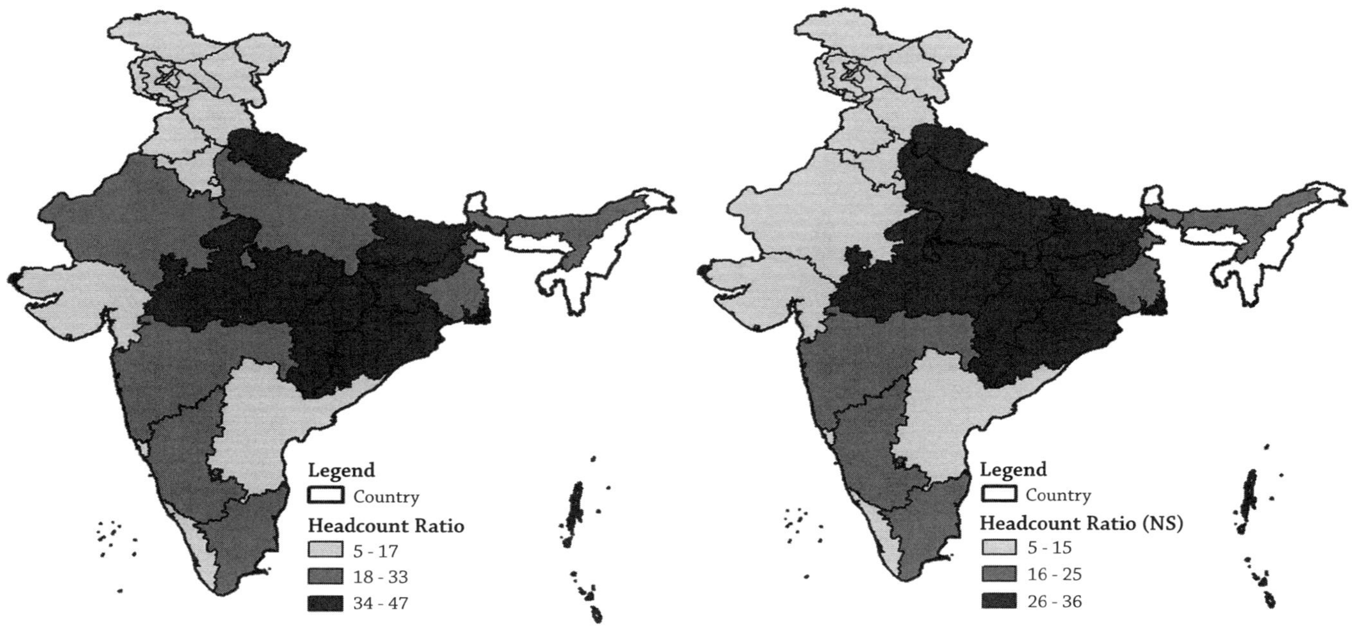

Figure 5.2. Poverty Rates by State in 2004–5 (All and NS)

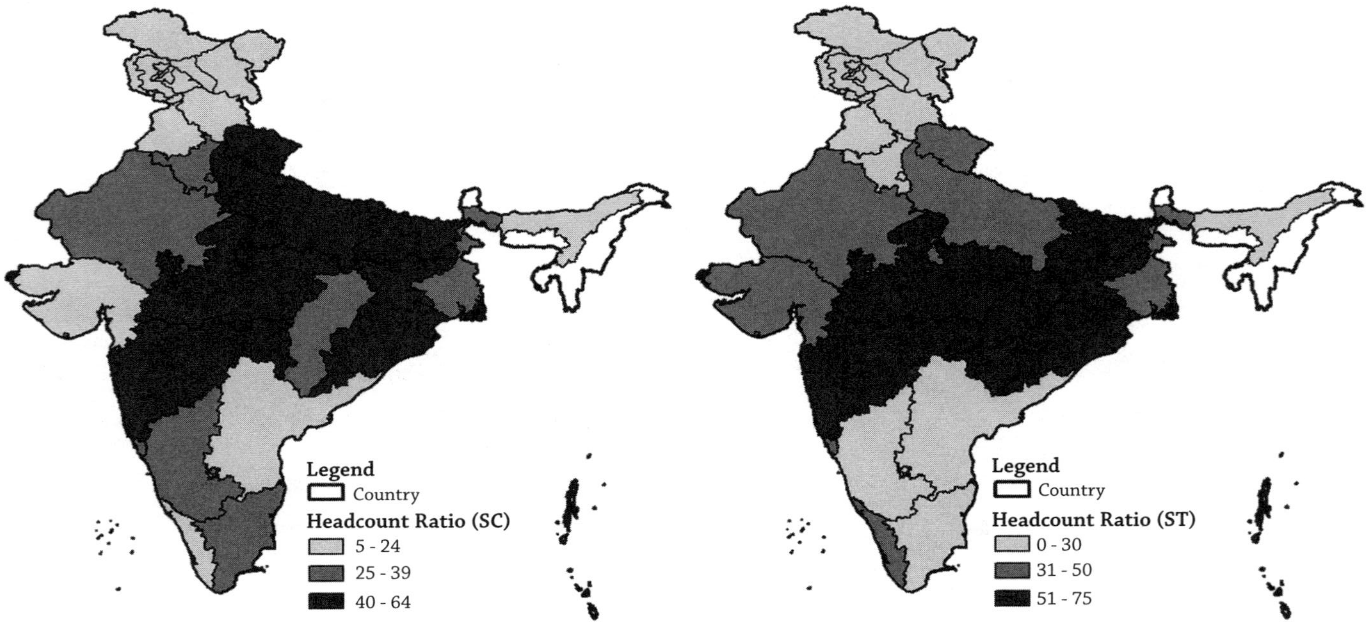

Figure 5.2. (continued). Poverty Rates by State in 2004–5 (SC and ST)

ST households. Five extreme cases are Goa, Haryana, Delhi, Punjab, and Jammu and Kashmir (J&K), which ended up with just 2, 11, 16, 18, and 20 ST households, respectively, in the 2004–5 survey. Poverty estimates based on such small number of households are unlikely to be precise. Unfortunately, there is no way around this, at least for the purposes of comparing the estimates across states and within states over time. Therefore, for now, we choose to report the estimates for all twenty-one states, while recognizing that the estimates are less precise in some cases than in others. Later, when we carry out regressions using state-level poverty estimates, we will conduct robustness tests by excluding states for which the number of ST household in the sample happens to be small.

With this caveat, we may now proceed to identify two features of the maps presented in Figure 5.2. First, the upper limits of poverty rate are higher for the SC and ST groups compared to those for the general population and the NS. And second, the overall (i.e., rural plus urban) rate of poverty is highest in central and northeastern states, with a few exceptions. The results for the general population and the NS are similar—poverty rates range between 5 and 47 percent for the general population and 5 and 36 percent for the NS, with states such as Orissa, Bihar, Jharkhand, Chhattisgarh, Uttarakhand, and Madhya Pradesh exhibiting the highest rates of poverty. On the other hand, the upper limit on poverty is 64 percent for the SC and 75 percent for the ST. However, the highest rates of poverty for the SC and ST are associated with the same states as the overall and NS rates. For the SC, states like Bihar, Uttarakhand, Jharkhand, and Orissa, and for the ST, states like Orissa, Madhya Pradesh, Bihar, and Maharashtra suffer from the highest rates of poverty. Thus, although the rates of poverty are higher for the SC and ST, there is substantial geographical overlap when considering high poverty rates among these groups and the NS.

Evolution of National Poverty Rates by Social Groups over Time

In the previous section, we provided snapshots of relative poverty rates across various groups at the national and state levels in 2004–5. Next, we turn to the evolution of poverty rates for various social groups over time at the national level. Since the OBC are identified only in 2004–5, for the purpose of comparison over time, the social groups must be limited to the SC, ST, and NS. Table 5.6 reports the relevant rate of poverty in rural, urban, and rural-plus-urban regions for various social groups for the years 1983, 1987–88, 1993–94, and 2004–5.

Perhaps the most remarkable feature of Table 5.6 is the declining rates of poverty over time for every single group in every region (rural, urban, and overall) between every pair of surveys. The results thoroughly counter any claims that the accelerated growth occurring since the early 1980s has failed to help disadvantaged groups. Most pointedly, poverty rates have declined significantly even for the ST, who are often said to be outside the mainstream of the economy. During the twenty years covered by the surveys, poverty declined by twenty percentage points for the SC and eighteen percentage points for both the ST and NS. Critics would no doubt like to argue that given the higher initial rates of poverty for the SC and ST, these reductions imply that the ratio of poverty rates for the SC and ST to that for the NS has gone up; however, the estimates in Table 5.6 refute the claim that growth has bypassed socially disadvantaged groups.

CROSS-STATE ANALYSIS: POVERTY AND PER CAPITA INCOME

We now move on to a more disaggregated analysis over time, focusing on individual states. We focus on two main issues: (1) How have SC and ST poverty rates evolved between 1983 and 2004–5 in states

Table 5.6 EVOLUTION OF POVERTY RATES BY SOCIAL GROUPS

Survey Year	*SC*	*ST*	*OBC*	*FC*	*NS*	*All Groups*
			RURAL			
1983	59	64.9			41	46.6
1987–88	50.1	57.8			32.8	38.7
1993–94	48.4	51.6			31.3	37
2004–5	37.2	47	25.9	17.5	22.8	28.2
			URBAN			
1983	56.2	58.3			40.1	42.5
1987–88	54.6	56.2			36.6	39.4
1993–94	51.2	46.6			29.6	33.1
2004–5	41.1	39	31.3	16.2	22.8	26.1
			RURAL + URBAN			
1983	58.5	64.4			40.7	45.7
1987–88	50.8	57.6			33.8	38.8
1993–94	48.9	51.2			30.8	36
2004–5	38	46.3	27.1	17	22.8	27.7

Source: Authors' calculations using the unit-level data the NSSO expenditure surveys

where they are highly concentrated? and (2) Are increases in average per capita income associated with declining rates of poverty at the level of the state?

Turning to the first question, we show that the trend of declining poverty rates for each group observed at the national level is broadly reproduced at the level of the states. Figure 5.3 shows the poverty rates for the SC for the ten largest states based on the statewise SC populations in 2004–5. States are arranged in declining order of SC population from left to right using data from the 61st round, conducted in 2004–5. Therefore, Uttar Pradesh has the largest SC population, West Bengal the second largest, and so on. For comparison, we also include the overall SC poverty rate in the eighteen largest states taken together. Note that we aggregate the three new states (Chhattisgarh, Jharkhand, and Uttarakhand) with their respective mother states (Madhya Pradesh, Bihar, and Uttar Pradesh).

Three observations follow from Figure 5.3. First, some of the states with large SC populations and above-average SC poverty rates are among some of the poorest states in India. Uttar Pradesh, Bihar, and Madhya Pradesh were the bottom three states by per capita income in 2004–5 and are also among the top five states in terms of SC population. They also have poverty rates well in excess of the average poverty rate of the eighteen largest states by population. These three states also experienced growth rates well below the national average between 1983 and 2004–5.

Second, comparing the rates between 1983 and 2004–5, poverty declined in every one of the ten states by at least ten percentage points. In some states, the decline was impressive. For instance, it fell from 70 to below 30 percent in West Bengal and from almost 70 to a little above 30 percent in Tamil Nadu between 1983 and 2004–5. By the same token, poverty reduction in some states has been extremely slow. In Bihar, the poverty rate only fell seven percentage points, from 70 percent in 1987 to 63 percent in 2004–5.

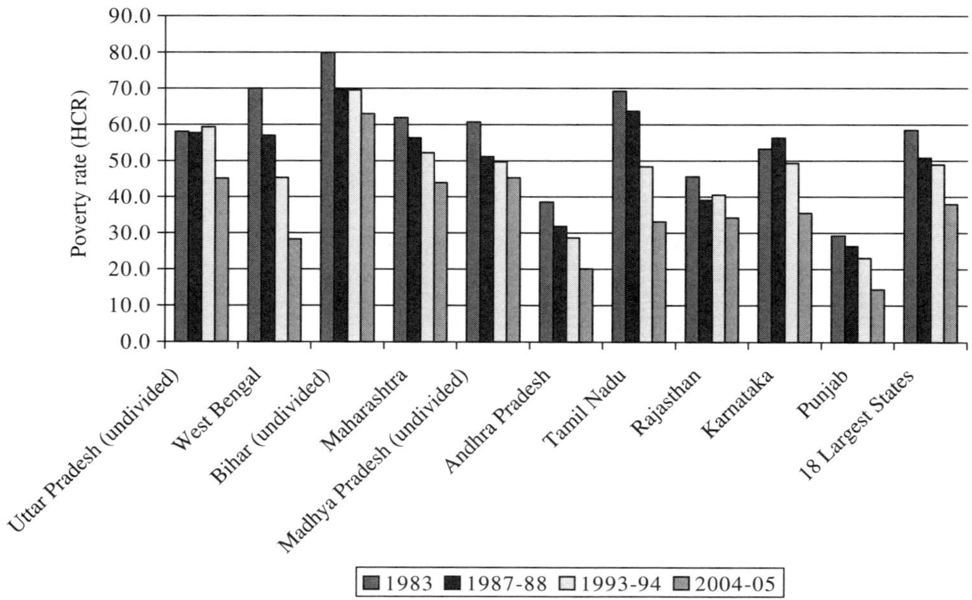

Figure 5.3. SC Poverty Rate from 1983 to 2004–5 in the Top Ten States by the SC Population

Finally, going by the sample surveys, the reduction in poverty has been monotonic in most but not all states. While progress between 1987–88 and 1993–94 was limited—there were even reversals in some states—visible reductions in poverty took place in each of these ten states between 1993–94 and 2004–5. This is especially interesting considering that 1991 was the year of the balance of payments crisis, and it took some years for the country to return to the 6 percent growth rate experienced between 1993–94 and 2004–5.

Next, we turn to the evolution of poverty rates for the ST by state. As in the case of the SC, we show the poverty rates associated with the four surveys in the top ten states according to the ST population in 2004–5 in Figure 5.4. The states are arranged in declining order of the ST population, from left to right. We note that the number of ST households underlying each estimate shown in the figure is well above two hundred. As such, the estimates shown are reasonably precise.

The pattern is similar to that for the SC, with one important difference. As in the case of the SC, there is a significant decline in poverty rates for all states between 1983 and 2004–5. But in contrast to the SC, there are several states in which ST poverty rates have seen a marginal increase between 1993–94 and 2004–5. This particular fact is contrary to the hypothesis of declining poverty rates with increasing per capita incomes.

Using poverty rates and per capita-income data, we can study more directly the relationship between poverty and growth for various social groups. For this purpose, we first present a set of graphs showing declining poverty rates for each group statewide with rising per capita incomes using cross-state data for 2004–5. We obtain similar graphs when we disaggregate the data by social group for rural and urban areas in 2004–5 and for 1983, 1987–88, and 1993–94 in rural, urban, and rural-plus-urban areas. We do not include these graphs here, to economize on space, but they are available on request.

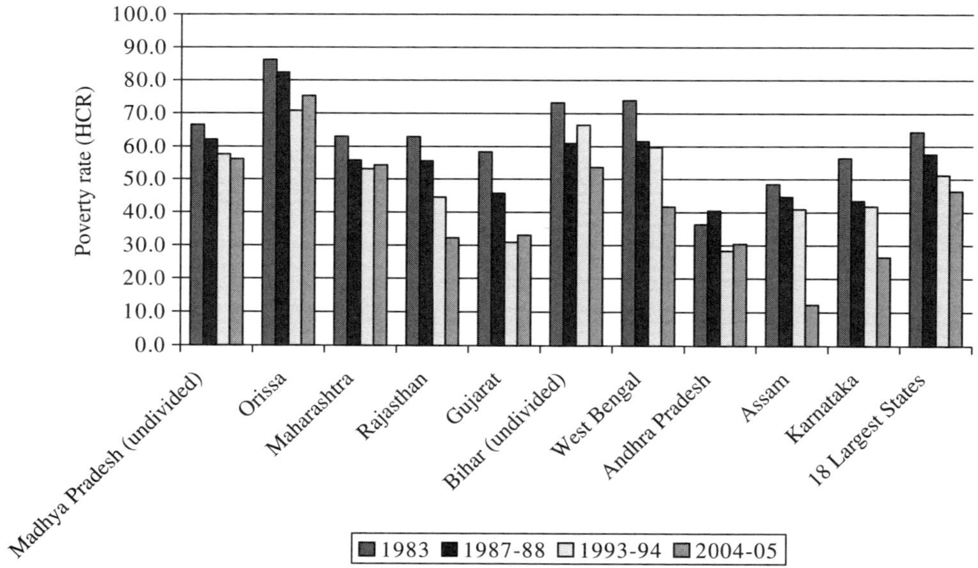

Figure 5.4. ST Poverty Rates in the Top Ten States by the ST Population. 1983 to 2004–5

Following the graphs, we present some econometric results relating poverty rates to per capita incomes for each social group.

Figures 5.5–5.8 show the groupwise scatter plots of poverty rates against per capita incomes and the associated best-fit lines. In each graph, we compare the relationship between poverty level and per capita income for an individual group such as the SC or ST to that for the entire population referred to as "All." In all cases, we combine Chhattisgarh, Jharkhand, and Uttarakhand with their respective mother states. This brings the total number of states in the sample down to eighteen. In Figures 5.5, 5.7, and 5.8, we use the observations from all of the eighteen states. But in Figure 5.6, which depicts poverty among the ST and that among all groups combined, we drop four states—Punjab, Haryana, Delhi, and J&K—from the sample because of the relatively small number of ST households picked up by the survey in these states.

Interestingly, the best-fit line between poverty rates and per capita incomes is uniformly negatively sloped in every single case. That is to say, poverty rates decline as per capita incomes rise for every social group. As we have already noted, poverty levels for the disadvantaged groups are generally higher than those for the general population.

We next turn to a more formal verification of the hypothesis that rising per capita incomes leading to declining poverty among various social groups. We carry out the regressions by pooling the data on poverty rates and per capita incomes for the four years for which we have survey data. For consistency, we continue to aggregate the three states (Chhattisgarh, Jharkhand, and Uttarakhand) that were created in 2000 and for which data are reported separately in the 61st round with their respective mother states (Madhya Pradesh, Bihar, and Uttar Pradesh).

We run an ordinary least squares (OLS) regression of the following form:

$$\ln pov_{it}^{k} = \alpha + \beta \ln PCI_{it} + \delta_{i} + \mu_{t} + \varepsilon_{ikt}$$

Here, the dependent variable is the poverty ratio for social group k residing in state i in year t, and the main explanatory variable is per capita income that varies by state (δ_i) and year (μ_t). Using the data for eighteen states for four years (1983, 1987–88, 1993–94, and 2004–5), we estimate equation (1) for the SC, ST, and NS. We measure per capita income by per capita Net State Domestic Product (NSDP). At this stage, we continue to use observations for all social groups, including the ST for all eighteen states. Later, we will consider the implications of dropping the ST observations associated with unacceptably imprecise estimates of poverty due to small number of households appearing in certain states.

We report the results from four sets of regressions in Table 5.7: without any fixed effects, with year-fixed effects, with state-fixed effects, and with both year- and state-fixed effects. In the first three sets of regressions, eight of the nine coefficients are statistically significant at the 99 percent level and show that poverty is indeed negatively related to per capita income. Even in the remaining case, the sign of the coefficient supports a negative relationship, but owing to a high standard error, it is not statistically significant. The magnitudes of the coefficients are all within the plausible range: a 100 percent increase in income leads to an eleven- to twenty-seven-percentage-point reduction in poverty.

But in the last case, where we allow for both state- and year-fixed effects, the results change dramatically. The coefficient for none of the social groups is significant any longer, the coefficient for the ST changes sign, and the remaining two coefficients see a drastic fall in magnitude. At first blush, this might appear to be a devastating blow to the hypothesis of a causal effect running from per capita income

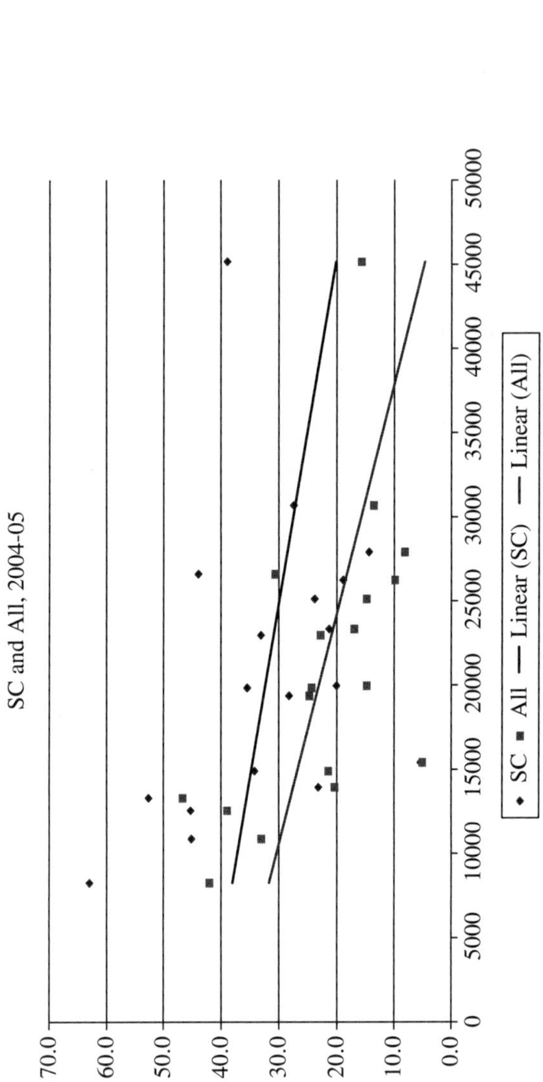

Figure 5.5. Poverty Rate and Per Capita Income: SC and All Groups, 2004–5

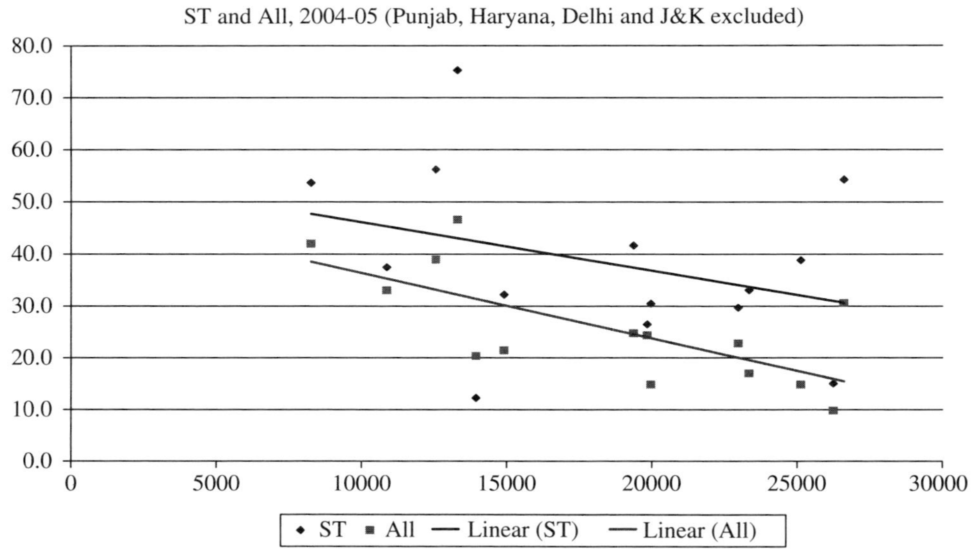

Figure 5.6. Poverty Rates and per Capita Income: ST and All Groups (with Haryana, Punjab, Delhi, and J&K removed from the sample due to small number of households), 2004–5

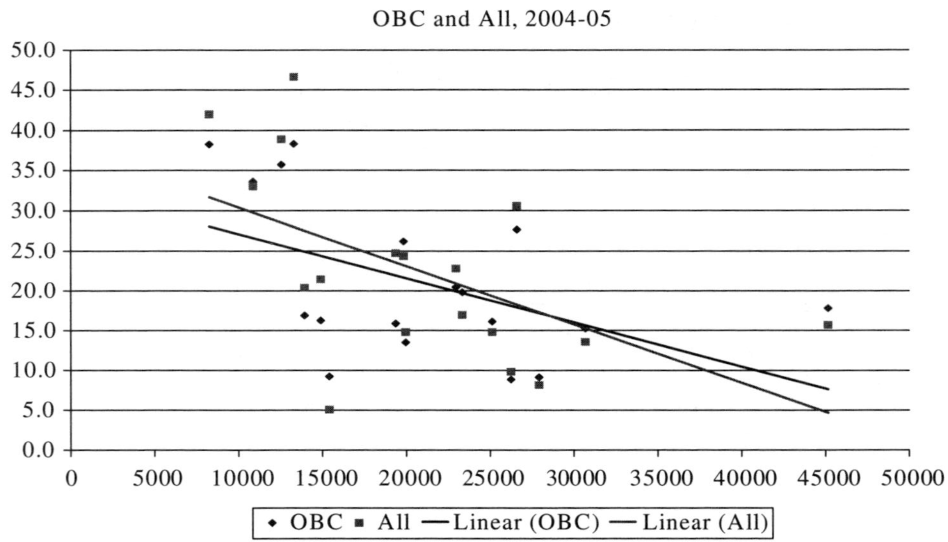

Figure 5.7. Poverty Rates and per Capita Income: OBC and All Groups, 2004–5

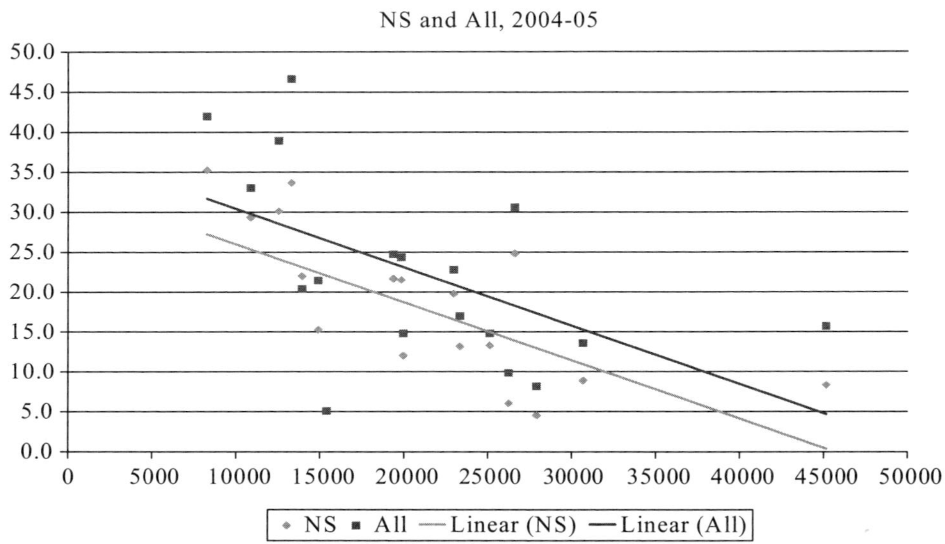

Figure 5.8. Poverty Rates and per Capita Income: NS and All Groups, 2004–5

Table 5.7 PER CAPITA INCOME AND POVERTY WITH AND WITHOUT YEAR- AND STATE-FIXED EFFECTS

Item	*SC*	*ST*	*NS*
(1) NO FIXED EFFECTS			
Coefficient	−16.0321**	−25.0258***	−19.6469***
Standard Error	6.0	5.92	3.13
R^2	0.24	0.31	0.51
(2) STATE-FIXED EFFECTS ONLY			
Coefficient	−23.2982***	−17.8310***	−19.2071***
Standard Error	3.7	4.89	2.37
R^2	0.85	0.78	0.9
(3) YEAR-FIXED EFFECTS ONLY			
Coefficient	−11.18	−27.0780***	−18.9509***
Standard Error	8.46	8.71	4.57
R^2	0.3	0.32	0.53
(4) STATE- AND YEAR-FIXED EFFECTS			
Coefficient	−1.67	4.72	−4.71
Standard Error	10.14	15.35	6.01
R^2	0.89	0.8	0.93

*** $p < 0.01$, ** $p < 0.05$ and * $p < 0.1$

to poverty. For example, there may be something specific to each state and each year other than the change in per capita income that accounts for the observed patterns in poverty as well as per capita income.

There remains the possibility, however, that with four years and eighteen states, the year- and state-fixed effects soak up all the variation in income, leaving the latter with no additional variation. We investigate this possibility by regressing per capita income on state and year dummies. The reported R^2 is .958, implying that state and year dummies account for 95.8 percent of the variation in per capita income. It is small wonder, then, that the inclusion of both sets of fixed effects leaves little extra variation in per capita income. By regressing per capita income separately on state and year dummies, we find that the former by themselves account for 63.3 percent of the variation in per capita income and the latter for 32.5 percent.

Based on these findings, we proceed to control for state-specific characteristics directly rather than through the introduction of dummy variables. We continue to use year-fixed effects to control for time-varying unobserved characteristics. We identify five state-level characteristics: lagging versus leading states, landlocked versus coastal states, the proportion of the SC and the ST in the state population in the first year of observation (1983), and the proportion of all poor in the state population in 1973–74.[8] Each of these variables varies across states and may impact poverty independent of per capita income. Thus, we modify the regression equation as below

$$\ln pov_{it}^{k} = \alpha + \beta \ln PCI_{it} + \gamma Controls_{it}^{k} + \mu_t + \varepsilon_{ikt}$$

Our results are shown in Table 5.8, where we also include a specification for poverty for all groups (i.e., the general population) in the last column. In all four cases, the coefficient of per capita income is

Table 5.8 PER CAPITA INCOME AND POVERTY WITH CONTROLS FOR STATE-LEVEL CHARACTERISTICS

Variable	*SC*	*ST*	*NS*	*ALL*
Ln PCI	–4.49	–13.7771**	–11.2362***	–9.5038***
	[3.841]	[5.791]	[2.784]	[2.894]
Year 1987–88	–6.9921**	–3.5	–5.6521***	–5.9004***
	[2.910]	[4.387]	[2.109]	[2.192]
Year 1993–94	–8.5048***	0.6	–5.5528**	–5.8985**
	[3.072]	[4.631]	[2.227]	[2.315]
Year 2004–5	–17.7032***	–6.43	–9.1933***	–10.7609***
	[3.921]	[5.911]	[2.842]	[2.954]
Lagging state	–7.2551*	10.1631*	0.25	0.29
	[3.977]	[5.996]	[2.883]	[2.997]
Landlocked	8.0156**	–18.2783***	–0.76	–0.36
	[3.333]	[5.025]	[2.416]	[2.511]
SC initial	0.5007**	0.6518**	0.15	0.4101***
	[0.204]	[0.308]	[0.148]	[0.154]
ST initial	0.02	0.8768***	0.08	0.3233***
	[0.159]	[0.239]	[0.115]	[0.120]
Poverty 1973–74	1.2598***	0.28	0.6518***	0.7325***
	[0.152]	[0.229]	[0.110]	[0.114]
Constant	13.02	123.4963***	83.4670***	64.6426***
	[29.625]	[44.663]	[21.472]	[22.321]

Table 5.8 (*continued*)

Variable	*SC*	*ST*	*NS*	*ALL*
Observations	72	72	72	72
R^2	0.74	0.68	0.8	0.81

Standard errors in square brackets
*** $p < 0.01$, ** $p < 0.05$, * $p < 0.1$

negative. In the case of ST, NS, and all groups taken together, it is also statistically significant at the 95 percent or higher level.[9] It is only in the case of the SC that the coefficient remains insignificant at the 90 percent or higher level of significance. The three statistically significant estimates are within the plausible range: a 100 percent increase in per capita income is associated with a poverty reduction of 13.8 percent for the ST, 11.2 percent for the NS, and 9.5 percent for the general population.

These results support the hypothesis that an increase in overall state-level per capita incomes leads to a reduction in the rates of poverty for the ST and NS. In the case of SC poverty there is no evidence that an increase in per capita income leads to any harm, but we would require additional data to claim with statistical confidence that an increase in per capita income has a positive impact. We remind readers that poverty estimates for the ST in some of the states included in our sample may be unacceptably imprecise due to the small number of ST households observed. We will return to this qualification later in a separate section devoted to robustness check.

POVERTY AND OPENNESS

Recent work by Hasan, Mitra, and Ural (2006–7) and Cain, Hasan, and Mitra (2010) has shown that there is a negative relationship between openness and poverty rates for all groups taken together in rural, urban, and rural-plus-urban regions. Their results reverse those obtained earlier by Topalova (2007) and reiterated in Topalova (2010). Both sets of papers exploit the variation in the degree of openness generated by India's trade liberalization in the 1990s across different administrative units of the country. A key difference between the approaches taken by them is with regard to the measurement of openness. Topalova treats nontraded sectors as the same as freely traded import-competing sectors, while Hasan et al. treat them (correctly, in our view) as nontraded. Naturally, the differences in the assumptions lead to differences in the numerical measures of openness employed in the two sets of papers. Hasan et al. and Topalova also differ with respect to the unit of analysis: whereas the former carry out their analysis at the level of the state and region as defined by the NSSO, the latter does so at the level of the district. While district-level analysis has the advantage of higher degrees of freedom in regressions, it also has the disadvantage of reducing the number of observations on which the poverty estimate itself is based. Hasan et al. discuss other problems with district-level analysis.

A common concern expressed truculently in Indian policy circles is that even if openness helps the population overall, it is detrimental to the interests of socially disadvantaged groups. We have already shown in the previous section the impact of growth on poverty among the socially disadvantaged groups is hardly different from that on remaining groups. While openness may work partially through growth, in the present section we consider its impact on poverty more directly.

Given that the sample size of the survey becomes much smaller when we restrict the counts to socially disadvantaged groups, we run a serious risk of large measurement errors in the estimation of poverty ratios at the level of the district. For this and other reasons discussed in Hasan et al. (2007) and Cain et al. (2010), we choose to carry out our analysis at the level of the state. This has the added advantage that it allows us to use their measures of protection. They construct state-level measures of trade protection for three regions—rural, urban, and rural plus urban. They weight industry-level tariff rates and nontariff barrier (NTB) coverage rates for two-digit agricultural, mining, and manufacturing industries by sector-specific employment shares in each state using the following formulas:[10]

$$Tariff_{it}^{j} = \sum_{k} \gamma_{ik,1993}^{j} * Ind\_Tariff_{kt}$$

$$NTB_{it}^{j} = \sum_{k} \gamma_{ik,1993}^{j} * Ind\_NTB_{kt}$$

Here $\gamma_{ik,1993}^{j}$ is the employment share of industry k in region j (j = rural, urban, and rural plus urban) of state i derived from the 1993–94 employment-unemployment survey.[11] Ind_Tariff_{kt} and Ind_NTB_{kt} represent tariff rates and nontariff coverage rates in industry k in year t where industries are measured at a two-digit classification. The employment share weights are defined such that they sum to unity. Stated simply, $\sum_{k} \gamma_{ik,1993}^{j} = 1$ where k represents tradable two-digit industries (comprising agricultural, mining, and manufacturing industries). Nontradable industries are excluded from the calculations.

Because tariff rates and nontariff barriers are highly correlated, they cannot be used simultaneously in the regressions. Therefore, we use the two measures separately and in succession. In addition, following Cain et al. (2010), we use a third measure, which combines these tariff and nontariff measures into a single measure using principal component analysis. Principal component analysis is commonly deployed to collapse the vector of correlated variables into a smaller set of variables containing much of the variation in the data. In the present case, the first principal component contains approximately 90 percent of the variation in the protection data for all industry groups.

The basic regression equation we estimate is

$$y_{ijt}^{k} = \alpha + \beta_1 protection_{ijt-1} + \beta_2 * Z_{it} + \delta_i + \mu_t + \varepsilon_{it}$$

In this equation, the dependent variable ykijt is the logarithm of poverty for social group k in sector j (urban, rural, and rural-plus-urban) in state i and year t. The principal variable of interest, $protection_{ijt-1}$, is one of the three measures of trade protection lagged once: nominal rate of protection (NRP), nontariff barriers (NTB), and the first principal component (FPC) of NRP and NTB.[12] Variable Z_{it} denotes a time-varying state-level control variable, which we choose to be per capita development expenditures. Vectors δ_i and μ_t represent state-fixed and year-fixed effects, respectively. Finally, ϵ_{it} is an error term and is assumed to satisfy the usual properties.

We note that all regression results we report in this section control for year- and state-fixed effects. Our first step is to reproduce the basic results of Cain et al. (2010), which relate to all groups taken together in rural, urban, and rural-plus-urban regions. Because the data on protection at the level of the states are available only from 1986 and for fifteen states, our analysis is based on forty-five observations relating to the 43rd, 50th, and 61st NSSO rounds, conducted in 1987–88, 1993–94, and 2003–4, respectively. While we have data on poverty rates for the 38th round, conducted in 1983, the protection series does not go that far back. Likewise, while we have protection data to include the 55th round, conducted in 1999–2000, we do not have the poverty levels by social groups on a comparable basis for this year.

Our results for all social groups combined closely correspond to those of Cain et al. (2010), although we do not include data from the 55th NSS round (1999–2000). For instance, they find that poverty declines by .57 percent for every percentage-point reduction in the weighted tariff rate (NRP). As shown in Table 5.9, the corresponding figure in our analysis is .67 percent. Our other results are similar; we describe these briefly without comparing them to those in Cain et al. (2010). Thus, according to our results, a 1 percent reduction in the NTB coverage ratio is associated with a 2.68 percent fall in the headcount ratio. The analysis for urban and rural regions shows that trade liberalization has affected them differentially. A 1 percent reduction in weighted tariff measures lowers poverty in the urban areas by 1.96 percent, but its effect on rural poverty, while having the hypothesized sign, is statistically insignificant. On the other hand, a fall in nontariff barriers in rural areas is associated with a whopping 3.7 percent reduction in poverty but their effect on urban areas is small and statistically insignificant.

An interesting point that emerges from our analysis of openness and poverty reduction for individual social groups, worthy of note at the outset, is that while the results for the SC closely track those for the NS group, those for the ST turn out to be much weaker. Tables 5.10–5.12 report our results for the SC, ST, and NS, respectively. Table 5.10 shows that a 1 percent reduction in nontariff barriers is associated with a 2.6 percent reduction in poverty in rural and urban regions combined and a 3.1 percent reduction when we consider only rural areas. Consistent with the results for all social groups, the effect of weighted tariff reductions is positive and significant (2.4 percent) for urban areas and we find a similar result for nontariff barriers in rural areas. These results are in line with the high correlation (0.7126) between the share of the general population and that of the SC across states.

Table 5.9 POVERTY AND TRADE OPENNESS (ALL SOCIAL GROUPS)

	Combined			*Urban*			*Rural*		
	NRP	NTB	FPC	NRP	NTB	FPC	NRP	NTB	FPC
VARIABLES	(1)	(2)	(3)	(4)	(5)	(6)	(7)	(8)	(9)
Protection	.0067**	.0268**	.3324**	.0191**	0.02	.9627**	0.01	.0368**	.3013**
	[.003]	[.012]	[.120]	[.007]	[.019]	[.361]	[.004]	[.014]	[.143]
Dev. Exp. Pc	0.14	0.2	0.13	.78807*	.7499*	.7209*	0.24	0.3	0.22
	[.235]	[.230]	[.223]	[.395]	[.437]	[.393]	[.299]	[.274]	[.286]
Constant	1.64	−0.85	1.72	−3.91	−3.13	−2.84	0.77	−2.83	0.88
	[1.568]	[1.959]	[1.487]	[2.798]	[3.295]	[2.668]	[1.983]	[2.316]	[1.901]
Observations	45	45	45	45	45	45	45	45	45
R^2	0.95	0.96	0.96	0.93	0.92	0.93	0.94	0.95	0.94

Standard errors in square brackets
*** $p < 0.01$, ** $p < 0.05$, * $p < 0.1$

The correlation of the distribution of the ST with that of the general population across states is much lower than of the SC; therefore one might expect the effect of trade liberalization and openness to be different for the former. Indeed, this is very much in keeping with what we find. In general, the statistical significance of the openness variables is much lower for the ST. In particular, reductions in nontariff barriers seem to have no significant effect on poverty. Reductions in tariffs in urban areas are associated with a large reduction in poverty (4.1 percent) and are also statistically significant at a high threshold, but recall that the ST population in urban areas is tiny. In rural areas, where the ST population is concentrated, openness measures do not have a statistically significant effect.

Finally, for completeness, we also carry out the analysis for the NS as a group. The results indicate that the relationship between poverty reduction and trade liberalization for those in the NS group closely mirrors those for the population as a whole. A percentage reduction in tariffs is associated with a .65 percent fall in poverty. Similarly, a 1 percent reduction in nontariff barriers leads to a 2.5 percent fall in poverty. In rural areas, the effect of nontrade barriers rises to 3.8 percent while it is insignificant in urban areas. On the other hand, a fall in tariffs is associated with a 2.2 percent fall in poverty in urban areas and has little effect on rural poverty.

In summary, our results find strong support for the positive relationship between trade liberalization and overall poverty reduction in India between 1983 and 2004. These results vary substantially across urban and rural areas. Most importantly, from the viewpoint of our focus on social groups, we find that poverty reduction for the NS and SC tracks that for the population as a whole reasonably closely, but the effect is weaker for the ST. In no case, rural or urban and SC, ST, or NS, do we find the effect of increased openness on poverty to be positive and statistically

Table 5.10 POVERTY AND TRADE OPENNESS (SCHEDULED CASTES)

	Combined			*Urban*			*Rural*		
	NRP	NTB	FPC	NRP	NTB	FPC	NRP	NTB	FPC
VARIABLES	(1)	(2)	(3)	(4)	(5)	(6)	(7)	(8)	(9)
Protection	0	.0258**	.2359*	.0242***	0.02	1.213***	0	.0300**	0.18
	[.004]	[.012]	[.135]	[.007]	[.019]	[.347]	[.004]	[.013]	[.132]
Dev. Exp. Pc	–0.09	–0.05	–0.1	1.0103**	.9625**	.9257**	–0.23	–0.2	–0.25
	[.251]	[.236]	[.243]	[.374]	[.441]	[.370]	[.267]	[.242]	[.261]
Constant	3.6533**	1.17	3.690**	–5.88**	–4.88	–4.528*	4.5747**	1.61	4.6309
	[1.676]	[2.012]	[1.621]	[2.654]	[3.326]	[2.517]	[1.775]	[2.048]	[1.731]
Observations	45	45	45	45	45	45	45	45	45
R^2	0.92	0.93	0.92	0.91	0.88	0.91	0.92	0.93	0.92

Standard errors in square brackets
*** $p < 0.01$, ** $p < 0.05$, * $p < 0.1$

Table 5.11 POVERTY AND TRADE OPENNESS (SCHEDULED TRIBES)

	Combined			*Urban*			*Rural*		
	NRP	NTB	FPC	NRP	NTB	FPC	NRP	NTB	FPC
VARIABLES	(1)	(2)	(3)	(4)	(5)	(6)	(7)	(8)	(9)
Protection	0	–0.01	–0.11	.040***	0.02	1.497**	0	0	0.02
	[.008]	[.031]	[.328]	[.013]	[.046]	[.631]	[.010]	[.040]	[.391]
Dev. Exp. Pc	0.75	0.73	0.75	–0.23	–0.28	–0.37	0.85	0.86	0.85
	[.607]	[.600]	[.605]	[.627]	[.769]	[.676]	[.790]	[.783]	[.789]
Constant	–2.14	–1.77	–2.47	4.56	5.62	9.7702*	–3.02	–3.06	–2.96
	[4.449]	[4.467]	[4.590]	[4.621]	[5.581]	[5.304]	[5.792]	[5.823]	[5.992]
Observations	44	44	44	41	41	41	44	44	44
R^2	0.72	0.73	0.73	0.91	0.87	0.9	0.64	0.64	0.64

Standard errors in square brackets
*** $p < 0.01$, ** $p < 0.05$, * $p < 0.1$

Table 5.12 POVERTY AND TRADE OPENNESS (NON-SCHEDULED INDIVIDUALS)

	Combined			*Urban*			*Rural*		
	NRP	NTB	FPC	NRP	NTB	FPC	NRP	NTB	FPC
VARIABLES	(1)	(2)	(3)	(4)	(5)	(6)	(7)	(8)	(9)
Protection	.0066*	.0262*	.326**	.0223**	0.02	1.1041**	0.01	.0375**	0.29
	[.004]	[.013]	[.134]	[.009]	[.023]	[.454]	[.005]	[.018]	[.175]
Dev. Exp. Pc	0.06	0.12	0.06	0.72	0.68	0.64	0.27	0.33	0.25
	[.262]	[.257]	[.251]	[.496]	[.543]	[.495]	[.363]	[.339]	[.353]
Constant	2.03	–0.4	2.11	–3.85	–2.83	–2.59	0.31	-3.37	0.42
	[1.747]	[2.191]	[1.677]	[3.514]	[4.095]	[3.365]	[2.409]	[2.871]	[2.342]
Observations	45	45	45	45	45	45	45	45	45
R^2	0.96	0.96	0.97	0.92	0.9	0.92	0.94	0.95	0.94

Standard errors in square brackets
*** $p < 0.01$, ** $p < 0.05$, * $p < 0.1$

significant. In this sense our results strongly support those of Hasan et al. (2006–7) and Cain et al. (2010) and refute those of Topalova (2007, 2010) for the population as a whole. On balance, the rising tide seems to have lifted all boats, even if some have been lifted more than others. Most importantly, it has lowered, let alone sunk, none.

SENSITIVITY ANALYSIS

Two characteristics of our data call for sensitivity checks. First, the year 1987–88 was subject to a drought that had a differential impact across states. In all probability, some of the states with large populations of the poor, SC and ST, were subject to greater adverse impact than others. Therefore, the observations from year 1987–88 may not follow the same pattern as those coming from other years. Second, in many states, our poverty estimates for the ST are based on relatively small number of ST households sampled by the survey. These estimates are likely to be imprecise and may bias our estimates of the relationships between poverty and per capita income and poverty and openness. In this section, we check the implications of correcting for these sources of biases.

In order to check whether the drought in 1987–88 may have contaminated the relationship between poverty and per capita income, we rerun equation (2) after excluding observations from the 43rd round conducted in 1987–88. We report the resulting coefficients and associated standard errors in Table 5.13. As can be seen, other than minor differences in the magnitudes, the coefficients and their statistical significance are virtually the same as in Table 5.8. We conclude that the inclusion of observations from the drought year of 1987–88 did not bias the direction of our coefficients and had marginal effects on the magnitudes.

The implications of dropping the observations that are based on small number of ST households are more mixed. A key problem in approaching this question is that we have no objective basis for defining a "threshold" number of ST households below which the poverty estimates are to be considered imprecise. As Appendix Table 5.A1 shows, the number of ST households picked up by the survey varies widely across states and survey years. As a result, whether we draw the line at 100, 50, or 30 households causes a considerable difference in the number of states that get included in the regressions.

We alleviate this problem by taking two alternative approaches to identifying the states to be excluded from the regression sample. First, we test whether the poverty estimate for a state in a given year can be identified as being statistically significantly different from that in any of the other years for which a sample survey was conducted. The idea here is to check whether the estimate is tight enough to be distinguished from another estimate in a statistical sense. The criterion is, of course, not foolproof, in that if the two poverty estimates being compared are indeed equal, the test will accept the null hypothesis of equality even when each of the estimates is based on a very large number of households. Conversely, if the estimates are vastly different, there is a possibility that the null will be rejected even when the two estimates are based on a small number of observations. Our second approach is to require the poverty estimate to be based on an arbitrarily chosen minimum number of ST households to be included in the sample used for the regressions.

When we consider the combined (rural-plus-urban) sample, the first criterion excludes only one observation: Delhi in 2004–5. Without reporting the estimated equations, we note that this exclusion does not change our results with respect to either the impact of per capita income or openness on poverty. Indeed, since Delhi was absent from the regression sample for openness and poverty (Tables 5.9–5.12) in

Table 5.13 PER CAPITA INCOME AND POVERTY (EXCLUDING 1987–88)

VARIABLES	*SC*	*ST*	*NS*	*All*
Ln pc	–5.35	–15.8489**	–10.9272***	-9.2894**
	[4.425]	[7.329]	[3.326]	[3.464]
Lagging state	-9.7863**	7.05	–1.15	–1.4
	[4.627]	[7.663]	[3.478]	[3.622]
Landlocked	10.6108***	–17.7410***	0.73	1.36
	[3.865]	[6.401]	[2.905]	[3.025]
SC initial	0.5436**	0.7869*	0.21	0.4764**
	[0.237]	[0.392]	[0.178]	[0.185]
ST initial	0.1	0.9275***	0.12	0.3599**
	[0.185]	[0.306]	[0.139]	[0.144]
Poverty 73–74	1.2993***	0.27	0.6955***	0.7808***
	[0.177]	[0.293]	[0.133]	[0.138]
Year 1993	-8.2817**	1.14	-5.6328**	-5.9540**
	[3.144]	[5.207]	[2.363]	[2.461]
Year 2004	–17.1131***	-5.01	-9.4050***	–10.9078***
	[4.214]	[6.979]	[3.167]	[3.299]
Constant	15.82	138.0587**	77.3844***	58.9949**
	[34.370]	[56.927]	[25.835]	[26.904]

(*continued*)

Table 5.13 (*continued*)

VARIABLES	*SC*	*ST*	*NS*	*All*
Observations	54	54	54	54
R^2	0.75	0.64	0.8	0.81

Standard errors in square brackets
*** p < 0.01, ** p < 0.05, * p < 0.1

the first place due to unavailability of protection measures for it, this regression remains unchanged.

The criterion is more discriminatory when we consider rural and urban samples separately. It reduces the number of observations to thirty-three for the urban sample and forty-two for the rural sample. Without reporting the regression results, we note that they remain qualitatively unchanged from Table 5.11. The two measures of protection (NRP and FPC) remain positively and statistically significantly associated with urban poverty, while protection shows no statistically significant effect on rural poverty for the ST.

Our second criterion leads to more serious deviations from our original results. For the combined (rural plus urban) sample, we set a threshold of a minimum sample of seventy or more ST households for inclusion in the regression. This leads us to drop Delhi, Haryana, J&K, Kerala, and Punjab from all rounds and Tamil Nadu from the 61st round. The change once again leaves the results in Table 5.7 largely unaffected, but those in Table 5.8 are altered: the coefficient of per capita income becomes positive and statistically insignificant.

Turning to the impact of openness on poverty, when we drop the observations based on a minimum number of ST households, surprisingly, our results are considerably strengthened. Keeping the trade-off between the number of households necessary to get a reasonably precise estimate of poverty and the number of observations necessary to get a meaningful regression fit, we proceed as follows:

(1) For the regressions involving combined samples of rural and urban households, we exclude all observations involving less than seventy households. This leads to the exclusion of Delhi, Haryana, J&K, Punjab, and Kerala from all rounds and Tamil Nadu from the 61st round.
(2) For the regressions involving rural households, we exclude Delhi, Haryana, J&K, Punjab, Kerala, and Tamil Nadu from all rounds. This ensures that the poverty estimates for the included states are based on seventy or more ST households.
(3) For the regressions involving urban households, the exclusions are much larger, since the surveys pick very small number of ST households in many states. Here we drop Delhi, Haryana, J&K, Punjab, Himachal Pradesh, Tamil Nadu, Rajasthan, and UP from all rounds. This list still includes two states with fewer than seventy observations, but cutting the list any further would have left us with too few observations.

Taking into account the fact that we have protection measures for only fifteen states and three survey rounds, the above restrictions reduce the sample size to thirty-five for the combined (rural plus urban) sample, thirty-three for the rural sample, and twenty-nine for the urban sample. Our results are reported in Table 5.14. Comparing these results to those in Table 5.11, we see that dropping the observations associated with poverty estimates based on small number of ST households strengthens the results. At least one measure of protection now leads to a positive and statistically significant effect on poverty for rural, urban, and combined poverty measures. In the case of urban poverty, each of the three measures of protection has a statistically significant effect.

CONCLUDING REMARKS

We begin the concluding remarks with an emphatic statement on the bottom line of what we have shown: there is absolutely no statistically significant evidence that rising incomes and increased openness have negatively impacted any of the three broad social groups. This does not preclude the possibility that specific individuals within these groups, including those belonging to the Non-Scheduled group, may fail to enjoy any benefits. But we find no evidence of any harmful impacts at the average level for each social group.

Beyond this bottom line, our chapter has offered the most up-to-date and comprehensive analysis of poverty among the socially disadvantaged groups in comparison to those without social handicaps. We offer compelling evidence of steadily declining poverty among all groups in rural as well as urban areas at the national level. We also provide the trends in poverty ratios in the top ten states by the SC and ST populations. The top ten SC states account for 85 percent of the total countrywide SC population, and the top ten ST states for more than 90 percent of the countrywide ST population. In the case of the SC, every one of the top ten states saw the poverty ratio decline between 1993–94 and 2004–5. This is not true of the ST states, however, where reversals were observed in some states.

We demonstrate that declining poverty rates are uniformly associated with rising per capita incomes. In the case of the ST, the Non-Scheduled, and all groups taken together, we show that rising per capita incomes have a statistically significant and negative effect on poverty at the 95 percent or higher level. Our sensitivity tests

Table 5.14 OPENNESS AND POVERTY FOR THE ST (ROBUSTNESS TESTS)

	Combined			*Urban*			*Rural*		
	NRP	NTB	FPC	NRP	NTB	FPC	NRP	NTB	FPC
VARIABLES	(1)	(2)	(3)	(4)	(5)	(6)	(7)	(8)	(9)
Protection	0.01	.1133***	0.79	.0287***	.0827**	1.4083***	0.01	.140***	0.8946
	[.013]	[.037]	[.479]	[.008]	[.031]	[.365]	[.014]	[.035]	[.527]
Dev. Exp. Pc	.8039*	.9021**	.7705*	0.38	0.15	0.3	1.1937**	1.1987***	.9978**
	[.401]	[.329]	[.379]	[.566]	[.624]	[.537]	[.480]	[.329]	[.452]
Constant	–2.58	–13.70***	–2.81	0.27	–5.34	4.64	–5.08	–18.423***	–2.063
	[2.747]	[4.390]	[2.559]	[4.173]	[5.004]	[4.029]	[2.995]	[4.016]	[3.950]
Observations	35	35	35	29	29	29	33	33	33
R^2	0.83	0.88	0.84	0.96	0.96	0.97	0.85	0.92	0.871

Standard errors in square brackets
*** $p < 0.01$, ** $p < 0.05$, * $p < 0.1$

dilute slightly the result for ST poverty, but do not alter our basic message. We also find that rising per capita incomes are accompanied by declining poverty rates within the SC, but the estimated coefficient is statistically insignificant at the 90 percent or higher level.

Finally, we also conduct an econometric test of the effect of openness on poverty for various social groups. In the case of the SC and NS, we find that one or more measures of openness have a statistically significant and negative effect on poverty in rural and urban areas as well as the two areas combined. In the case of the ST, the coefficient is statistically significant in urban areas only when we use the entire sample. But once we exclude the observations associate with poverty estimates based on small numbers of ST households, the results for the ST are further strengthened. After this correction, we find that at least one measure of protection is associated with a statistically significant increase in poverty in rural, urban, and combined regions and, moreover, that all three measures have a positive and significant effect on poverty in the urban regions.

APPENDIX

Appendix Table 5.A1 NUMBER OF ST HOUSEHOLDS BY STATE AND BY SURVEYS

State	61st Round		50th Round		43rd Round		38th Round	
	Rural	Urban	Rural	Urban	Rural	Urban	Rural	Urban
Andhra Pradesh	446	80	373	85	390	73	350	60
Assam	674	110	496	46	497	75	641	17
Bihar	35	7	557	109	979	93	806	109
Chhattisgarh	651	135						
Dadra and Nagar Havel	137	13	205	34	274		239	
Delhi	0	16	2	18	1	23	4	19
Goa	2	0	3	5	33		25	4

State	61st Round		50th Round		43rd Round		38th Round	
Gujarat	443	129	483	112	544	135	532	74
Haryana	6	5	18	6	22	11	7	8
Himachal Pradesh	149	10	107	10	93	14	85	14
Jammu and Kashmir	13	7	15	13	31	18	5	7
Jharkhand	665	124						
Karnataka	207	63	212	96	168	73	237	56
Kerala	54	10	37	17	55	16	56	14
Madhya Pradesh	863	157	1,561	202	1,896	207	1,939	175
Maharashtra	577	208	563	202	719	227	820	201
Orissa	908	121	816	111	765	144	736	100

Punjab	8	10	32	15	25	25	29	15
Rajasthan	530	64	483	46	514	53	494	50
Tamil Nadu	15	20	82	43	42	31	45	54
Uttar Pradesh	40	26	83	27	81	105	156	35
Uttarakhand	74	14						
West Bengal	366	48	374	59	394	62	417	63
Total	6,863	1,377	6,606	1,291	7,647	1,435	7,694	1,113

NOTES

* The authors are, respectively, at the London School of Economics and Columbia University and can be reached at m.mukim@lse.ac.uk and ap2231@Columbia.Edu. They thank Rajeev Dehejia, Devashish Mitra, and Rana Hasan for extremely helpful interactions in the course of writing this chapter and K. Sundaram for his excellent comments at the Columbia-NCAER conference held in New Delhi on March 31–April 1, 2011. Work on this chapter has been supported by Columbia University's Program on Indian Economic Policies, funded by a generous grant from the John Templeton Foundation. The opinions expressed in the chapter are those of the authors and do not necessarily reflect the views of the John Templeton Foundation.

1. The SC and ST classifications have their origin in the Indian Constitution, which lists in separate schedules castes and tribes that are officially recognized as having suffered discrimination for centuries and therefore requiring special affirmative action. A program of reservation in public sector jobs and public schools, colleges, and universities for the SC and ST in India has existed since the early 1950s. Reservation in government jobs was extended to the OBC in 1990 and in central government educational institutions in 2006.
2. The document containing the statement by the National Campaign on Dalit Human Rights is posted at http://www.publications.parliament.uk/pa/cm201011/cmselect/cmintdev/writev/616/m02.htm (accessed June 3, 2011). The statement by Bidwai can be found in the article "Equity, Not Growth, Is the Key" posted at http://www.mydigitalfc.com/op-ed/equity-not-growth-key-359 (accessed June 3, 2011).
3. A recent study by Shukla, Jain, and Kakkar (2010) also focuses on the prevailing inequality among various social groups, offering rich set of indicators drawn from the National Survey of Household Income and Expenditure conducted by the National Council on Applied Economic Research. Additional references to earlier studies on inequalities between Scheduled and Non-Scheduled groups can be found in the reference lists in Kijima (2006) and Hnatkovska, Lahiri, and Paul (2010).
4. An earlier paper by Meenakshi, Ray, and Gupta (2000) provided statewise poverty estimates for the SC and ST for a single year, 1993–94, but did not deal with the issue of the evolution of poverty among these groups over time and how it may have been impacted by growth and reforms. These authors also refer to Dubey and Gangopadhyay (1998) as having provided the estimates of poverty by social groups in 1993–94 and perhaps earlier years.
5. Thick surveys are typically in the field from July 1 of the beginning calendar year to June 30 of the ending calendar year. For example, the 2004–5 survey was in the field from July 1, 2004, to June 30, 2005. The 38th round followed a different schedule, staying in the field from January 1 to December 31, 1983.

India has had a long tradition of conducting sample surveys; the first expenditure survey took place as early as the period from October 1, 1950, to March 31, 1951.

6. The poverty rate for each of these entities is calculated by recourse to one or another special assumption. For the six northeastern states and Sikkim, the poverty ratio is assumed to be the same as for Assam. In the case of Goa, its expenditures are combined with the poverty line of Maharashtra to calculate the poverty ratio. Similar assumptions are made for the UTs.
7. Targeted assistance is often provided based on the location of individuals. Rural employment guarantee schemes or subsidized food prices available to the rural poor, for instance, have this attribute. Such policies inadvertently impede migration, which may be detrimental to development in the long run.
8. For lagging and leading regions, we use the definition by the World Bank, which classifies the states into these regions according to per capita income. With respect to the 1973–74 poverty levels, ideally, we would like to have the proportion of the poor within SC population for SC regression, within ST population for ST regression, and so forth. Unfortunately, we do not have unit-level data for the quinquennial survey conducted in 1973–74 to carry out these calculations. The aggregate poverty rates are available from the Planning Commission website (http://planningcommission.gov.in/data/datatable/), however.
9. These coefficients remain significant if we replace the 1973–74 poverty levels with those from 1977–78, but the level of significance declines: upon replacement, the coefficients of SC and all groups pass the 90 percent threshold but not the 95 percent or higher threshold, while that of NS continues to pass the 99 percent threshold.
10. Cain et al. take the industry-level tariff rates and NTB coverage rates between 1988 and 1998 from Pandey (1999) and those for the subsequent years, until 2003, from Das (2008). The latter constructs the rates using the same methodology as the former. Because these sources do not provide the protection rates for every single year between 1988 and 2003, Cain et al. use simple linear interpolation to obtain the relevant rates. The rates for 1986, necessary to include the data from the 1987–88 survey, are estimated by assuming that tariff and NTB coverage rates grew at the same annual rate from 1986 to 1988 as they did from 1988 to 1989. The NTB coverage rates are of course bounded at 100 percent.
11. Cain et al. choose employment weights from the year 1993–94 because it is one of the middle years in the data and is therefore a good candidate to serve as the base (reference) year in the construction of state-level openness index. As with any good index, the weights are not held fixed over time.
12. Hasan et al. (2006–7) experimented with contemporaneous protection but it did not affect the results in any substantive manner. As such, we work exclusively with lagged protection measures here.

REFERENCES

Cain, Jewel, R. Hasan, and D. Mitra (2010). "Trade Liberalization and Poverty Reduction: New Evidence from Indian States." Working Paper no. 2010-3, Columbia Program on Indian Economic Policies, School of International and Public Affairs, Columbia University.

Das, D. (2008). "Trade Barriers Measurement: A Methodological Overview." Mimeo.

Dubey, Amaresh, and S. Gangopadhyay (1998). *Counting the Poor: Where Are the Poor in India?* Sarvekshana Analytical Report no. 1. New Delhi: Ministry of Statistics and Program Implementation, National Sample Survey Organization.

Hasan, R., D. Mitra, and B. Ural (2006–7). "Trade Liberalization, Labor Market Institutions, and Poverty Reduction: Evidence from Indian States." *India Policy Forum* 3, 70–135.

Hnatkovska, Viktoria, Amartya Lahiri, and Sourabh B. Paul (2010). "Castes and Labor Mobility." Department of Economics, University of British Columbia, October.

Kijima, Yoko (2006). "Caste and Tribe Inequality: Evidence from India, 1983–1999." *Economic Development and Cultural Change* 54(2), 369–404.

Meenakshi, J. V., R. Ray, and S. Gupta (2000). "Estimates of Poverty for SC, ST and Female-Headed Households." *Economic and Political Weekly*, 35(31), July 29, 2748–54.

Panagariya, Arvind (2008). *India: The Emerging Giant.* New York: Oxford University Press.

Pandey, Mihir (1999). *NCAER Report on Trade Protection in India.* National Council of Applied Economic Research, New Delhi, India.

Shukla, Rajesh, Sunil Jain, and Preeti Kakkar (2010). *Caste in a Different Mould.* New Delhi: Business Standard.

Sundaram, K., and S. Tendulkar (2003). "Poverty among Social and Economic Groups in India in 1990s." *Economic and Political Weekly* 38(50), December 13, 5263–76.

Topalova, Petia (2007). "Trade Liberalization, Poverty and Inequality: Evidence from Indian Districts." In Ann Harrison (ed.), *Globalization and Poverty.* Chicago: University of Chicago Press, 291–336.

——— (2010). "Factor Immobility and Regional Impacts of Trade Liberalization: Evidence on Poverty from India." *American Economic Journal: Applied Economics* 2(4), 1–41.

Chapter 6

Trade and Inequality in India*

PRAVIN KRISHNA AND GURU SETHUPATHY

A central aspect of the public debate over the economic policy reforms undertaken in India in the early 1990s[1] was the anxiety that the greater market orientation of the economy and its openness to international trade would widen the inequality between regions, states, urban and rural areas, and households across the country.[2,3]

Basic international trade theory predicts that trade will increase the returns to the abundant factors in an economy. For unskilled-labor-abundant countries, such as India, this could be good news: the implication is that trade will raise the incomes of low-skilled workers, thus generating a reduction in poverty and likely in income inequality as well. However, it is sometimes argued that this outcome may not obtain for a number of practical reasons. First, different regions may have different levels of access to international trade—lagging regions may not benefit from trade because transportation and other trade costs may be too high for these regions to interact with international markets. Second, an important source of the gains from trade comes from the improvement in the allocation of productive resources in the economy. However, this improvement in production efficiency may be diminished if factors of production, such as labor and capital are not mobile across sectors. Specifically, factors of production that are stuck in declining sectors may be hurt by trade liberalization. Third, insights from the literature on economic geography suggest that increases in regional disparities may be a natural feature of the economic development process. Specifically, if production is subject to economies of scale, market forces may induce production to agglomerate in a few areas. In this case, the economic development process can be a lumpy one—with some regions growing faster than others. Trade itself may affect agglomeration patterns and the location of economic activity. Trade liberalization may lead to an increase in the geographic concentration of economic activity—thus, possibly increasing (or decreasing) the extent of regional differences within a country. Thus, despite the aggregate benefits that openness to international trade and a greater market orientation are expected to bring, there remains the theoretical possibility that inequality is widened as a result.

Nearly two decades after the introduction of market-oriented economic reforms in India, the consequences of these reforms for inequality are being vigorously debated, with different empirical studies reaching different conclusions concerning the evolution of inequality subsequent to the reforms. For instance, Bhalla's (2003) study of inequality trends between 1983 and 1999 concludes that "the claim that inequality has worsened" over this time period is "somewhat erroneous," while Singh et al. (2003) find evidence of modest increases of regional and within-state inequality.[4]

One reason behind these equivocal findings is that the different studies that have examined inequality have analyzed quite different sample aggregates. For instance, Bhalla (2003) examines within-state inequality in rural and urban areas separately, while Singh et al. (2003) study the overall within-state inequality without separately considering the rural and urban components. Comparing inequality measures using data obtained at different levels of aggregation is especially problematic because the inequality measures used in the vast majority of inequality studies, such as the Gini coefficient, are unfortunately not additive across subgroups. For instance, the total Gini coefficient of a society is not equal to the sum of the Gini coefficients for its subgroups.

Our interest is in the evolution of total inequality as well as inequality within and across subgroups (such as states or urban and rural areas within states). It would therefore be desirable to use an inequality index that is additively decomposable (i.e., one that can be neatly expressed as the sum of across-group inequality and within-group inequality). Conceptually, the across-group component would be the value of the inequality index when all within-group inequalities were zero due to the hypothetical assignment of the group average to each member of the same group. Similarly the within-group component would be the value of the inequality index when all the across-group inequalities are suppressed by a hypothetical equalization of group means to the overall mean (by the equiproportionate change for every unit within each of these groups). The particular measure of inequality that we will use is Theil's entropy index, which, as is well known, is characterized by its property of additive decomposability.[5] Furthermore, as we will discuss, the Theil index has less stringent data requirements and is particularly useful when only group data are available rather than individual data or when individual data are subject to random measurement errors (which average out in larger samples). The Theil index enables us to explore in a consistent manner the evolution of inequality over different levels of aggregation.

This chapter measures inequality using Theil's inequality index constructed using Indian household expenditure survey data from 1988 to 2005. Our findings are as follows. The extent of inequality between states or between urban and rural areas is much lower than the inequality across households within these aggregates, which accounts for more than 90 percent of overall inequality and persists in this magnitude throughout the period of our study. Overall inequality shows some variation over the period, falling between 1988 and 1994, rising between 1994 and 2000, but falling again by 2005. A similar pattern is observed when inequality is measured using other inequality measures, such as the Gini coefficient and the variance of log expenditures. Furthermore, a similar inequality trend is seen within most Indian states. Thus, the evolution of inequality in the postreform period has been a nonmonotonic one. Finally, the change in inequality across households within states is found to be uncorrelated with the change in state-level measures of tariff and nontariff protection.

The rest of the chapter proceeds as follows. The second section describes the data that we use in this chapter. The third section describes the Theil index and its use in inequality measurement. The fourth section presents results on inequality and its association with international trade. The fifth section concludes.

DATA

Consumer Expenditure Surveys

The Indian National Sample Survey (NSS) is the primary source of information on household-level expenditures in India. The NSS provides household-level information on expenditure patterns, occupation, industrial affiliation (at the three-digit NIC level), and various other household and individual characteristics. The surveys cover all Indian states, and urban and rural areas within states are identified separately. Data are collected on about 75,000 rural and 45,000 urban households. Furthermore, within a state, the surveys indicate the region, district, and urban block or rural village within which the surveyed households are located. For our analysis, we use data from the 1987–88, 1993–94, 1999–2000, and 2004–5 rounds of the NSS.

The household expenditure surveys conducted by the NSS contain detailed information on consumption expenditures undertaken by the household. The surveys include information on food consumption, nonfood consumption on items such as energy and transportation, consumer durables expenditures, and housing.

The monetary estimates of total consumption for a household must be adjusted to reflect the different prices that different households face. The price variations that we are concerned with are less temporal than spatial: people who live in different parts of the country pay different prices for comparable goods. For example, prices tend to be lower in rural than in urban areas, at least for some goods and services. Such spatial differences can be quite large in both absolute and relative prices, so it is important to take them into account. In our analysis, we use household-level price data (obtained from the NSS consumption surveys) on a core set of consumption items (food items and energy) to determine a price index which is then used to deflate household expenditures to make them comparable across households. Specifically, our price index (Paasche) is constructed as a weighted sum of price ratios of different commodities:

where k denotes commodities; p^h denotes the price faced by household h; p^0 denotes the reference price, chosen to be the median price for the commodity in our sample; and w_k^h, the weight, is the

$$P^h = \left[\sum_k w_k^h \left(\frac{p_k^0}{p_k^h} \right) \right]^{-1},$$

share of each household's budget that is devoted to the particular good. Clearly the budget shares vary across households, implying a different weighting of the price ratios for each household. But, as Deaton and Zaidi (2002) argue, this formulation better reflects welfare changes than an index that uses the same weights across households (such as the Laspeyeres index).

One final point regarding the data on household consumption merits mention. As Deaton (2003) and others have noted, the design of the NSS survey questionnaire for the year 1999–2000 (the 55th round) was different from that in earlier rounds, raising questions regarding the comparability of the data from this survey with previous surveys. The comparability problem arises because the 55th round of the NSS required households to report their expenditure levels over different recall periods than the previous rounds.[6]

To account for the effect of the discrepancy in recall periods, we implement the solution suggested by Deaton (2003). Specifically, we exploit the fact that there were a subset of goods (accounting for more than 20 percent of consumer expenditures) for which the survey questionnaire had the same recall period (thirty days) across all rounds of the NSS and the expenditure on which is highly correlated with total expenditure. Assuming that the Engel curve relating the logarithm of expenditures per capita on thirty-day goods to the logarithm of total household expenditures per capita is stable over time, the total expenditures of the households can be backed out of expenditures on the thirty-day goods. While the validity of this assumption cannot be checked, Deaton (2003) confirms the robustness of the adjustment procedure.

Trade Protection

We use Hasan, Mitra, and Ural's (2007) data on state-level measures of trade protection. In particular, industry-level tariff rates and non-tariff barrier (NTB) coverage rates for agricultural, mining, and manufacturing industries are weighted by state- and sector-specific employment shares as follows:

where $\gamma^{j}_{ik,1993}$ is the employment share of industry k in state i derived from the 1993 employment survey. Ind_Tariff_{kt} and Ind_NTB_{kt} are

$$Tariff_{it} = \sum_{k} \gamma_{ik,1993} * Ind\_Tariff_{kt}$$

$$NTB_{it} = \sum_{k} \gamma_{ik,1993} * Ind\_NTB_{kt}$$

industry-specific tariff rates and nontariff coverage rates that are measured at the two-digit level for each year t.

MEASURING INEQUALITY

We measure inequality using Theil's T statistic, which, when used in the context of individual data, is given by:[7]

where n is the number of individuals in the population, c_p is the real consumption of the person indexed by p, and μ_c is the population's average consumption. If every individual has exactly the same

$$T = \sum_{p=1}^{n} \left\{ \left(\frac{1}{n} \right) * \left(\frac{c_p}{\mu_c} \right) * \ln \left(\frac{c_p}{\mu_c} \right) \right\}$$

consumption level, T will be zero; this represents perfect equality and is the minimum value of Theil's T. If one individual has all of the consumption, T will equal $\ln(n)$; this is the highest level of inequality and is the maximum value of Theil's T statistic.

If members of a population can be divided into mutually exclusive and completely exhaustive groups, then Theil's T statistic is made up of two components, the between-group element (T^b_g) and the within-group element (T^w_g).

When aggregated data is available instead of individual data, T^b_g can be used as a lower bound for the population's value of

$$T = T^b_g + T^w_g$$

Theil's T statistic. The between-group element of Theil's T can be written as:

where i indexes the groups, p_i is the population of group i, P is the total population, c_i is the average consumption in group i, and μ is the

$$T_g^b = \sum_{i=1}^{m} \left\{ \left(\frac{p_i}{P} \right) * \left(\frac{c_i}{\mu} \right) * \ln \left(\frac{c_i}{\mu} \right) \right\}$$

average consumption across the entire population. T^b_g is bounded above by the natural logarithm of the total population divided by the size of the smallest group (a value that is attained when the smallest group consumes all the resources).

As Conceição and Ferreira (2000) note, when data are hierarchically nested (e.g., every district is in a state and each state is in a country), Theil's T statistic must increase or stay the same as the level of aggregation becomes smaller (i.e., $T_{population} > T_{state} > T_{district}$). Theil's T statistic for the population equals the limit of the between-group Theil component as the number of groups approaches the size of the population.

The additive decomposability of our inequality index, which allows us to neatly express inequality as the sum of between-group inequality and within-group inequality, enables us to examine inequality at different levels of aggregation in our study. Furthermore, the Theil index has less stringent data requirements and is particularly useful when only group data are available rather than individual data or when individual data are subject to random measurement errors (which average out in larger samples). In our case, inequality measures may be biased by the infrequent household consumption of durable goods or other lumpy expenditures (such as on weddings and funerals). As we will discuss in greater detail, we will sometimes group households into centiles and use consumption levels averaged across different centiles of the sample to construct the Theil index, thus exploiting the advantages of using the Theil index with aggregated data.

Finally, to ensure the robustness of our findings, we also measure inequality using other well-known inequality measures such as the Gini coefficient and the variance of log consumption.

RESULTS

We use household survey data from four NSS rounds—1987–88, 1993–94, 1999–2000, and 2004–5—to construct measures of per capita expenditure inequality that may be compared over time and which, exploiting the decomposability of the Theil index, convey information about the contribution of the different subnational aggregates (states and urban and rural areas within states) to overall inequality. Since the Theil index is sensitive to a changing number of subgroups (and thus a changing number of households in the sample), comparability of inequality over time requires that we work with aggregated groupings of the data while fixing the number of subgroups. Thus, we aggregate household expenditures into percentile groups within each subgroup. For instance, we aggregate households into 20,000 percentile groups to calculate overall inequality. For the decompositions, we aggregate households into 300 percentile groups within each state and 150 percentile groups with each rural or urban area within each state.[8] This also allows us to smooth consumption of durables and other lumpy expenditures and to also smooth out any random measurement error in the survey data. We present here results using only data on expenditures on nondurable goods (food items, energy and transportation, education, medical, and housing). Additional findings, not reported here, for overall consumption expenditures (including durable goods consumption) are very similar to the findings presented below.

Inequality Overall

We compute first the values of overall inequality over time. As mentioned in the previous section, in order to compare the evolution of inequality over time, we must use a fixed number of final elements, thus necessitating the use of percentile groups in our analysis.

Figure 6.1 plots overall Theil inequality levels for the years 1988, 1994, 2000, and 2005. For each of these years, we also obtain bootstrapped estimates of the sampling variances associated with the inequality estimates. This is done using the methodology suggested and implemented in the statistical package STATA by Jollife and Krushelnytskyy (STATA command *ineqerr*). Specifically, the chart indicates the inequality estimate along with a two-standard-deviation height (reflecting a 95 percent confidence interval band) marked above and below this mean estimate. Figure 6.1 reveals an interesting pattern in the data. Inequality rises after the implementation of the economic reforms until 2000 but falls back by 2005 to being slightly above the prereform 1988 level. Figure 6.2 provides a corresponding set of estimates using the Gini inequality measure, and Figure 6.3 provides inequality estimates using the variance of log expenditures as the inequality measure instead. Clearly, the different inequality measures provide a rather similar picture: while inequality rose in the immediate postreform period, there was a drop in inequality between the years 2000 and 2005. Thus, inequality has not risen monotonically since the economic reforms.

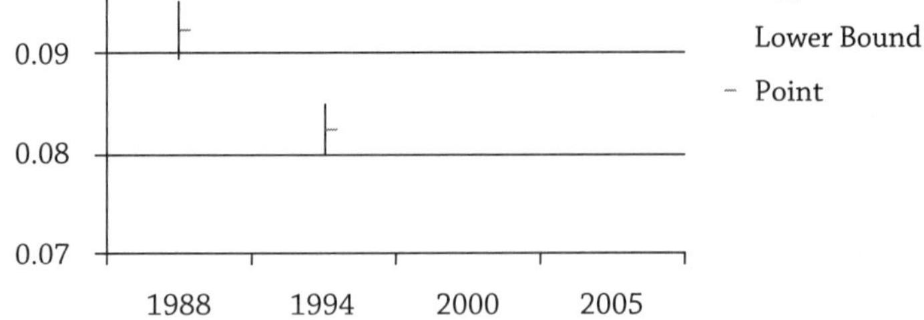

Figure 6.1. Theil Inequality—Adjusted

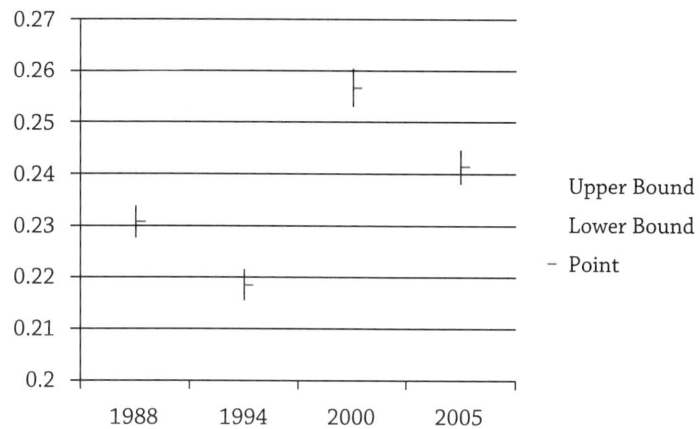

Figure 6.2. Gini Inequality—Adjusted

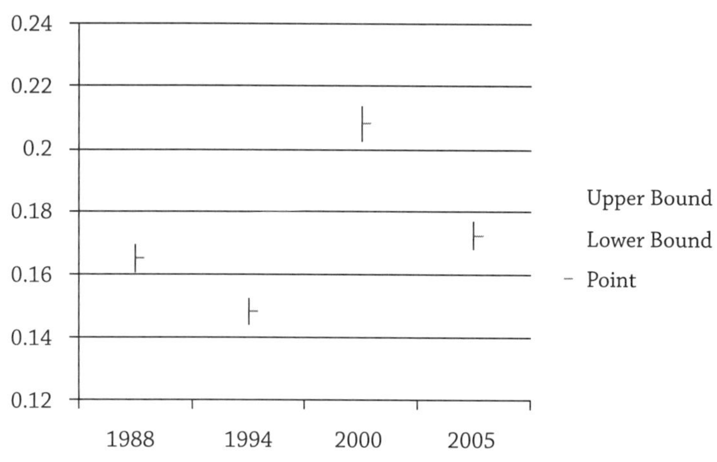

Figure 6.3. Variance of Log Consumption—Adjusted

For the results presented in Figures 6.1, 6.2, and 6.3, we have used the Deaton (2003) "adjusted" measure of income for the year 2000 (see the discussion in second section above). Figures 6.4, 6.5, and 6.6 present the corresponding inequality trends (for the Theil, Gini, and variance of log expenditure measures, respectively) without adjusting the inequality measure for the year 2000. The Deaton (2003) adjustments clearly raise the measured inequality in the year 2000, as can be seen by comparing Figures 6.1 with 6.4, 6.2 with 6.5, and 6.3 with 6.6. Without the adjustment, the rise in inequality between 1994 and 2000 is therefore smaller. Nevertheless, the overall inequality trend without the adjustment to 2000 consumption seems to be roughly as it was before. The point estimate of inequality falls between 1988 and 1994, then rises between 1994 and 2000 and then falls again by 2005, again implying a nonmonotonic evolution of inequality over time.[9]

Inequality Decomposition

Next, we decompose the Theil index to assess the contribution of various subnational aggregates to overall inequality. We consider several decompositions. We begin by decomposing overall inequality into the sum of inequality across urban and rural areas and inequality across household percentile groups within these urban and rural areas. Also, we consider inequality across states and across household percentile groups within these states. We then consider a more detailed decomposition with overall inequality

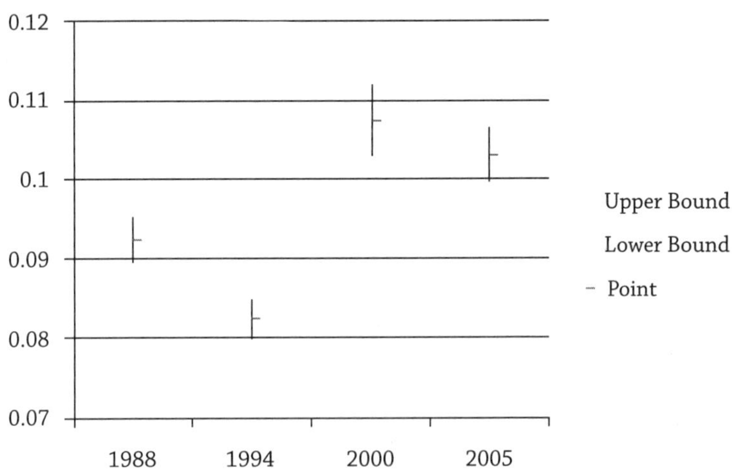

Figure 6.4. Theil—Unadjusted

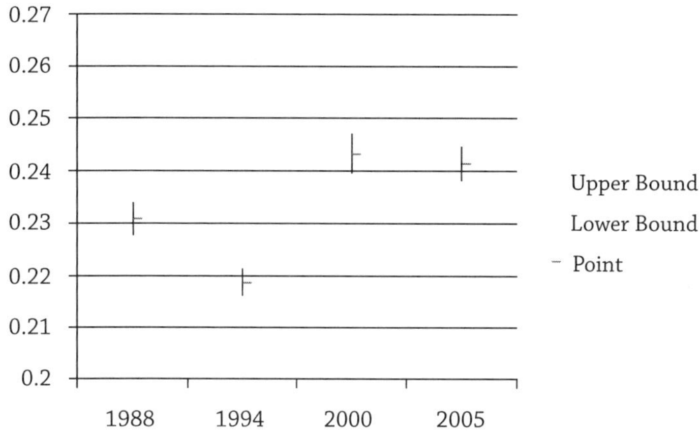

Figure 6.5. Gini—Unadjusted

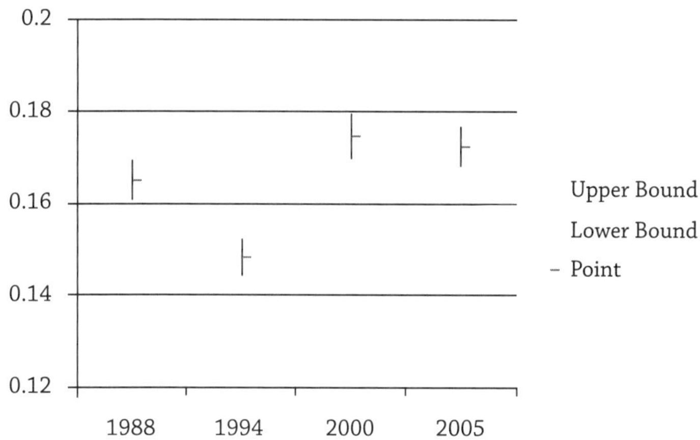

Figure 6.6. Variance of Logs—Unadjusted

split into inequality across states, across rural and urban areas within states and across household percentile groups within these urban and rural aggregates. Finally, in an even more detailed decomposition, inequality within urban and rural aggregates (within states) is now decomposed into inequality across different first-stage units (FSUs) that are either villages or collections of urban blocks and inequality across households within FSUs.

INEQUALITY ACROSS URBAN AND RURAL AREAS

Figure 6.7 presents the evolution of inequality decomposed as the sum of inequality between urban and rural areas and across household percentile groups within these areas. Figure 6.8 is similar but presents the shares of across-group and within-group inequality where the groups are urban and rural. From Figure 6.7, we see that urban-rural inequality has increased from 1994 onward. However, both figures clearly depict that most of the inequality lies at a level below that of the urban/rural aggregate. Indeed, the decomposition in Figure 6.8 tells us that much of the inequality seen here is inequality with in rural or urban areas, which accounts for more than 90 percent of overall inequality.

INEQUALITY ACROSS STATES

Next, we decompose overall inequality into across-state and within-state inequality. Figure 6.9 presents the evolution of this decomposition, and Figure 6.10 presents the decomposition in shares. As Figure 6.9 indicates, inequality across states rose between 1994 and 2000 and again between 2000 and 2005. However, again, most of inequality lies within states. Hence, as wide as is the gap in per capita expenditures

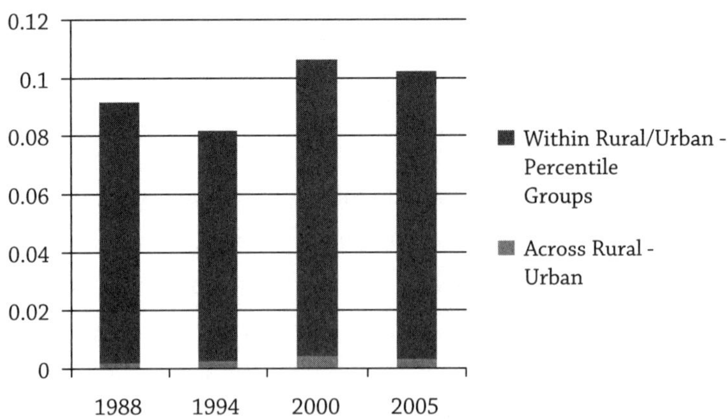

Figure 6.7. Inequality—Rural/Urban

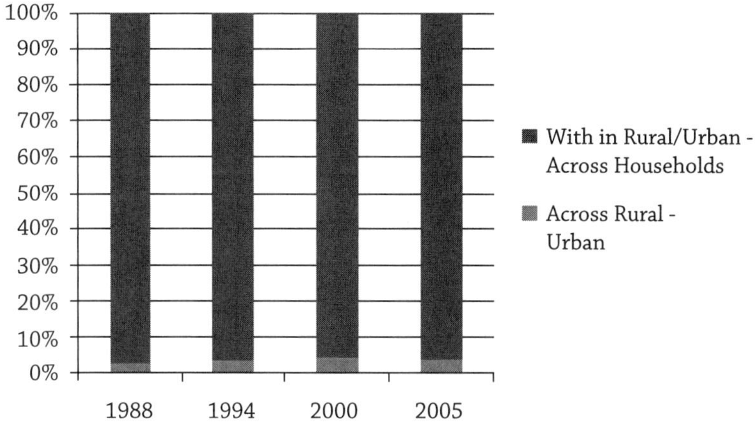

Figure 6.8. Inequality Decomposed—Rural/Urban

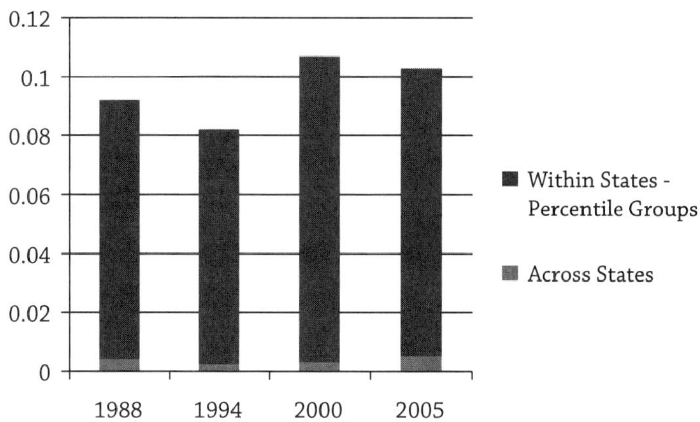

Figure 6.9. Inequality—across and within States

between Indian states, inequality within states is much larger, accounting for more than 90 percent of overall inequality in all years.

Figures 6.11 and 6.12 add one level of disaggregation to Figures 6.9 and 6.10, respectively. Inequality within states is further disaggregated into inequality across urban and rural areas within states and within these urban and rural areas within states. Once again, most of the inequality lies at a level below that of the urban and rural areas within states. An even more detailed decomposition is pre-

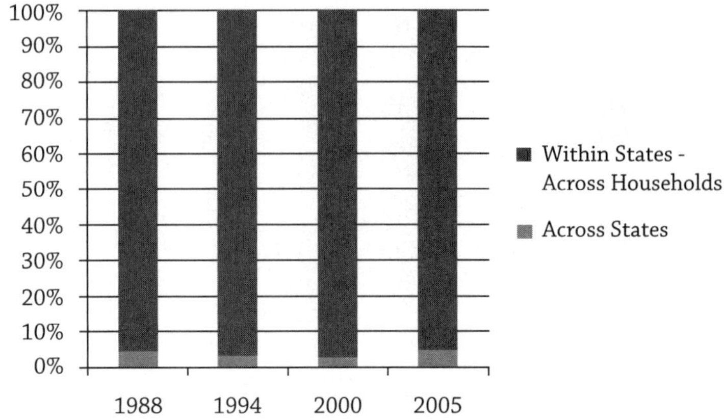

Figure 6.10. Inequality Decomposed—across and within States

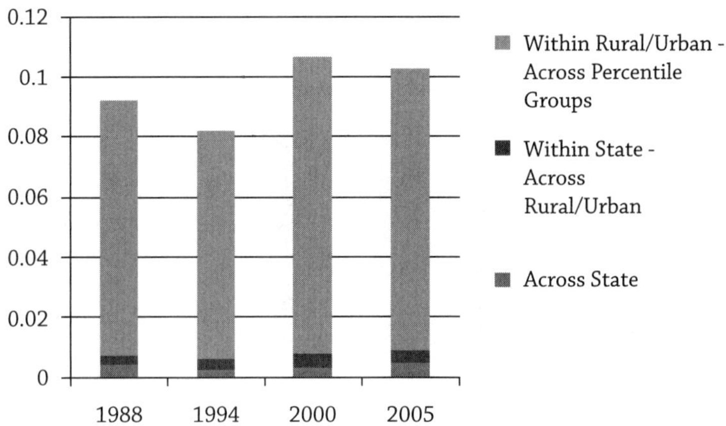

Figure 6.11. Inequality Decomposed

sented in Figure 6.13, where inequality within urban and rural areas (within states) is now decomposed into inequality across different FSUs and inequality across households within FSUs. As Figure 6.13 indicates, more than 60 percent of the overall inequality is accounted for by inequality across households within FSUs, with significant inequality also between FSUs within urban and rural areas within states. Consistent with earlier figures, most of the inequality is observed below urban and rural areas within states.

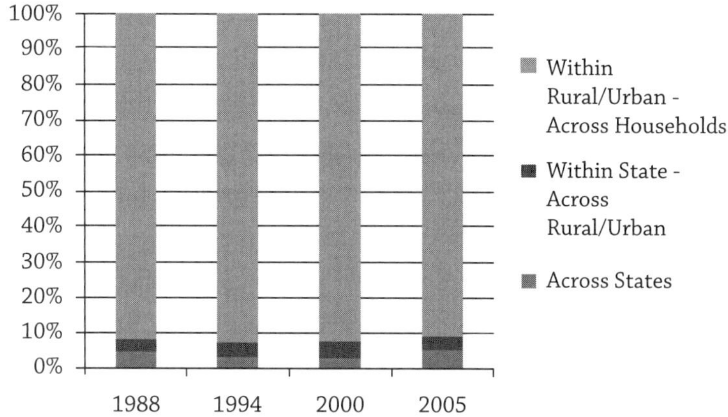

Figure 6.12. Inequality Decomposed

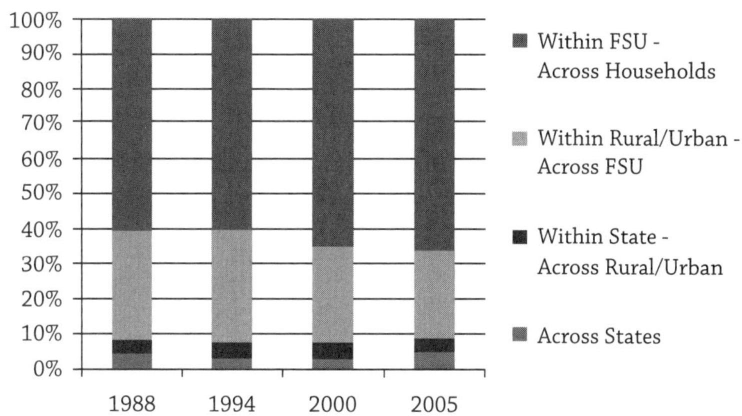

Figure 6.13. Inequality Decomposed

INEQUALITY WITHIN STATES

Table 6.1 presents within-state inequality measures calculated for each state—overall and separately for urban and rural areas. We note first that the inequality ranking of states is quite similar, although not identical, to the inequality rankings (measured using the variance of log expenditures) reported by Deaton and Dreze (2002). From Table 6.1, Kerala, Tamil Nadu, Maharashtra, and Andhra Pradesh appear in the top third of states with the highest rural inequality in 1994. This is consistent with Deaton and Dreze (2002). Likewise, Assam, Jammu and Kashmir, West Bengal, and Orissa appear in the bottom third, with the lowest levels of rural inequality. For urban areas, again as in Deaton and Dreze (2002), Kerala, Tamil Nadu, Maharashtra, and Himachal Pradesh appear in the top third of the group, while Rajasthan, Jammu and Kashmir, and Assam appear within the bottom third.[10]

Turning to changes in overall inequality, we can see from Table 6.1 that inequality trends within states mirror the national experience. Thus, inequality seems to have risen between 1994 and 2000 in the vast majority of states, but also fallen between 2000 and 2005 in most states. Indeed, between 2000 and 2005, only four states—Mizoram, Maharashtra, Orissa, and Haryana—show significant increases in inequality. The picture is almost exactly the same for rural and urban areas within states, with the majority of states experiencing rising inequality between 1994 and 2000, but falling inequality between 2000 and 2005.

Distribution of Consumption Expenditures

To study in greater detail the evolution of the overall level of inequality reported above, we examine next the distribution of growth in household per capita consumption over the time period 1988–2005. Figures 6.14, 6.15, and 6.16 illustrate the growth in real per capita consumption by centile groups across the years 1988–94, 1994–2000, and 2000–2005, respectively (with the expenditure data from the year 2000 being "unadjusted," as discussed in note 9). Figure 6.14, spanning the initial reform period, clearly indicates a slightly higher per capita consumption growth rate for the lower centiles. This corresponds to the reduced inequality in 1994 relative to 1988 that we have discussed earlier. Figure 6.15 reveals the opposite trend, with a slightly higher per capita consumption growth rate for upper centiles corresponding to increasing inequality over the 1994–2000 period. Finally, in Figure 6.16, representing the period 2000–2005, we see a higher growth rate for lower-centile households as well as for households in the upper half (above median) of the distribution. This corresponds to the slight fall in inequality from 2000–2005 (indicated in Figure 6.4).

Trade Openness and Inequality

We turn, finally, to the links between exposure to international trade and inequality. Our analysis is conducted at the level of the state. As discussed in the second section, we use measures of tariff and non-tariff protection constructed by Hasan, Mitra, and Ural (2007). Specifically, the state-level measures for protection are constructed by using industry-level tariff rates and nontariff barrier (NTB) coverage rates for agricultural, mining, and manufacturing industries, weighted by state- and sector-specific employment shares.

To this end, we would like to compare how trade reforms during the 1988–94 period affected inequality in the subsequent 1994–2005 period. Figure 6.17 plots the changes in inequality within states over the time period 1994–2005 against changes in state-level tariff protection between 1988 and 1994. No pattern can be discerned between the magnitude of tariff reductions and the changes in inequality. Figure 6.18 plots the changes in inequality within states (for the time period 1994–2005) against changes in state-level nontariff protection between 1988 and 1994. Once again, there is no clear pattern that can be discerned in the data.

Nevertheless, to test formally for the presence of a statistically significant association between changes in inequality and trade policy changes, we examine regression estimates from the following econometric specifications:

Table 6.1 EVOLUTION OF THEIL INDEX INEQUALITY WITHIN STATES (1988–2005)

	States	Overall				Rural				Urban			
		1988	1994	2000	2005	1988	1994	2000	2005	1988	1994	2000	2005
1	Andhra Pradesh	0.094	0.087	0.114	0.107	0.087	0.076	0.081	0.097	0.102	0.092	0.127	0.115
2	Arunachal Pradesh	0.135	0.126	0.206	0.134	0.142	0.128	0.186	0.130	0.088	0.102	0.279	0.141
3	Assam	0.065	0.053	0.098	0.068	0.060	0.043	0.073	0.053	0.071	0.077	0.148	0.102
4	Bihar	0.076	0.071	0.087	0.077	0.069	0.059	0.071	0.059	0.092	0.085	0.115	0.106
5	Gujarat	0.084	0.082	0.100	0.101	0.069	0.059	0.094	0.082	0.091	0.091	0.098	0.105
6	Haryana	0.071	0.075	0.082	0.089	0.069	0.071	0.074	0.081	0.076	0.081	0.093	0.101
7	Himachal Pradesh	0.083	0.082	0.113	0.105	0.072	0.070	0.079	0.091	0.103	0.094	0.123	0.110
8	Jammu & Kashmir	0.062	0.061	0.074	0.066	0.059	0.048	0.068	0.060	0.066	0.077	0.080	0.072
9	Karnataka	0.122	0.093	0.118	0.104	0.104	0.071	0.096	0.069	0.121	0.100	0.125	0.118
10	Kerala	0.114	0.115	0.137	0.138	0.103	0.102	0.125	0.128	0.139	0.131	0.147	0.154

11	Madhya Pradesh	0.094	0.072	0.111	0.095	0.078	0.058	0.095	0.080	0.113	0.081	0.119	0.107
12	Maharashtra	0.110	0.102	0.102	0.113	0.081	0.081	0.080	0.088	0.115	0.098	0.104	0.119
13	Manipur	0.043	0.047	0.124	0.083	0.044	0.050	0.107	0.073	0.041	0.043	0.137	0.098
14	Meghalaya	0.076	0.063	0.087	0.059	0.047	0.052	0.065	0.045	0.102	0.060	0.086	0.069
15	Mizoram	0.052	0.063	0.103	0.132	0.043	0.056	0.090	0.123	0.050	0.058	0.105	0.128
16	Orissa	0.078	0.066	0.084	0.094	0.071	0.054	0.062	0.084	0.081	0.082	0.116	0.108
17	Punjab	0.080	0.082	0.101	0.096	0.073	0.070	0.095	0.084	0.092	0.096	0.107	0.110
18	Rajasthan	0.085	0.068	0.092	0.084	0.079	0.061	0.083	0.077	0.095	0.077	0.103	0.091
19	Sikkim	0.062	0.068	0.148	0.090	0.054	0.050	0.139	0.083	0.056	0.072	0.108	0.086
20	Tamil Nadu	0.123	0.102	0.139	0.125	0.119	0.085	0.112	0.098	0.119	0.109	0.143	0.130
21	Tripura	0.056	0.077	0.102	0.090	0.051	0.062	0.092	0.068	0.076	0.098	0.102	0.110
22	Uttar Pradesh	0.083	0.075	0.089	0.091	0.075	0.065	0.078	0.079	0.099	0.092	0.111	0.117
23	West Bengal	0.078	0.065	0.096	0.092	0.067	0.050	0.076	0.073	0.094	0.085	0.115	0.115

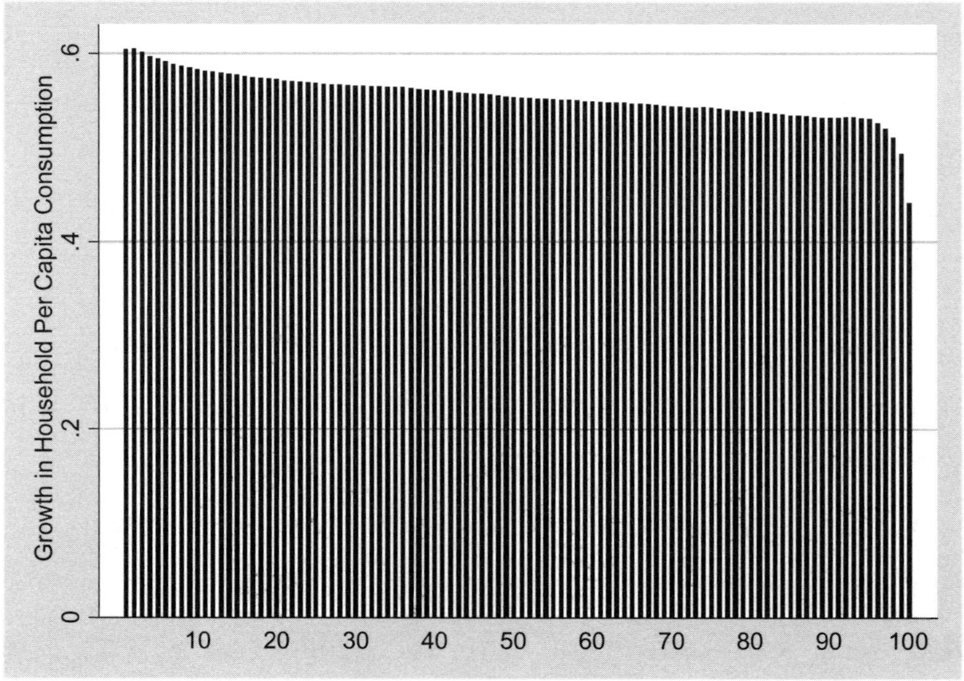

Figure 6.14. Per Capita Consumption Growth by Decile: 1988–1994

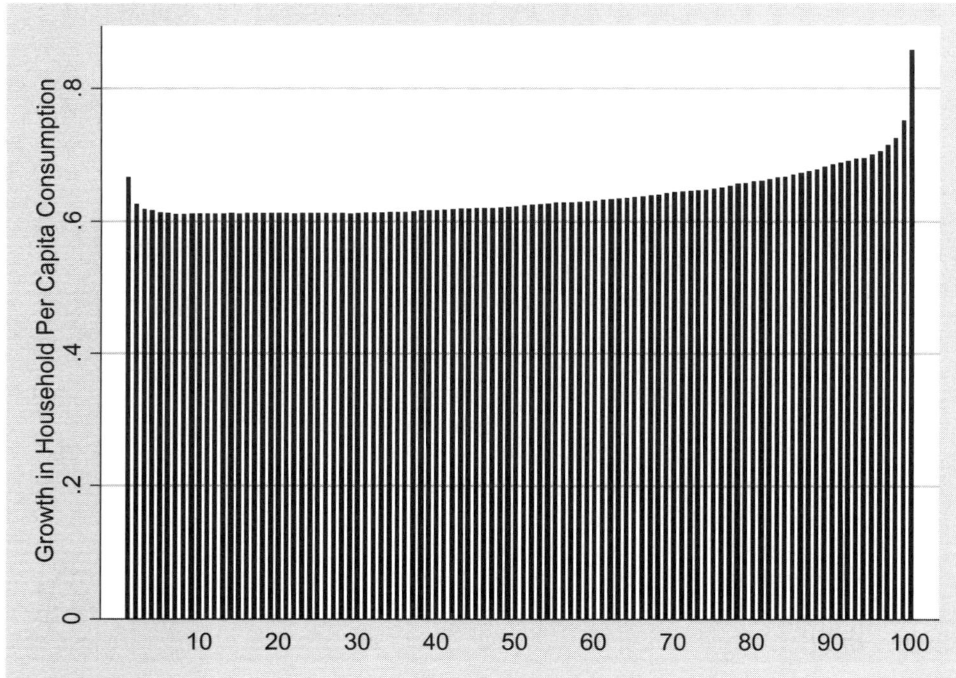

Figure 6.15. Per Capita Consumption Growth by Decile: 1994–2000

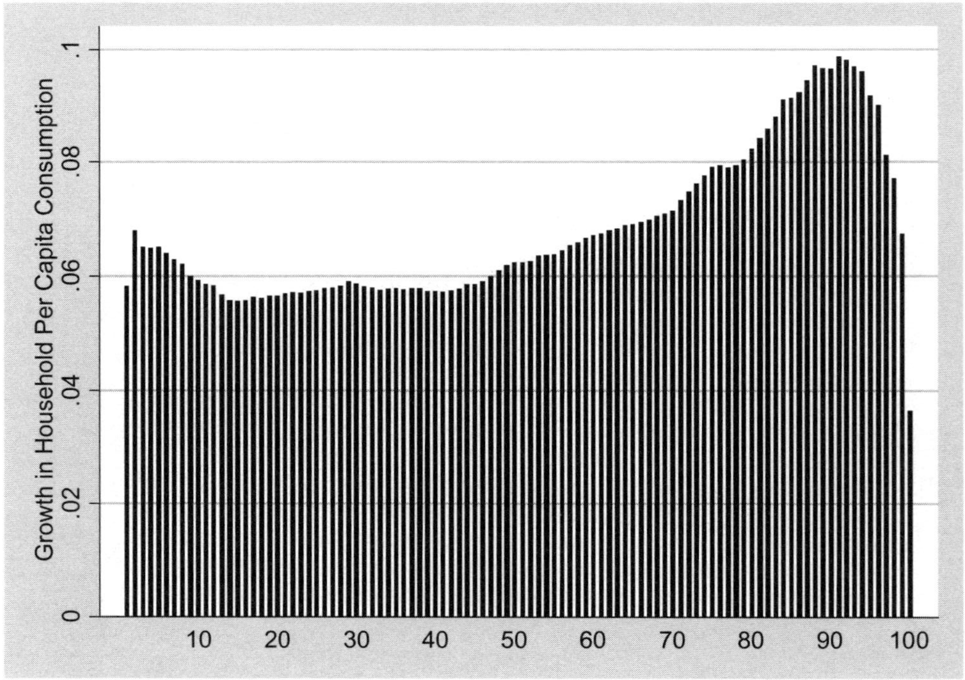

Figure 6.16. Per Capita Consumption Growth by Decile: 2000–2005

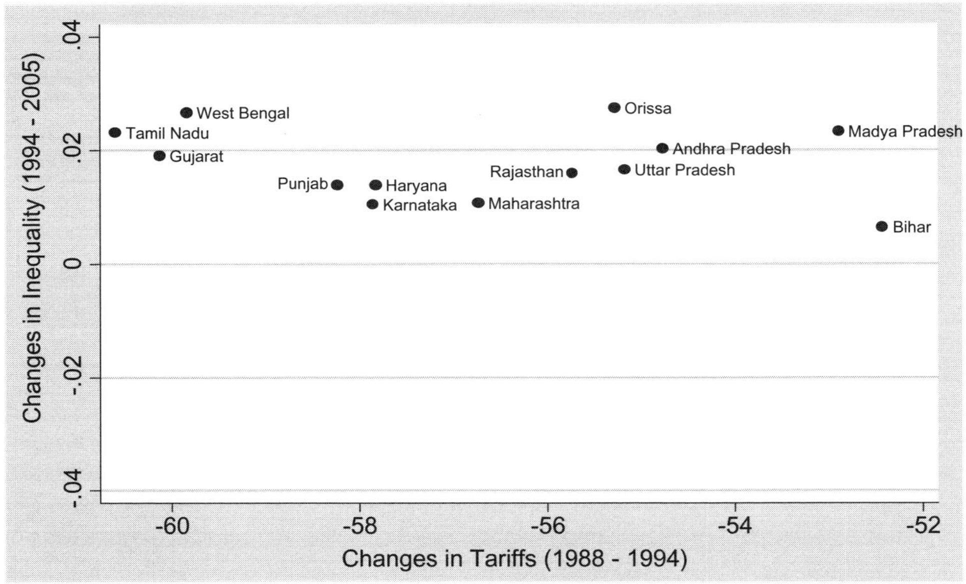

Figure 6.17. Changes in Inequality and Tariff Protection

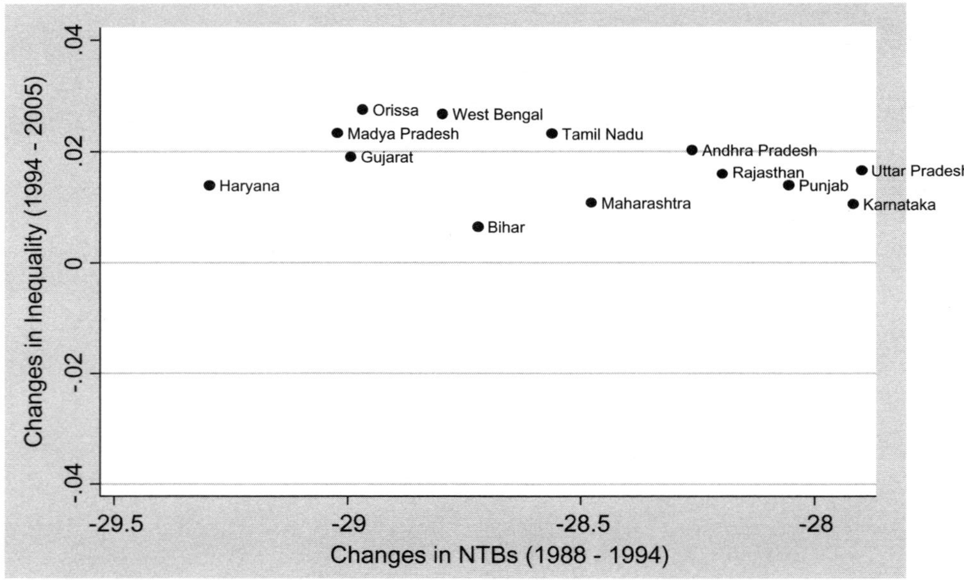

Figure 6.18. Changes in Inequality and Nontariff Protection

and

$$\Delta Inequality_{2005-1994} = \alpha + \beta(\Delta Tariff_{1994-1988}) + \varepsilon$$

Table 6.2 presents the results from ordinary least squares (OLS)

$$\Delta Inequality_{2005-1994} = \alpha + \beta(\Delta NTB_{1994-1988}) + \varepsilon$$

estimation of the specifications above. As suggested by the scatter plots in Figures 6.17 and 6.18, OLS estimates of the parameter β measuring the association between changes in inequality and trade policy changes are insignificantly different from zero.[11]

The finding of the lack of any significant association between trade openness and inequality is robust to many changes to the econometric specification we have considered above. Specifications involving levels rather than differences of the dependent and independent variables and the use of different lag structures all

Table 6.2 INEQUALITY AND TRADE PROTECTION

Inequality Change (2005–1994)	*Tariffs*	*NTBs*
Change in trade protection (1994–1988)	–0.00056 (0.00076)	–0.00489 (0.00337)
Constant	–0.01453 (0.04390)	–0.12222 (0.09522)
N	13	13
R^2	0.05	0.12

yield essentially the same outcome: a statistically insignificant association between trade openness and inequality. Furthermore, considering income inequality changes over different time periods rather than the 1994–2005 period and focusing separately on urban and rural inequality do not materially alter the results. Thus, the hypothesis of an association between trade and inequality does not find support in our analysis of the data.

CONCLUSIONS

The consequences of the economic reforms in India for inequality have been vigorously debated. To study the evolution of inequality subsequent to the economic reforms, we have used the Theil inequality index and other inequality measures using household expenditure data from the Indian National Sample Survey. As we have discussed in this chapter, the Theil index is additively decomposable: it can be expressed as the sum of across-group inequality and within-group inequality, thereby enabling a consistent examination of inequality at different levels of aggregation.

Our main findings are that overall inequality varied modestly over the period of our study, falling between 1988 and 1994, rising between 1994 and 2000, but falling again by 2005. Hence, the evolution of inequality since 1994 has been nonmonotonic. Furthermore, a similar nonmonotonic inequality trend has been seen within most states. While rural-urban inequality and across state inequality have risen slightly from 1994 to 2005, they constitute an extremely small portion of overall inequality. More than 60 percent of overall inequality is found at the micro level within urban blocks and rural villages. The change in inequality across households within states is found to uncorrelated with the change in state-level measures of tariff and nontariff protection. Considered alongside the evidence concerning the reduction in poverty in this time period, our findings should allay concerns regarding the adverse impact on equity of the economic reforms undertaken in India.

NOTES

* Prepared for the Columbia-NCAER Conference on Trade, Poverty, Inequality and Democracy, held in New Delhi, March 31–April 1, 2011. Work on this chapter was supported by Columbia University's Program on Indian Economic Policies, funded by a generous grant from the John Templeton Foundation. For many helpful comments and suggestions, we are grateful to our discussants, Jagdish Bhagwati, Rana Hasan, and Amartya Lahiri. The opinions expressed in the chapter are those of the author(s) and do not necessarily reflect the views of the John Templeton Foundation.

1. For detailed discussion of the post-Independence history of the Indian economy and the context in which these reforms were eventually undertaken, see Bhagwati 1993 and Panagariya 2008.
2. Income inequality here refers simply to differences in incomes. As Kuznets (1953) stated, this is "without regard to their desirability as a system of reward or undesirability as a scheme running counter to some type of equality." It is important to note, as Atkinson (1983, pp. 1–10) does, that "in order to assess the implications of differences in income, we need to first establish that the people involved are comparable in other relevant respects" and that "once we have established that people have comparable circumstances, the inferences depend upon the underlying principles of social justice." Different ideas about social justice can lead to quite different views regarding inequality. Separately, the question of whether trade liberalization (or economic globalization more generally) has benign or malign effects on the distribution of income has been widely debated. See Bhagwati 2005 for a comprehensive discussion.
3. It is, of course, possible that openness to a global economy alters the patterns of income mobility in society as well, a question that we do not study in this chapter. See, however, recent work on this interesting topic by Hnatkovska, Lahiri, and Paul (2010), Jalan and Murgai (2009), and Munshi and Rosenzweig (2009).
4. For comparative discussions of the evolution of inequality subsequent to the reforms and prior to the 1999–2000 period survey of household incomes by the Indian National Sample Survey, see Pal and Ghosh 2007 and Panagariya 2008 (chap. 8).
5. See Conceição and Ferreira (2000) for a detailed exposition of the theoretical and practical merits of the Theil index over other indices measuring income inequality.

6. More specifically, as Deaton (2003) notes, the issue is as follows: the 55th round differed both from earlier rounds and from either of the schedules in the experimental rounds. For the high-frequency items, households were asked to report their expenditures for both recall periods. The questionnaires were printed with the list of goods down the leftmost column, with the next four columns requesting quantities and expenditures over the last seven days and over the last thirty days, respectively. Such multiple reporting periods are often used in household expenditure surveys, and may well produce excellent estimates in their own right. But the results are unlikely to be comparable with those from a questionnaire in which only the thirty-day questions are used. For example, when they are asked both questions, respondents are effectively being prompted to reconcile the rates of consumption across the two periods. Indeed, there is some evidence that is consistent with this sort of reconciliation.
7. Our discussion in this section of Theil index methodology is based on the more detailed description of the Theil index and its use provided by Conceição and Ferreira (2000).
8. Changing the number of subgroups has no material effect on the results. We want to maximize the number of subgroups to get a more accurate estimate of household inequality while at the same time maintaining the same number of subgroups over time to make comparisons.
9. Having noted the similarity in inequality trends with and without the Deaton (2003) adjustment to the data for the year 2000, we used unadjusted data for the remainder of the analysis.
10. We should note that the study by Deaton and Dreze (2002) reported inequality estimates for fifteen states, in contrast to the twenty-three reported on in Table 6.1. Our comparison of inequality rankings with those reported in Deaton and Dreze 2002 is therefore just an indicative one. We should also note that a major exception is Punjab, which indicates reasonably high levels of urban inequality in our study while appearing at the bottom of the list in Deaton and Dreze 2002.
11. Kerala and Assam, outlier states due to the magnitude of the change in their trade barriers, have been dropped from these figures and the regression results. However, our results are robust to adding Kerala and Assam to the regression; β is still statistically insignificant from zero.

REFERENCES

Atkinson, A. B. (1983). *The Economics of Inequality*. 2nd ed. New York: Oxford University Press.

Bhagwati, J. (1993). *India in Transition: Freeing the Economy*. New York: Oxford University Press.

——— (2005). *In Defense of Globalization*. New York: Oxford University Press.

Bhalla, S. (2003). "Recounting the Poor: Poverty in India, 1983–1999." *Economic and Political Weekly* 38(4), January 25, 338–49.

Conceição, P., and P. Ferreira (2000). "The Young Person's Guide to the Theil Index: Suggesting Intuitive Interpretations and Exploring Analytical Applications." University of Texas Inequality Project (UTIP), Working Paper no. 14.

Deaton, A. (2003). "Adjusted Poverty Estimates for India for 1999–2000." *Economic and Political Weekly* 38(4), January 25, 322–26.

Deaton, A., and J. Dreze (2002). "Poverty and Inequality in India: A Re-Examination, Center for Economic Development." Working Paper no. 107, Princeton University, Princeton, NJ.

Deaton, A., and S. Zaidi (2002). "Guidelines for Constructing Consumption Aggregates for Welfare Analysis." Living Standards Measurement Study, Working Paper no. 135, World Bank, Washington, DC.

Hasan, R., D. Mitra, and B. Ural (2007). "Trade Liberalization, Market Institutions and Poverty Reduction, India Policy Forum." *Brookings Institution* 3, 71–110.

Hnatkovska, V., A. Lahiri, and S. Paul (2010). "Castes and Labor Mobility." Working Paper, University of British Columbia, Vancouver.

Jalan, J., and R. Murgai (2009). "Intergenerational Mobility in Education in India." Working Paper, Indian Statistical Institute, Delhi.

Kuznets, S. (1953). *Share of Upper Income Groups in Income and Savings*. New York: National Bureau of Economic Research.

Munshi, K., and M. Rosenzweig (2009). "Why Is Mobility in India So Low? Social Insurance, Inequality, and Growth." Working Paper, Department of Economics, Brown University, Providence, RI.

Pal, P., and J. Ghosh (2007). "Inequality in India: A Survey of Recent Trends." United Nations, Department of Economic and Social Affairs, Working Paper no. 45, New York, NY.

Panagariya, A. (2008). *India: The Emerging Giant*. New York: Oxford University Press.

Singh, N., L. Bhandari, A. Chen, and A. Khare (2003). "Regional Inequality in India: A Fresh Look." *Economic and Political Weekly* 38(11), March 15, 1069–73.

INDEX